Economic Crisis and Structural Reforms in Southern Europe

In recent years the countries of southern Europe have undergone, with varying intensity, a serious and prolonged economic crisis. Most have had to implement comprehensive economic adjustment programmes, including a wide range of structural reforms. Economic Crisis and Structural Reforms in Southern Europe examines these reforms, drawing policy lessons from their successes and failures.

This book employs two basic strands of analysis: issues of policy design, and political economy considerations. It considers the choice of timing and sequencing of reforms, the choice of the appropriate policy instruments, the pressure of interest groups and the political calculations involved in reforms. Featuring chapters in which contributors explore both national cases of specific structural reforms, and a comparative approach in order to evaluate similar reforms across countries, this important and topical work explores ongoing issues within the economy.

Focusing on the challenges of designing and implementing structural reforms under conditions of crisis, this book will be of interest to policy makers and researchers from national and international organizations as well as academics and members of research institutes interested in the economics and politics of the Eurozone crisis.

Paolo Manasse is a Professor of Macroeconomics and International Economic Policy at the University of Bologna. He has previously worked for the OECD, the World Bank and the Inter-American Development Bank and belongs to the expert Roster of the Fiscal Affairs Department, IMF and the Expert Panel on Capital Markets of the Centre for Economic Policy Studies in Brussels.

Dimitris Katsikas is Lecturer of International and European Political Economy at the Department of Political Science and Public Administration, National and Kapodistrian University of Athens and Head of the Crisis Observatory at the Hellenic Foundation for European and Foreign Policy (ELIAMEP). He has coordinated a number of Greek and European research programmes related to the economic crisis.

Routledge Studies in the European Economy

Economic Crisis and Structural Reforms in Southern Europe

Policy Lessons

Edited by
Paolo Manasse and
Dimitris Katsikas

LONDON AND NEW YORK

First published 2018
by Routledge
2 Park Square, Milton Park, Abingdon, Oxon OX14 4RN

and by Routledge
52 Vanderbilt Avenue, New York, NY 10017

First issued in paperback 2020

Routledge is an imprint of the Taylor & Francis Group, an informa business

British Library Cataloguing-in-Publication Data
A catalogue record for this book is available from the British Library

Library of Congress Cataloging-in-Publication Data
A catalog record for this book has been requested

ISBN 13: 978-0-367-66730-6 (pbk)
ISBN 13: 978-1-138-28033-5 (hbk)

Typeset in Times New Roman
by Apex CoVantage, LLC

Dedication by Dimitris Katsikas
"In memory of my father, Christoforos"

Contents

Contributors

Turrini Alessandro, Head of Unit "Macroeconomic Imbalances and Adjustment", European Commission, DG Economic and Financial Affairs.

Terzi Alessio, Affiliate Fellow, Bruegel and Visiting Fulbright Fellow, Harvard, Kennedy School of Government.

Petralias Athanassios, Statistical Analyst, Statistics Department, Bank of Greece.

Cuerpo Carlos, Head of Division, Economic Analysis Division, Spanish Independent Authority for Fiscal Responsibility.

Herrero Carlos, Ph.D. Student, University of Valencia.

Katsikas Dimitris, Lecturer of International and European Political Economy, National and Kapodistrian University of Athens and Head, Crisis Observatory, Hellenic Foundation for European and Foreign Policy (ELIAMEP).

Panagiotarea Eleni, Senior Economist, Piraeus Bank, Onassis Scholar and Research Fellow, Hellenic Foundation for European and Foreign Policy (ELIAMEP).

Geli Federico, Analyst, Economic Analysis Division, Spanish Independent Authority for Fiscal Responsibility.

Steinberg Federico, Professor of Economics at Universidad Autónoma de Madrid and Senior Analyst at the Elcano Royal Institute (Spain).

Catao Luis, Senior Economist, Research Department, International Monetary Fund.

Anastasatou Marianthi, Economist, Economic Analysis and Research Department, Bank of Greece.

Otero-Iglesias Miguel, Senior Analyst in International Political Economy, Elcano Royal Institute (Spain), Senior Research Fellow, ESSCA School of Management (France), and Adjunct Professor at IE University (Spain).

Manasse Paolo, Professor of Macroeconomics and International Economic Policy, University of Bologna.

Clerides Sofronis, Professor of Economics, University of Cyprus.

Aksoy Tolga, Assistant Professor, Department of Economics, Yildiz Technical University.

Figures

Tables

Preface and acknowledgements

In recent years, the countries of southern Europe went through an economic crisis of extraordinary intensity and duration. Now, after a long period of economic malaise and uncertainty, some of them are on the way to recovery, having though many hurdles to overcome yet, while others are still struggling to turn a new leaf. The Eurozone, which these countries joined the previous decade with much promise for a better economic future, did not shelter them from the crisis; indeed, its own faults nurtured the conditions that ultimately led to the crisis, and the way it confronted the crisis probably made its consequences more painful than necessary.

The crisis produced severe economic and social consequences in the countries of southern Europe, which upset their politics and in some cases led to a complete reshaping of their political systems. As residents in two of the countries at the epicentre of the crisis, we have experienced its consequences up close. Accordingly, we have devoted a large part of our recent professional lives to the study of its various aspects. While we are critical of the way the crisis was confronted, we cannot escape the conclusion that the countries of southern Europe urgently need to proceed with a range of structural reforms if they want to improve the performance of their economies. Indeed, it is the mere size of the fiscal consolidation effort needed in some of these countries that requires that structural reforms be an integral part of their adjustment programmes: their absence would render the task of fiscal consolidation inefficient, unjust and ultimately unsustainable, both economically and politically. The design and implementation of structural reforms is by itself a challenging task, but becomes extremely difficult in conditions of crisis, under tight fiscal constraints and when the proposed reforms are perceived as imposed from outside the country. This is why the details of the reforms are of utmost importance during crises.

The idea of this book is to examine the structural reforms that have taken place, or have been attempted in these countries, to evaluate their progress and to draw policy lessons from their success and/or failure. We are fortunate to have a great team of collaborators in this project, which includes academics, researchers and economists working in national and international institutions, the European Commission and the IMF, some of whom had first-hand experience in the process of dealing with the crisis in the countries involved. We would like to thank them for their great effort to produce new and original work for this volume. We would also like to thank the Stavros Niarchos Foundation for funding a workshop on the 19th of February 2016 in Athens, organized by the Crisis Observatory of the Hellenic Foundation for European and Foreign Policy (ELIAMEP), which allowed the contributors to meet, present and discuss their work. We are truly thankful to Kyriakos Filinis, Fenya Lymperopoulou and Sophia Tsaroucha for their work in organizing the workshop and to Pery Bazoti for her help with the preparation of the manuscript. Finally, we would like to thank Routledge and in particular Emily Kindleysides, Elanor Best, Natalie Tomlinson and Anna Cuthbert for their support and their patience.

Paolo Manasse and Dimitris Katsikas

1   Introduction

Dimitris Katsikas and Paolo Manasse

1.1 Southern Europe in crisis

The Eurozone debt crisis was, for the most part, a crisis of the European periphery and in particular of the European south. Southern European countries underwent, with varying intensity, a serious and prolonged economic crisis. Many of them (Greece, Portugal and Cyprus) had to resort to bailout agreements, which entailed the implementation of comprehensive economic adjustment programmes, while Spain negotiated a more limited and targeted financial package for its ailing financial sector, at the price of the latter's comprehensive restructuring. Even countries that did not enter a financing agreement, like Italy, came under intense pressure to adjust their economies.

Most analysts would now agree that the principal direct causes of the crisis in these countries were sluggish productivity growth coupled with easy credit conditions. These translated into low international competitiveness and led to unsustainable current account deficits (see for example Baldwin and Giavazzi 2015). With the partial exception of Italy, which also suffered from low competitiveness, but where the major imbalance was the fiscal one, the other southern European countries exhibited very high current account imbalances during the years that preceded the crisis. These deficits, which mirrored high current account surpluses of northern European countries, were very persistent: the real exchange rate could only adjust via price movements, since these countries were members of the Eurozone. These imbalances did not raise particular concerns at the time, as it was thought that they reflected a positive and indeed, sought after, 'catch-up' process. According to this rationale, investors from the capital-rich North directed their funds to profitable investments in the relatively capital-poor South, increasing the latter's growth potential and promoting convergence in the Eurozone. As it is now clear however, these capital flows did not fund productive investment that could foster convergence; they were instead directed towards the non-tradable sectors of these countries' economies, raising wages and inflation, thereby undermining further their already weak international competitiveness, and boosting asset and real estate prices, thereby creating financial bubbles; in some countries, they were also used to fund mounting fiscal deficits. When, in the aftermath of the global financial crisis, there was a 'sudden stop' of the capital flows, these countries had to face the harsh adjustment of a credit crunch.

This narrative of mounting imbalances and sudden stops is a familiar one, as it describes a pattern often encountered in previous crises (Reinhart and Rogoff 2009). A key question then is, why weren't these imbalances addressed before they led to crisis? After all, that these countries could end up in trouble was hardly surprising. Already before the euro came into being, some of these countries were considered EU's economic weak links. Indeed, according to several studies, they should not have been part of the first wave of the Economic and Monetary Union (EMU); in theory at least, the potential for a successful monetary union was limited to the countries of the core (e.g. Bayoumi and Eichengreen 1993). However, the EMU was in essence a political project, and a variety of factors, beyond the scope of this volume, ultimately led to the decision to allow all countries to participate from the beginning.

The failure to prevent the crisis can be attributed to two main factors. First, it is not always easy to discern good from bad current account deficits (Eichengreen 2012). Experts can disagree for years over such issues, and at the time, it was not immediately clear what these deficits entailed. Still, given that a few years after the launch of the EMU, evidence was increasingly becoming available about the growing imbalances, this argument becomes increasingly tenuous as we move in time towards the crisis. A second factor that could explain inaction even in the face of mounting evidence of unsustainable imbalances, are the politics and institutional architecture of the EMU. It is commonly acknowledged by now that EMU's architecture was seriously flawed; its monetary pillar was the only one with any real substance, built around the European Central Bank (ECB), with its clear institutional framework, strong policy mandate and statutory independence from political interference. The economic pillar on the other hand was very weak. The so-called 'preventive arm' of the Stability and Growth Pact (SGP) lacked enforcement powers, and more to the point, only regarded individual fiscal imbalances. There was no real supranational coordinating mechanism to tackle the EU-wide stance of fiscal policy and thus current account imbalances. Multilateral surveillance was supposed to be carried over at the Council, but its Broad Economic Policy Guidelines proved completely ineffective (Pisani-Ferry 2006). As a result, the EU lacked effective institutions with a clear mandate to prevent excessive imbalances. Finally, the ability of economic coordination to address growing international imbalances is limited in any case, because current account imbalances are not under the direct control of governments, so addressing them is not an easy task. With hindsight, it is not difficult to see that, lacking an international framework, domestic interests and politics dictated inaction in a situation where everybody was profiting: banks and other financial players from northern Europe enjoyed substantial profits from their investments, while governments, and the financial and construction sectors of the economy in particular, in southern European countries, were enjoying the benefits of easy money (Eichengreen 2012).

Before EMU, imbalances of such magnitude would not easily occur, as higher inflation rates in a country would lead to periodic exchange rate devaluations in order to restore competitiveness. In turn, expectations of a potential depreciation served to keep interest premia high and capital flows at moderate levels in inflation-prone countries. Once these countries joined the EMU, things changed: they lost national monetary policy and the privilege to issue money, the SGP constrained their fiscal policy, and devaluation was no longer an option. In this context, their tactic of using the exchange rate as a substitute for market-based productivity growth was not a viable option any more (Hall 2014). There was no easy alternative to a long and politically costly effort of major reforms. However, the incentive to undergo politically painful reforms was attenuated by the influx of capital after joining the EMU. Spreads declined to historically low levels and markets effectively dismissed national-specific risk, leading to the imbalances described above. The failure of Eurozone's architecture was due to the fact that the external constraint did not bind: to the contrary, the pressure for reforms was weakened further.

Once the crisis hit, the discussion on reforms came back with a vengeance. Structural reforms formed the second pillar of Eurozone's strategy to handling the crisis in countries receiving bailout funds, the first pillar being austerity, promoted through ambitious fiscal consolidation programmes. Fiscal discipline was also at the core of a new set of measures designed to reinforce the governance of Eurozone. A revised SGP and an intergovernmental treaty on fiscal discipline, the so-called Fiscal Compact, formed the core of the new fiscal regime. The design of both bailout programmes and governance reforms reflected an 'individual responsibility' approach to budget discipline: every country needs to get its house in order, with little consideration for the economic and social costs (Katsikas 2012). EU-wide growth-funding initiatives, such as the Compact for Growth and Jobs, were agreed at the European Council of June 2012, but were never implemented. This approach effectively resulted in an adjustment process, whose burden was entirely borne by the deficit countries.

Structural reforms were thought to be necessary to remedy some of the underlying drivers of the major imbalances that led to the crisis. In other words, fiscal consolidation and labour and product market reforms were considered complementary. As will be shown later in this volume however, the combination of structural reforms and fiscal consolidation may not be as harmonious as some believed. Although there is considerable consensus that structural reforms yield positive results in the long run, evidence is much more mixed in the short term, particularly when reforms are implemented in a negative economic environment. Since austerity policies are bound to lead to economic slowdown, the appropriateness of their combination with structural reforms is far from evident, and if decided upon, reforms should be designed carefully in order to avoid reinforcing the adverse effects of austerity.

Despite the lack of conclusive evidence, this policy mix was the dominant approach to handling the crisis. The reasons were mainly political. An individual responsibility approach did not require any burden-sharing mechanisms, such as requiring surplus countries to pursue expansionary policies in order to facilitate Eurozone's recovery. Their reluctance to assume a more active role stemmed primarily from the primary domestic goal of keeping a balanced budget and from a 'moral hazard' preoccupation concerning deficit countries: facilitating the recovery of crisis-hit countries would ease the pressure for fiscal adjustment and reforms.

Moreover, it was dictated by the politics of the time: bailing out crisis-hit countries that were depicted in the press as spendthrift and/or corrupt was not a particularly popular proposition, especially following the public bailouts of banks during the financial crisis only a couple of years earlier. The rationale of the austerity plus reforms approach was facilitated and domestically legitimated by the narrative of the first incident of the wider Eurozone crisis, the Greek crisis.

Greece was a country evidently in need of major economic reforms and guilty of unparalleled fiscal laxity. As the crisis spread and real estate bubbles started bursting elsewhere, it became evident that the other southern European countries also faced serious structural weaknesses. However, not all of them faced the same structural weaknesses and not all of these weaknesses were on a scale comparable to that of Greece. Moreover, not all of these countries faced fiscal problems. Spain for example, throughout the early 2000s recorded very low fiscal deficits and from 2004 ran fiscal surpluses until 2008, when, due to the financial crisis and the accompanying economic stimulus package, its budget balance turned negative. Likewise, in 2007, the Spanish public debt was only 36 percent of GDP. Spain's performance in terms of debt and deficit was substantially better than that of Germany at the time. Similarly, the fiscal deficit in Cyprus from the mid – 2000s was well within SGP limits, recording a significant surplus in 2007, while the public debt to GDP ratio was on a downward trend reaching 45 percent of GDP in 2008.

This 'individual' responsibility approach to crisis management produced a number of problems. First, for some of the crisis-hit countries, the pursuit of harsh front-loaded fiscal consolidation and the emphasis on labour rather than product market measures resulted in deep recessions and very high unemployment, sparking a social crisis (see for example Manasse (2015) for the case of Greece); second, the economic crisis in these countries worsened their debt dynamics (not least because of the link between troubled banks and sovereign debt), and third, the social crisis that followed the recession undermined the popular support for the reforms and generated political instability. These developments kept uncertainty at high levels in sovereign bond markets for these countries. To make matters worse, core countries also underwent a fiscal tightening at the same time, in an effort to reduce increased fiscal deficits due to their own banking bailout and stimulus packages employed to address the effects of the global financial crisis in 2008. The combination of these policies led Eurozone to a double-dip recession in 2012 and an anaemic recovery for a number of years thereafter.

Despite these problems, many European and national officials from the surplus countries still consider the handling of the crisis as a success. The following account of the Managing Director of the European Stability Mechanism (ESM), Klaus Regling, summarizes this narrative (2016, p. 3):

> Europe has shown a willingness to provide financial solidarity. But countries can only get ESM money on strict conditions. They have to go through a process of often painful economic reforms. It is not something any government takes lightly. But this bitter medicine works. Four countries have successfully exited their programmes and are now success stories.

On the other hand, this policy mix has received strong criticism from many economists (e.g. De Grauwe 2015; Eichengreen and Wyplosz 2016; Krugman 2015). However, even within the economics profession, views are often divergent, as to the appropriate design and duration of the necessary policy recipe. For example, in its annual report 2016/17, the German Council of Economic Experts, stress the importance of continuing the pace of ongoing structural reforms (2016, p. 2): 'further structural reforms are needed that facilitate more flexible wage and price formation and increase labour mobility'.

All in all, it seems that consensus over the appropriate policy response to the crisis is still elusive.

1.2 Economic crises and structural reforms

The moral hazard argument is essentially an argument about the timing of structural reforms. A crisis is thought to be a good time to implement reforms because it exerts pressure on the governments to take measures that would otherwise be politically difficult to take. The idea is not new; the proposition that crises beget reforms has dominated academic research for many years. Already in the mid-1990s the role of economic crises as a significant trigger for reforms was accepted as common wisdom in the literature (Drazen and Grilli 1993; Tommasi and Velasco 1996). This should come as no surprise, since scholarly interest on the issue of reforms became particularly intense following the Latin American debt crisis and the collapse of the Soviet Union during the 1980s; these two events led many countries in Latin America and Eastern Europe to implement (or attempt to implement) a host of reforms to change their economies (Rodrik 1996). The origins of the scholarly interest for reforms notwithstanding, the link seems obvious; we would expect reforms to be pursued when things have gone bad (therefore, a crisis has occurred).[1] It is for this reason that Rodrik complained that this hypothesis is to a large degree tautological and therefore non-falsifiable, since failure to reform may be always attributed to the lack of a crisis 'severe enough' to justify it (1996, p. 27).

Irrespective of which side of the epistemological debate one is positioned,[2] empirical findings seem to somewhat contradict this intuition, as they have produced mixed results; some studies have found evidence of strong support for the hypothesis that economic crises produce reforms (e.g. Pitlik and Wirth 2003), others have found that economic crises do not result in reforms (e.g. Campos et al. 2010),[3] while most studies have reproduced the finding that some types of crises and some types of reforms seem to be related (e.g. Abiad and Mody 2003; Lora and Olivera 2004; Galasso 2014). On the whole, the evidence seems to point to the existence of some sort of positive association between crises and reforms, which however is quite complicated and diverse.[4]

The reasons for this outcome are two-fold: (a) methodological difficulties of measuring and evaluating reforms, and (b) substantive issues that affect the implementation and impact of reforms. Simply put, the findings of the empirical literature could be the result of our inadequate methods to identify and measure reforms in the aftermath of a crisis, or could simply reflect the fact that reforms do not happen as often as we think, following a crisis.

Concerning methodology, despite the fact that a variety of techniques have been employed in the empirical literature, these are not always well suited to the study of reforms. For example, many researchers deduce the implementation of reforms by observed changes in macroeconomic variables (e.g. Drazen and Easterly 2001; Alesina et al. 2006) in the aftermath of a crisis. However, it is obvious that the improvement of macroeconomic indicators may be caused by factors other than the adoption of a reform programme by the government (such as macroeconomic policies, or exogenous positive shocks) and therefore such an approach cannot provide conclusive evidence that reforms were actually implemented and were successful. Other studies employ more direct measures for assessing the promotion of reforms, such as indices based on regulations in particular policy areas. However, this approach may also produce unsatisfactory outcomes, because structural reforms are implemented over time; a change in the regulatory framework may not be enough, as lack of material and institutional resources to implement a reform and supervise it may result in reforms, existing only 'on paper'. Finally, even if a reform is implemented, it is not easy to make a conclusive assessment on its effects, as the reform may need some time to produce results.

The discussion above highlights the difficulty of defining, measuring and evaluating reforms. Indeed, part of the literature confirms the crisis hypothesis, by considering stabilization policies (e.g. Drazen and Easterly 2001). However, stabilization policies are much simpler to design and measure than structural reforms. Accordingly, it is very important for the purposes of this volume to define reforms clearly so as to identify them and distinguish their effects from those stemming from macroeconomic stabilization. According to the International Monetary Fund (IMF), structural reforms (IMF 2015, p. 15):

> typically concern policies geared towards raising productivity by improving the technical efficiency of markets and institutional structures, and by removing impediments to the efficient allocation of resources [. . .] structural reforms may also involve actions to address market failures.

Extrapolating from IMF's list of structural reform objectives, it becomes clear that structural reforms have four main characteristics: (a) they entail lasting changes in the functioning of markets and/or the state, (b) they are not one-off, single measures, but comprise a package of policy interventions, (c) they take some time to design and implement and their full effects are only observable in the medium to long-run, and (d) they typically require consensus from a wide array of affected parties, in order to be implemented and function properly.

The second reason for the ambiguous relation between crises and reforms is that the implementation and effectiveness of reforms can be severely affected by the adverse economic circumstances occurring at times of crisis, by the stabilization policies adopted to address them and by the political and institutional characteristics of the country undergoing the crisis. Moreover, the evidence suggests that some reforms have adverse effects in the short run, and that it takes some time before they produce benefits (e.g. Bouis et al. 2012; Cacciatore and Fiori 2016; OECD 2016). This increases the importance of short-term political factors on policy makers' choices. Governments have to deal with the opposition of interest groups which stand to lose from the reforms (Olson 1982; Alesina and Drazen 1991; Drazen and Easterly 2001), or may have difficulties gathering a required pro-reform majority simply because uncertainty over the distribution of the gains/losses creates a pro status quo bias in the public opinion and its political representatives (Fernández and Rodrik 1991).

These complications during times of crisis reveal the importance of designing policy carefully when contemplating the introduction of reforms. Policy makers should take into consideration the aforementioned problems and employ a strategy of sequencing and calibrating the policy measures that achieve the best results *subject* to the political constraints, so that reforms are not abandoned or reversed.

1.3 Rationale and outline of the book

Finding the appropriate policy design is not an easy task, and as we saw above, the debate on the appropriate policy response to the Eurozone crisis is still ongoing. The idea behind this collective volume is to contribute to this debate by examining the structural reforms that have taken place, or have been attempted in the countries of southern Europe, in order to evaluate their progress and draw policy lessons from their success and/or failure. We believe that this is an important and topical task, not least because structural reforms in most of the countries under examination are still ongoing and will be for some time yet.

We propose two basic dimensions of analysis which in our view determine to a significant degree the success or failure of structural reforms: (a) issues of design and (b) political economy considerations. Even when policy makers are assumed to be 'benevolent' and free from political calculations and pressures, issues of policy design play a critical role in getting structural reforms right. Past experience has shown that factors such as the choice of timing (e.g. upfront vs back-loaded measures), the sequencing of reforms (i.e. their order), the choice and the balance of the appropriate policy instruments, are crucial for the success or failure of reforms. Matters are even more complicated, because in reality, policy makers do make political calculations when designing and/or implementing reforms and they are the recipients of substantial pressure from interest groups that stand to lose and/or gain from a change in the status quo, and whose electoral support they may need to keep their office.

In this context, the contributors to this volume explore the two different rubrics of policy design and political economy analysis either by analyzing individual national cases of specific structural reforms, or by following a comparative approach across countries, with the aim of drawing empirically based lessons for the design and implementation of structural reforms. The methodological approach is flexible so as to accommodate both quantitative and qualitative analyses, which we believe are equally well suited to the study of structural reforms, particularly when the two different angles of analysis described above are taken into consideration.

The book comprises three parts. Part I provides a background for the empirical chapters through a review of the literature on structural reforms both on a general level, and as applied to the Eurozone crisis more specifically. In his chapter, Dimitris Katsikas provides a critical review of the literature on the design of structural reforms in times of crisis, covering topics such as the initial conditions on the ground, the policy mix between fiscal consolidation and structural reforms, the timing (sequencing and pacing) and scope of a reform programme, as well as political economy considerations, in order to identify the factors that account for the success or failure of structural reforms during crises. Additionally, he reviews the literature on the role of the IMF, given that this institution has been a key player in the resolution of the economic crises of the past 40 years, including the Eurozone crisis. The conclusions derived from this exercise forms the theoretical background against which many of the findings of the empirical papers are evaluated.

In the second chapter of Part I, Alessio Terzi applies John Williamson's (1994) framework for identifying the political conditions necessary for the implementation of reforms, to the southern European countries' polities during the crisis. The Eurozone crisis exposed the fragility of the economies of Europe's south. Governments mostly knew what was to be done, but in the majority of cases, they did not know how to garner sufficient political momentum behind their policies. This chapter is thus written as a handbook for reformist governments, identifying the political elements that made reform possible (or impossible) in Europe's South. A comparison with past crisis experiences from the rest of the world allows to draw some general lessons on how to achieve the necessary political conditions for maintaining the pace of reforms.

Part II offers an empirical analysis and evaluation of the design of structural reforms implemented in southern European countries during the crisis. The section includes comparative analyses of similar reforms across crisis-hit countries, as well as reviews of national efforts to promote specific structural reforms. In the first chapter of Part II, Tolga Aksoy and Paolo Manasse study the effects of the crisis on southern European countries' labour markets, by focusing on two important aspects of the latter's response: the impact effect of the recession on the rate of unemployment, and the persistence of high unemployment rates. The authors find that countries lie on a trade-off between 'resilience' and 'persistence': in countries where the labour market institutions, such as employment protection legislation and centralization of wage bargaining, make it more 'rigid (flexible)', the rate of unemployment is less (more) affected on impact by output shocks; but more 'flexible (rigid)' labour markets also imply a faster (slower) recovery from high unemployment rates. Thus, reforming labour market institutions towards less employment protection and more decentralized bargaining reduces the persistence of high unemployment rates over time, at the cost of increasing its short-run response to a recession. As a consequence, implementing front-loaded 'structural reforms' alongside fiscal consolidation may enhance the rise in unemployment and possibly undermine the political support for the reforms. When the authors estimate the contribution of product and labour market reforms to the short-term rise of unemployment in southern Europe, they find positive, albeit small, effects, that are quickly reversed.

In the following chapter, Luis Catao identifies current account imbalances as the main driver of the crisis in southern Europe and pursues a comparative analysis of the main determinants of the external deficits of Greece, Ireland, Portugal and Spain. In particular, his contribution looks at how the mix of macroeconomic adjustment and structural reforms implemented in the last few years has affected the evolution of those countries' external positions. The analysis combines theories of the current account and real exchange rate behaviour with panel data regressions to shed light on the standing of those economies' external 'competitiveness'. The results show that fiscal adjustment and credit tightening were the main factors behind the current account dramatic recovery, but that they cannot entirely account for the sizable current account improvement experienced by these countries. Structural reforms in product and labour market seem to have also played a role in the external adjustment process, by fostering productivity growth and improving unit labour costs, although this did not immediately translate into price competitiveness.

In the first of the three national case studies that follow, Alessandro Turrini discusses labour market reforms in Portugal during the crisis. Because many of the macroeconomic challenges faced by Portugal were rooted in the inefficiencies of labour, product and credit markets, the adjustment programme contained a wide set of measures aimed at increasing the resilience and responsiveness of the economy and at raising its growth potential. Labour market measures received particular attention in the Portuguese bailout agreement. The case of Portugal is peculiar in that many of these reforms had already been discussed extensively among policy makers and experts in the years preceding the crisis. This allowed them to be legislated and implemented in a relatively short time. The focus of the chapter is on the design and execution of reforms of the institutions of the labour market. Turrini shows that a key element for the success of a reforms' programme is 'ownership': the domestic government and the public opinion must perceive that the measures are in the interest of the country and not just external impositions aimed at ensuring repayment of the loan. Moreover, reforms need to be carefully designed, particularly with regard to timing (when to launch a structural reforms' programme) and phasing (how fast should the reforms be implemented) aspects.

In the following chapter, Carlos Cuerpo, Federico Manzano Geli and Carlos Herrero review and analyze the 2012 Spanish labour market reform. The chapter analyzes the impact of the reforms from both a partial and a general equilibrium perspective. First, the paper describes the main pillars of the reform and compares its objectives with the actual labour market outcomes. Second, the authors estimate key labour market relationships, such as Okun's law, the Beveridge Curve and the Philips Curve, as well as other structural measures of wage flexibility and productivity growth, and assess whether these show significant changes between the pre- and post-reform period. Finally, they calibrate a New Keynesian model with search and matching frictions, and find evidence suggesting that the reform has encouraged wage moderation, reduced labour market frictions and has increased the resilience of the labour market to negative shocks. However, their results also show that the reforms had an unintended negative effect: they seem to have worsened the duality between temporary and permanent workers, with the latter bearing most of the employment consequences of the adjustment.

The last chapter of Part II, written by Athanassios Petralias, Marianthi Anastasatou and Dimitris Katsikas, examines the policy mix adopted in Greece. The focus is on the impact of reforms in the business environment and the product markets. The authors try to identify whether reforms, which have lowered barriers to entry, reduced competition obstacles, simplified procedures for start-ups and lowered capital requirements for new businesses, have significantly affected output prices and employment. They control for the effects of fiscal consolidation measures such as increases in VAT and consumption taxes, as well as for 'internal devaluation' measures such as the reduction of minimum wages and the relaxation of employment protection. By relying on model selection methods which allow the authors to measure the time lag of the reforms' effects, they show that structural reforms, particularly in product markets, have reduced inflation and raised employment. However, these positive effects were swamped by the contractionary effects of the depression which engulfed the country, partly due to austerity policies. Moreover, due to their late introduction and lags of their effect, the reform effort could be characterized as 'too little, too late'.

Part III of the book includes three chapters that are devoted to the political economy of structural reforms. Sofronis Clerides describes the build-up of the crisis in Cyprus and its culmination in the dramatic collapse of Cyprus's banking system in 2013. The decision to bail in private deposits in the two largest Cypriot banks was unprecedented in both conception and scale. The paper focuses on the domestic and international political economy factors that helped shape this catastrophic outcome. Clerides's analysis shows that politics played a key role first in the mismanagement of the banking sector which led to banks' default, and later in the way the crisis was confronted. In particular, domestic politics was responsible for delaying the necessary action, and this led to the progressive deterioration of banks' balance sheets that ultimately put the option of the deposits' 'haircut' on the table. In combination with the harsh economic reality, political constraints at the European and international level, such as the widespread opposition against using taxpayers' money to rescue banks, and the considerable presence of Russian depositors, ensured that this option would eventually win out. This choice had an immense impact on the distribution of the burden associated with the collapse of Cyprus's banks.

In the next chapter, Eleni Panagiotarea reviews the experience of Greece and Portugal in reforming their financial sectors. Portugal represents, overall (but not without problems) a success story, while Greece's effort has been less successful. The author compares the measures taken for clearing banks' balance sheets from Non-Performing Loans (NPLs). After reviewing the reforms undertaken during the crisis, which include changes in the financial sector regulation and institutions, the author examines how political economy factors have conditioned the policy choices, mix and success of the reforms. The stark differences observed in the way the two countries confronted a similar problem and their relative success allows a number of conclusions to be drawn. The most important reasons behind the Portuguese relative success were stronger technical capacity, a more favourable economic environment, a more stable political environment and wider political consensus ('ownership') over the reforms.

In the section's final chapter, Federico Steinberg and Miguel Otero examine the political economy of Spain's financial restructuring in the period 2008–14, from the beginning of the Global Financial Crisis to the completion of the Spanish bailout programme. Their analysis confirms a long-standing tenet. Financial systems collapse when they take on too much risk and when they do not have sufficient reserve capital to absorb the losses associated with their risky investments. The Spanish case illustrates what happens when regulators and policy makers fail to act decisively as soon as economic and financial indicators show unsustainable imbalances, and perhaps more importantly, what happens when they face strong political pressures that protect the status quo. Their political economy analysis highlights how the presence of different actors with divergent preferences and objectives can worsen the crisis and delay reform, at a huge cost for society. In the end, the political deadlock, which delayed reform, was only broken when the severity of the crisis threatened to have European and international repercussions and spurred the intervention of the International Institutions. Thus, the Spanish case illustrates how the 'external constraint' can be useful as a means to promote reform.

Finally, in the concluding chapter, the editors of the volume distil the main findings of the evidence-based chapters in the second and third parts, and relate them to the main themes discussed in the chapters of Part I. The aim is to test and improve our understanding of the economics and politics of reforms on the basis of the new empirical evidence presented. This allows us to identify a few lessons on how to design and manage structural reforms in times of crises so as to maximize their economic benefits subject to the political constraints and avoid overwhelming political backlash. Given the ongoing effort in the countries of southern Europe, we hope that this is a timely and useful contribution.

Notes

1 The reasons given in the literature are numerous and they include among other things a sense of urgency, increased costs from the status quo and a change of perceptions and/or the power of significant interest groups. For a review of the arguments, see Drazen and Easterly (2001).
2 In a reply to Rodrik's critique, Drazen and Easterly (2001) argued that the crisis hypothesis could be formulated in a falsifiable form and went on to perform the first comprehensive empirical test of the hypothesis.
3 Nonetheless, their findings show that reforms often follow from political crises.
4 A recent IMF study using structural reform indices for 108 countries for the period 1970–2011, also documented patterns of reform, which are closely associated with international economic crises; however, they alone are not enough to explain all reforms, as globalization and country idiosyncratic factors also seem to play a role (IMF 2015).

Bibliography

Abiad, M. A., and Mody, M. A. (2003) *Financial Reform: What Shakes It? What Shapes It?* IMF. Working Paper No. 03/70.

Alesina, A., Ardagna, S., and Trebbi, F. (2006) *Who Adjusts and When? The Political Economy of Reforms.* IMF. Staff Papers No. 53, pp. 1–49.

Alesina, A., and Drazen, A. (1991) Why Are Stabilizations Delayed? *American Economic Review*, 81(5), 1170–1189.

Baldwin, R., and Giavazzi, F. (eds.) (2015) *The Eurozone Crisis: A Consensus View of the Causes and a Few Possible Solutions*, London: CEPR Press, A VoxEU.org eBook.

Bayoumi, T., and Eichengreen, B. (1993) Shocking Aspects of European Monetary Unification. In: Torres, F. and Giavazzi, F. (eds.) *Adjustment and Growth in the European Monetary Union*, Cambridge: Cambridge University Press, pp. 193–229.

Bouis, R., Causa, O., Demmou, L., Duval, R., and Zdzienicka, A. (2012) *The Short-Term Effects of Structural Reforms: An Empirical Analysis.* OECD Economics Department. Working Paper No. 949.

Cacciatore, M., and Fiori, G. (2016) The Macroeconomic Effects of Goods and Labor Markets Deregulation. *Review of Economic Dynamics*, 20, 1–24.

Campos, N. F., Hsiao, C., and Nugent, J. B. (2010) Crises, What Crises? New Evidence on the Relative Roles of Political and Economic Crises in Begetting Reforms. *The Journal of Development Studies*, 46(10), 1670–1691.

De Grauwe, P. (2015) *Secular Stagnation in the Eurozone.* VoxEU. [Online]. Available from: http://voxeu.org/article/secular-stagnation-eurozone.

Drazen, A., and Easterly, W. (2001) Do Crises Induce Reform? Simple Empirical Tests of Conventional Wisdom. *Economics & Politics*, 13(2), 129–157.

Drazen, A., and Grilli, V. (1993) The Benefit of Crises for Economic Reforms. *The American Economic Review*, 83(3), 598–607.

Eichengreen, B. (2012) European Monetary Integration With Benefit of Hindsight. *Journal of Common Market Studies*, 50(S1), 123–136.

Eichengreen, B., and Wyplosz, C. (2016) *How the Euro Crisis Was Successfully Resolved.* VoxEU. [Online]. Available from: http://voxeu.org/article/how-euro-crisis-was-successfully-resolved.

Fernández, R., and Rodrik, D. (1991) Resistance to Reform: Status Quo Bias in the Presence of Individual-Specific Uncertainty. *American Economic Review*, 81(5), 1146–1156.

Galasso, V. (2014) The Role of Political Partisanship During Economic Crises. *Public Choice*, 158(1–2), 143–165.

German Council of Economic Experts. (2016) *Executive Summary of the Annual Report 2016/17.* [Online]. Available from: https://www.sachverstaendigenrat-wirtschaft.de/fileadmin/dateiablage/gutachten/jg201617/kurzfass_eng_2016_17.pdf.

Hall, P. A. (2014) Varieties of Capitalism and the Euro Crisis. *West European Politics*, 37(6), 1223–1243.

IMF (2015) *Structural Reforms and Macroeconomic Performance: Initial Considerations for the Fund.* IMF. Staff Report, November.

Katsikas, D. (2012) The Power of Credit: Germany and the Leadership Deficit in Eurozone. *Greek Review of Political Science*, 39(May–November), 59–83 (in Greek).

Krugman, P. (2015) 'The Austerity Delusion', The Long Read. *The Guardian.* [Online]. Available from: www.theguardian.com/business/ng-interactive/2015/apr/29/the-austerity-delusion.

Lora, E., and Olivera, M. (2004) What Makes Reforms Likely: Political Economy Determinants of Reforms in Latin America. *Journal of Applied Economics*, 7(1), 99.

Manasse, P. (2015) *What Went Wrong in Greece and How to Fix It*. VoxEU. [Online]. Available from: http://voxeu.org/article/what-went-wrong-greece-and-how-fix-it.

OECD (2016) Short-Term Labour Market Effects of Structural Reforms: Pain Before the Gain? In: *OECD Employment Outlook 2016*. Paris: OECD Publishing.

Olson, M. (1982) *The Rise and Decline of Nations: Economic Growth, Stagflation, and Social Rigidities*, New Haven, CT: Yale University Press.

Pisani-Ferry, J. (2006) Only One Bed for Two Dreams: A Critical Retrospective on the Debate Over the Economic Governance of the Euro Area. *Journal of Common Market Studies*, 44(4), 823–844.

Pitlik, H., and Wirth, S. (2003) Do Crises Promote the Extent of Economic Liberalization? An Empirical Test. *European Journal of Political Economy*, 19(3), 565–581.

Regling, K. (2016) *Lessons From the Crisis and the Next Steps for EMU, Finland Conference*, Helsinki, 9 December. Available from: www.esm.europa.eu/sites/default/files/2016_12_09_kr_speech_helsinki.pdf.

Reinhart, C. M., and Rogoff, K. S. (2009) *This Time Is Different*, Princeton and Oxford, Princeton University Press.

Rodrik, D. (1996) Understanding Economic Policy Reform. *Journal of Economic Literature*, 34(1), 9–41.

Tommasi, M., and Velasco, A. (1996) Where Are We in the Political Economy of Reform? *The Journal of Policy Reform*, 1(2), 187–238.

Williamson, J. (ed.) (1994) *The Political Economy of Policy Reform*, Washington, DC: Institute for International Economics.

Part I

The economics and politics of structural reforms

Theoretical considerations and historical experience

2 Designing structural reforms in times of crisis

Lessons from the past

Dimitris Katsikas

2.1 Introduction

Structural reforms are, by definition,[1] complex policy projects with extensive and long-lasting effects. As such, they require technical expertise, institutional capacity and political and social consensus in order to be properly designed and implemented. The latter is also important for their long-term sustainability, since political and/or social dissent can lead to a reversal of structural reforms (Grüner 2013). In times of crisis the pursuit of structural reforms can become an extremely challenging task. There are three main reasons why this is so:

(1) Crises produce adverse economic effects for households and businesses. From a political economy point of view, agents who have already been negatively affected by a crisis will oppose structural reforms if these entail further losses. The lack of social consensus in turn, may undermine the implementation and sustainability of structural reforms, not least by affecting the political will to pursue them.
(2) Crises typically produce a stabilization policy response from incumbent governments. To the extent that stabilization policies target public expenditures and income, the ability of the public administration (due to diminished resources, including personnel) and the incentives of public servants (due to lay-offs, wage and benefit reductions) to design and implement structural reforms may be negatively affected.
(3) The combination of a crisis and stabilization policies increases uncertainty about the effects of structural reforms and consequently about the distribution of costs and benefits that will result from them. This may create problems both for the design of reforms,[2] but also for their acceptance by economic agents who may prefer the 'safety' of the status quo over uncertain future economic outcomes (Fernández and Rodrik 1991).

It is clear that crises affect all the factors mentioned above (technical expertise, institutional capacity, political/social consensus) as prerequisites for successful structural reforms. Given these complications, how should policy makers go about designing structural reforms in times of crisis? The aim of this chapter is to critically review the theoretical and empirical literature in order to identify key issues and lessons for the successful design, implementation and sustainability of structural reforms. This will provide the historical and theoretical context, against which the findings of the empirical chapters of this volume can be assessed, with a view to reaching a number of policy relevant proposals. In the remainder of this chapter, the literature will be discussed under three headings:

(1) The design of structural reforms. As noted above, structural reforms are complex and technically challenging policy projects. Even assuming benign policy makers seeking only to maximize social welfare, issues of policy design play a critical role in getting structural reforms right. Past experience has shown that factors such the choice of timing and sequencing of reforms, the use of the appropriate policy instruments and the balance of the policy mix, may prove crucial for the success or failure of reforms.
(2) The political economy of structural reforms. Relaxing the hypothesis that politicians seek only to maximize social welfare makes the discussion more realistic. Policy makers do make political calculations when designing reforms and they are the recipients of substantial pressure from interest groups that stand to lose or gain from a change in the status quo. This admission introduces, ex ante, the incorporation of distributional consider-ations into the design of reforms.
(3) The external constraint – the role of the International Monetary Fund (IMF).[3] Typically, countries undergoing a crisis seek economic assistance from the IMF, which comes at the cost of policy conditionality and supervision. Countries in this position are expected to face pressure concerning the implementation of reforms. However, this does not guarantee success for many of the reasons addressed previously, but also because the intrusion of international organizations in the formulation of economic policy in sovereign states raises democratic legitimacy issues, which undermine political and social consensus.

2.2 The design of structural reforms

The literature has identified a number of design issues that affect the successful implementation and sustainability of reforms. Below, we examine the most sig-nificant of these under three headings: (a) initial conditions, (b) the balance between stabilization policies and structural reforms and (c) the timing and scope of structural reforms.

2.2.1 Initial conditions

Researchers have time and again pointed to the significance of the initial condi-tions on the ground when designing structural reforms. This is particularly impor-tant in times of crisis, because adverse economic conditions in the aftermath of a crisis may undermine the effectiveness of the reforms. In this context, there are two types of initial conditions that are particularly relevant for the design of structural reforms. The first refers to *institutional conditions*, that is, the status of the institutional framework of both the markets and the polity in a country undergoing an economic crisis.[4] The initial market and polity institutional conditions are important for a variety of reasons: (a) they determine the magnitude and scope of the reforms required; in a country with well-functioning institutions, structural reforms can be quite limited and focused on specific problem areas, in contrast to countries whose institutions are characterized by widespread inefficiency and/or corruption. This affects not only the scope and complexity of the reforms to be pursued, which translates into both longer periods of design and implementation and more pronounced political economy considerations, but also complicates the stabilization policies that need to be adopted, as the potential benefits of the reforms may be delayed; (b) related to the last point, the initial market institutional conditions in particular, affect the nature and intensity of the outcomes of the reforms themselves. This may hold true for reforms both within a policy area (e.g. employment protection and unemployment income support in the labour market) and for reforms in different areas, which demonstrate some degree of complementarity (e.g. labour and product market reforms) (Bouis et al. 2012);[5] (c) the efficiency of the public administration dictates the capacity of the state to implement structural reforms. It is the public administration that is typically called upon to design and implement structural reforms; accordingly, a public administration that is inadequately (in terms of numbers) and poorly (in terms of quality) staffed, is burdened with bureaucratic red tape, faces low incentives to perform, lacks the necessary resources (both material and in terms of know-how) and is often paralyzed by political considerations, either formally (that is through officially sanctioned politicization of the administration), or informally, is unlikely to be able to design and implement successful reforms; (d) research has shown that solid initial market institutional conditions, such as for example competitive product markets, or a well-capitalized and efficient financial system can increase an economy's resilience to economic shocks, by facilitating adjustment to the new conditions. This in turn translates into a faster and comparatively less painful exit from crises, which facilitates the implementation of reforms (OECD 2010; IMF 2015).

The second type of initial conditions refers to *macroeconomic and fiscal conditions*. These can also produce important impediments for structural reforms. One reason for this is the short-term effects of reforms. Some types of reforms (e.g. product market and mainly labour market reforms) although beneficial for the economy in the long-term, may have adverse effects in the short-term (e.g. Cacciatore and Fiori 2016). Recent empirical research has showed that typically the manifestation and severity of these adverse effects depend on two conditions: (a) the initial market institutional conditions (see (b) above), which may delay the positive effects of the reforms and or even cause adverse effects (Bouis et al. 2012; OECD 2016) and (b) the overall economic conditions, particularly in the case of labour market reforms (Bordon et al. 2016; OECD 2016). For example, a reduction of employment protection is thought to produce positive results in terms of employment as it stimulates demand for labour. However, this positive potential is only realized when the economy is on the upward side of the economic cycle; during a downturn, given the low demand for labour, due to the adverse economic conditions, such a reform may simply facilitate employee dismissals, thereby increasing unemployment. Moreover, research has shown that the effects of the reforms during a crisis and when monetary policy is at the zero lower bound, may be contractionary, as they create expectations of prolonged deflation, raise the real interest rate, and depress aggregate demand (Eggertsson et al. 2014).

More generally, adverse economic conditions may undermine the operation of crucial mechanisms through which the positive effects of structural reforms occur. Thus, for example, the role of well-functioning financial markets is stressed as a prerequisite for translating the expectations of future productivity gains to an increase in today's asset prices, leading thus to positive wealth and collateral effects, which could spur spending by companies and households (OECD 2009; Bouis et al. 2012). Also, well-functioning financial markets relax the liquidity constraints of households and companies, which may be substantial during a crisis (Mishkin 2007). However, it is often the case that a crisis, irrespective of its origins, also affects the operation of the financial system and its ability to provide credit to the economy, delaying or even completely negating the positive effects of reforms.

Finally, the initial fiscal conditions are particularly important, as they affect both the government's willingness and ability to implement reforms. Their impact operates through two channels: (a) the availability of resources for the government to compensate the potential losers of the reforms, and (b) the possibility for the government to implement policies to counter the negative short-term effects of some reforms. The first channel is important for political economy reasons; compensation to groups that are adversely affected by reforms is often necessary to achieve a broad consensus for reforms. This makes reforms easier to implement and more sustainable (Helbling et al. 2004; OECD 2010; Grüner 2013). The second channel is also important, because as we saw above, the short-term effects of some reforms can be recessionary. Accommodating fiscal policy can be used to sustain demand, thereby limiting the adverse impact of these reforms on the economy (Bordon et al. 2016). It follows that in cases where there is no available fiscal space to pursue accommodating and/or compensating fiscal policies, the drive for reforms may stall and their implementation may cause adverse effects in the short-term and backfire. In a similar vein, a large public debt coming due may restrict the ability of the government to pursue discretionary fiscal policy, as a result of large interest payments on both the past and the new debt (Tanzi 2015).

2.2.2 The balance between stabilization policies and structural reforms

The initial fiscal conditions are closely related to the second issue that affects the design of reforms: the balance between stabilization policies and structural reforms. An economic crisis is manifested as the simultaneous deterioration of some macroeconomic or fiscal indicators. Accordingly, the typical response of governments is to introduce some kind of stabilization policy.[6] The problem here is that these policies may complicate significantly the drive for reforms, their implementation and their effectiveness.

The reason is that stabilization policies may have substantial recessionary effects on the economy. Pursuing reforms in an economy in recession is difficult, particularly if the intended reforms have adverse short-term effects, which as noted before is more likely to occur during a recession. Given that the full effects of structural reforms take some time to materialize (Bouis et al. 2012; Duval et al. 2016), we could end up with a vicious cycle of recessionary stabilization policies, which undermine the effectiveness of structural reforms, which in turn intensify the recession, at least in the short-term, thereby reducing the appetite for reforms.[7]

The possibility of such dynamics strengthens the argument about the role of discretionary fiscal policy, discussed above. Following an empirical overview of structural reforms in industrial countries, an IMF report concludes that 'reforms are more likely when there is room for budget accommodation' (Helbling et al. 2004, p. 115). This in turn could go some way towards explaining the mixed empirical results we saw in the introduction concerning the occurrence of structural reforms after crises; whereas the evidence on the relation between crises and stabilization policies is clear-cut, the evidence on structural reforms is more ambiguous, with some types of reforms (e.g. labour market reforms) proving particularly difficult. Given that labour market reforms are likely to produce negative effects in the short-term and are affected negatively by adverse macroeconomic conditions, they typically require some form of compensation, which in the case of a fiscal crisis will not be forthcoming.

More generally, a fiscal crisis,[8] which is followed by fiscal consolidation, may lead to a deep and prolonged recession (Romer 2012); this in turn may stem the drive for reforms and reduce their effectiveness. In effect, the fundamental question that emerges from this discussion is whether fiscal consolidation and structural reforms should be treated as substitutes or complementary policies. The debate on this issue has intensified in recent years as it touches on the core strategy employed by the Eurozone to deal with the debt crisis, that is, fiscal consolidation, accompanied by structural reforms; consensus is still elusive.

The view that structural reforms and fiscal consolidation are (at least partial) substitutes starts with the premise that fiscal consolidation can be contractionary, especially in the near term (IMF 2010; Romer and Romer 2010; Anderson et al. 2014). This finding has been further supported by recent research on fiscal multipliers; these were found to be substantially larger than previously thought, leading to much-reduced growth in countries implementing a fiscal consolidation programme (Blanchard and Leigh 2013). Moreover, the situation seems to be further aggravated when monetary policy is also at the zero lower bound, which means that it has limited scope to offset the negative effects of the consolidation (Christiano et al. 2011). This may explain why the debt dynamics in the countries that pursued strong fiscal consolidation programmes in the Eurozone periphery deteriorated further: the negative growth effects exceeded the direct effects of fiscal deficit reduction (Romer 2012). If this is the case, the policy advice offered is that countries which face a fiscal crisis and are in need of structural reforms, such as the countries of Southern Europe, should undertake the latter immediately, and accompany them by a back-loaded fiscal consolidation policy (Romer 2012).

On the other hand, the view that structural reforms and fiscal consolidation are complementary is first of all based on a matter-of-fact argument, which simply posits that for countries with significant fiscal constraints the need to adjust cannot be postponed since there is no fiscal space to adopt a more accommodating fiscal policy (Tanzi 2015). Pressure for monetary policy to substitute fiscal policy, through for example quantitative easing, cannot solve all the problems that adverse initial fiscal conditions pose and may also create distortions of its own (e.g. in the allocation of capital towards sectors with larger availability of collateral) (Tanzi 2015). In this case, structural reforms, necessary to tackle the structural rigidities of the economy, should go hand in hand with fiscal consolidation. Another argument in favour of this view, is that fiscal consolidation does not always result in economic contraction, and that in some cases it is even possible to have an 'expansionary fiscal consolidation' (Giavazzi and Pagano 1990; Alesina and Perotti 1995; Alesina and Ardagna 2010, 2012). To a large degree, this result is dependent on the composition of the fiscal consolidation package; relying more on reducing expenditure is less recessionary, more likely to reduce the debt-to GDP ratio and more likely to produce an expansionary consolidation (Alesina and Ardagna 2012). In this context, structural reforms that accompany spending reducing policies could be instrumental for reducing the adverse economic impact of consolidations (Alesina and Ardagna 2012; Anderson et al. 2014).[9,10]

2.2.3 The timing and scope of structural reforms

Most studies acknowledge a significant role for the time and scope dimensions in the design of structural reforms. Four issues seem to be of particular importance:

(1) The timing of reforms

While most analysts seem to agree that following a crisis, reforms should be pursued as soon as possible in order to address the structural rigidities of the economy and boost productivity and long-term growth, this view is somewhat qualified by the considerations regarding the initial macroeconomic and fiscal conditions, as noted above. Accordingly, while empirical results show that governments implement structural reforms even in 'bad years', the drive for structural reforms is even more pronounced during the recovery phase, when conditions become more favourable (Helbling et al. 2004, pp. 114–115).[11] Moreover, while there is consensus that reforms should start as soon as possible, how many and which reforms is a matter of debate.

(2) The pacing of reforms

In effect, this aspect concerns the speed of reforms, or as it is often encountered in the literature, the choice between a 'big-bang' or 'shock' treatment, or a more gradual approach. This is an old area of dispute, which developed along with the wider literature on crises and reforms since the 1980s. From a standard economic theory point of view, the swift and simultaneous implementation of reforms is the first-best strategy; however, market distortions may make gradualism a second-best strategy, while political economy considerations complicate things further (Martinelli and Tommasi 1993). The debate became particularly heated during the 1990s due to disagreements on the appropriate pace for the transition of Eastern European economies (e.g. Sachs 1994; Desai 1995). Consensus is lacking, with proponents of the two approaches giving different evaluations on a range of related considerations such as the size of the adjustment costs, credibility, feasibility and associated risks (for a review see, Nsouli et al. 2002). Thus, for example, credibility may be enhanced during a gradual approach if short-term results are favourable (Rodrik 1989), or following a drastic approach, if this is interpreted as a sign of the determination of the government to change the direction of the economy (Funke 1993).

Empirical evidence on this issue seems to lend support to a carefully planned pacing of reforms, even when many of them are undertaken during the same period. According to a recent report by the IMF, 'differences in the post-reform productivity growth underscore the need to calibrate the pace of reform depending on the reform type and the country group' (2015, p. 23). Previous research by the IMF did not address this question directly but found that there are important spillovers across policy areas of reforms, supporting an ambitious approach (package of reforms), which however is appropriately sequenced over time (Helbling et al. 2004). This latter conclusion is supported by more recent research, which shows that a gradual and carefully sequenced approach may produce better results, especially in mitigating potential adverse economic effects in the short-term (Bordon et al. 2016). Finally, the speed of the reforms can be influenced by the nature of the market in question; for example, Boeri (2005) argues and provides related empirical evidence, that labour markets are more prone to partial reforms, for political economy reasons, but also because it is possible to introduce reforms for different parts of the labour market (e.g. new entrants compared to incumbents). In contrast, partial product market reforms are more difficult due to the characteristics of the market and therefore more radical reforms are observed in this area.

(3) The sequencing of reforms

From the previous discussion it is evident that pacing and sequencing are interrelated, since a gradual approach to reforms typically involves a sequencing strategy, while a big-bang approach means that many reforms are implemented simultaneously. While there are many different views on the appropriate sequencing of reforms, a degree of consensus has been reached in a number of policy areas (for detailed reviews, see Funke 1993; Nsouli et al. 2002).[12] For example, stabilization policies and major institutional reforms are generally thought to be prerequisites for most structural reforms (Nsouli et al. 2002). Also, there are theoretical arguments suggesting that reforms in product markets tend to facilitate or drive reforms in the labour market (e.g. Blanchard and Giavazzi 2003; Boeri 2005; Fiori et al. 2007). This would suggest that product market reforms should precede (at least some) labour market reforms, an idea which has received empirical support, as most studies find that product market reforms are more likely to produce positive effects in the short-term than labour market reforms, and these effects are likely to be higher in a more regulated labour market environment (Fiori et al. 2007; Bouis et al. 2012; Bouiset al. 2016). The conclusion that all analyses seem to agree on, is that the appropriate sequencing of reforms differs from country to country depending on a variety of idiosyncratic factors, including the initial institutional and macroeconomic conditions.

(4) The scope of reforms

This aspect is typically encountered in the debate about the 'bundling' or 'unbundling' of structural reforms. What this really refers to is the extent to which reforms should be combined in big package or 'wave', or be pursued in a more gradual and limited way. Obviously, this is an issue which overlaps with both the pacing and sequencing dimensions and some of the arguments discussed above apply to this case as well. Nonetheless, there are some arguments and evidence which speak more specifically to the scope and composition of the reforms to be implemented.

Apart from credibility arguments, reviewed previously, which often tend to cut both ways, the most used theoretical argument for going for an extensive package of reforms is the existence of complementarities between them (e.g. Coe and Snower 1997; Blanchard and Giavazzi 2003; Bassanini and Duval 2009). In this sense, implementing a set of reforms as part of a comprehensive strategy may be argued to deliver better results than piece-meal reforms. Indeed, this effect may be more pronounced in the short-term when the positive impact of reforms may be reduced or even completely reversed, depending on the institutional conditions prevailing in other policy areas (Bouis et al. 2012; OECD 2016). The negative impact of partial reforms, particularly if these remain incomplete can also be seen in a number of crises in the past, where unbalanced reform strategies left countries exposed to significant downside risks (OECD 2010).[13] On the other hand, Rodrik argues that previous experience from developing countries shows that selective targeting of reforms thought to have a big impact is more likely to be effective, rather than an ambitious reform package, which is typically implemented in a short period of time (the big-bang approach) (Rodrik 2016).

Empirical studies seem to suggest that 'bundles' or waves of reform tend to produce better results than isolated reforms (Tommasi and Velasco 1996; Helbling et al. 2004; Bassanini and Duval 2009; IMF 2015). This however, does not mean that all types of reforms should be lumped together or undertaken simultaneously; pursuing reforms in waves is consistent with gradualism and sequencing, both across and within waves. Indeed, according to IMF's recent report, 'successful reforms were typically implemented in sequence and as part of a 'wave' of reforms intended to reinforce and complement one another' (2015, p. 26). Besides, bundling too many reforms together at the same time may stretch institutional capacity to its limits, with negative effects on both their design and implementation. Finally, bundling may entail political economy risks, as political capital can be 'squan-dered' across many reforms, with limited effect, instead of being spent more effec-tively on the reforms that 'matter most' (Rodrik 2016).

2.3 The political economy of structural reforms

The literature on the political economy of reforms is a broad and diverse literature that engages with a number of different subjects, not all of which will be covered in this section. More specifically, it is often the case that the literature discusses indis-criminately stabilization policies and structural reforms, while often political factors (e.g. ideological positioning of incumbent governments, majority vs. representative electoral systems, etc.) are referred to as political economy issues. The discussion that follows focuses on structural reforms and political economy considerations.

Political economy considerations are defined as (typically ex ante) consider-ations regarding the distribution of costs and benefits of structural reforms. The distributional consequences of reforms preoccupy economic agents (households and companies), but also politicians, who are assumed to be self-interested. Accordingly, increasing their reelection probability is considered a key (although not the only) motivation behind politicians' decisions. Political economy dynamics may explain the fundamental puzzle in the debate over reforms: given that struc-tural reforms are supposed to increase efficiency and ultimately social welfare, why is there often so much opposition to them? In the remainder of this section, the principal sources of opposition to structural reforms are identified and then alternative approaches to overcome it are discussed.

2.3.1 Sources opposition to reform

(1) Social opposition[14]

A first, obvious obstacle to reform is the opposition of large social groups. If large parts of the electorate believe that a certain reform will affect them adversely, they are likely to resist it.[15] The political costs associated with such opposition may lead governments to abandon or modify scheduled reforms. Resistance is likely to be even stronger if large parts of the populace perceive the reform to provide benefits to a privileged minority or interest group (such as large companies in the case of a labour market reform, for example), or when it entails the loss of past privileges, which are not sustainable anymore and is therefore typically combined with 'pain-ful' adjustment policies. In the latter case, the uneven distribution of costs and benefits over time, with costs being borne in the short term and the benefits becom-ing manifest in the long term, is bound to increase opposition.

(2) Lobbies

One of the factors long identified in the literature as crucial for the progress of reforms is the role of particular interest groups. Interest groups may block structural reforms if the post-reform environment is worse than the status quo in absolute or even in relative terms (e.g. compared to competing interest groups). The analysis of interest groups' power to lobby policy makers goes back to collective action theory (Olson 1965); interest groups have higher per capita interest in the object of reform and enjoy fewer collective action (free-rider) problems compared to the general public, attributes which make them more effective lobby players. The influence of these groups can be so pervasive that policy makers can be 'captured' over time (Bernstein 1955), or their activity can even influence the design of regulation to accommodate their interests ex ante (Stigler 1974; Peltzman 1976). In this context, interest groups that benefit from a particular status quo will oppose socially beneficial reforms if these entail redistribution from them to the rest of society or other groups. The dominance of such groups has been used to explain lack of reform and more generally economic progress in many societies (Olson 1982), especially when their comparative advantage to influence policy is embedded in economic and political institutions (Acemoglu and Robinson 2012).

(3) Uncertainty over outcomes

Uncertainty over the outcome of reforms and in particular over the identity of winners and losers and the distribution of their respective benefits and losses may become an obstacle for reforms, in the case of both specific interest groups and society at large. Two classic accounts which address the impact of these two sources of uncertainty on the progress of reforms, are those by Alesina and Drazen (1991) and Fernández and Rodrik (1991). The first account presents a 'war-of-attrition' model where two different groups in society disagree about the allocation of the costs of a necessary and beneficial stabilization following a crisis, with each group having a preference for the other group to bear most of the adjustment costs.[16] Given the uncertainty about the other group's evaluation of costs, each group holds out against stabilization hoping to 'wear down' the other group and stabilization is thus delayed, leading to a Pareto inferior result.[17] In the second account, the authors present an argument for the rational rejection of reforms by an electorate, even if it is known, ex ante, that the reforms will benefit a majority of the voters. Uncertainty at the individual level over the identity of the winners will drive voters to reject the reforms.

2.3.2 Overcoming reform resistance

(1) Crisis

Reform resistance may dissipate when reforms are pursued in the aftermath of a crisis. This applies to all the sources of resistance outlined above, as well as politicians' own reluctance to promote reforms that may entail political costs. A severe enough crisis can alter economic agents' cost-benefit calculus by raising the costs of the status quo (Drazen and Grilli 1993); this is likely to make them more amenable to reforms. Similarly, the greater the uncertainty about the post-reform environment, the greater the deterioration of the status quo must be to overcome such resistance (Drazen and Easterly 2001).

However, even a crisis may not be enough. First, people's acceptance of a change in the status quo, especially when this has been institutionalized, may be more difficult than suggested by the crisis hypothesis. New institutional theory in political science has demonstrated the tendency of institutional arrangements to persist in time once they have been set up, even if the original conditions in which they were established have ceased to exist (e.g. Thelen 1999; Pierson 2004). This is due to path dependence; once an institutional arrangement has been put in place, its operation through time shapes the path to be followed in the future by anchoring actors' interests and even their ideas and beliefs to the established institutional order, through processes such as increasing returns, self-reinforcement, positive feedbacks and lock-in (Page 2006). This implies an expanded set of interest-defining parameters, which enter the cost-benefit calculus of economic agents when weighing reforms against the status quo. This is particularly relevant for reforms in areas characterized by fragmentation[18] (e.g. labour markets, product markets and pension systems), where the costs of adjustment may be pushed on to the system's 'outsiders'.[19]

Second, as we saw previously, uncertainty over the expected outcomes of structural reforms may be heightened during times of crises. Moreover, it is often the case that consensus over the origins of a crisis and the best ways to address it is lacking; even expert assessments do not necessarily coincide to produce a consensus view, especially when it comes to structural reforms (Rodrik 1996). Also, even if there is an expert consensus this does not necessarily translate into a consensus for the public. This may be so for a variety of reasons: (a) low credibility of politicians and/or experts. This may be related either to their past record, or to a general lack of trust in a society (Heinemann and Tanz 2008); (b) limited information and (c) behavioural biases including cognitive biases, status quo bias and time inconsistent preferences (Heinemann and Grigoriadis 2013).

Empirical evidence seems to confirm the reservations expressed above; as we saw in the introductory chapter, the crisis hypothesis has produced mixed results in the empirical literature, especially in the case of structural reforms. Moreover, evidence for various measures (e.g. number of parties, majoritarian vs. proportional systems, etc.) meant to capture the impact of political fragmentation on reforms (as a way to test for the war of attrition model) have also produced inconclusive results with some studies suggesting a positive association (e.g. Alesina et al. 2006 (for stabilizations), Helbling et al. 2004; OECD 2010), others rejecting the hypothesis (e.g. Pitlik and Wirth 2003; Lora and Olivera 2004; Agnello et al. 2015) and still others finding no significant relation (e.g. Høj et al. 2006).

(2) Compensation

In principle, political economy issues could be dealt with by adopting an appropriate compensation scheme. If the parties that are expected to incur losses from a proposed reform are adequately compensated they should accept the reform.

Typically, compensation schemes can take two forms: (a) direct compensation (payments) to losers and (b) complementary reforms that compensate losers in one area with benefits in another (Grüner 2013).

The first approach is more straightforward but not without problems. First of all, it is costly; it entails either direct payments paid for by the public budget, or some form of distortionary taxation on the winners of the reforms. In the first case, fiscal space becomes a key condition for successful compensation. Governments with restricted fiscal space and/or in need of fiscal consolidation will be hard-pressed to find the necessary funds for direct payments. In the second case, the cost comes in terms of lost efficiency, since some of the efficiency gains from the reform will be consumed by the compensation scheme (Grüner 2013). Moreover, direct compensation may not work for reasons related to other-regarding preferences (see Grüner 2013 for a discussion of related work).

The design of complementary reforms essentially refers to bundling. The typical argument in favour of bundling reforms together is that it facilitates compensation to losers in one area with gains from other areas, thereby building larger public support. In a similar argument, Rodrik (1996) argues that bundling is a way for reformist governments to bypass opposition and push through structural reforms with distributional implications, by binding them together with reforms and stabilization policies that raise welfare for everyone. Obviously, this approach provides a way out for governments that are fiscally constrained and cannot use direct payments. Another argument in favour of bundling is the time inconsistency problems inherent in gradual reforms. These problems emerge because time affects the credibility of compensation packages. For example, in the case of individual uncertainty discussed above, promises for ex post compensation of losers will not be credible ex ante, since once the reform is passed, a majority (the winners) will back the reform even without compensation (Fernández and Rodrik 1991). Likewise, in a setting with different distributional outcomes for differently sequenced reforms, ex ante knowledge of the possibility that winners of early reforms may block ex post further reforms, will drive the losers of early reforms to block the entire process from the beginning (e.g. Martinelli and Tommasi 1993). In such cases, bundling may offer a way out, to the extent that it introduces concurrently complementary (in the compensatory sense) reforms, thereby rendering compensation more credible. From this, it is obvious that a key factor for the success of compensation schemes is the credibility of the government.

Empirical evidence does not provide clear answers on the political economy of bundling. While, as documented in the previous section, there is evidence that seems to provide support for the bundling strategy as a means to promote reforms, the relevance of political economy factors for such decisions has not been systematically tested. One exception is Lora and Olivera (2004) who find no evidence that political economy considerations affect the bundling of reforms. On the other hand, evidence that product market and labour market reforms tend to occur together in OECD countries (Helbling et al. 2004), seems to indirectly lend support to the idea that complementarities between reforms may reduce resistance, not least because of better compensation opportunities.

(3) Create pro-reform constituencies

Opposition to reforms could also be overcome by building support for them. Obviously, one way to encourage the formation of pro-reform constituencies is compensation. However, governments could also generate support through the design of structural reforms. For example, contrary to the bundling approach outlined above, two oft-cited arguments concentrate on the potential of unbundling strategies to facilitate reforms, by expanding the pro-reform constituencies. First, unbundling may be preferable when reforms are complementary, because people may be willing to accept new reforms in order to avoid losing the benefits of previous reforms (Dewatripont and Roland 1992); second, unbundling may be used to overcome a dissenting majority, if it helps build gradual support for reforms by (growing) constituencies who have benefited from previous reforms (Wei 1997).

Moreover, 'gradualists' argue that time should be allowed for the building of a safety net to smooth the potential adverse effects of some reforms, especially in terms of unemployment. In a gradual approach adverse effects are smaller and thus more manageable, while part of the gains of early reforms could be used as compensation for subsequent reforms (Lian and Wei 1998). Moreover, a gradual approach allows for the building up of a social consensus, through policy dialogue and the proper functioning of democratic institutions (Przeworski 1991). The absence of these elements in shock therapy risks the long-term sustainability of reforms.

Finally, the sequencing of reforms could also be used to create pro-reform constituencies. For example, structural reforms could start in areas where the affected constituencies are politically weaker (e.g. workers in non-typical forms of employment – 'outsiders') and then move to the more politically sensitive constituencies (e.g. workers with regular employment – 'insiders'), once positive results have raised public support for reform (Høj et al. 2006). In a similar vein, reforms could start first in sectors where strong pro-reform constituencies are present (e.g. trade and financial sectors) compared to sectors where reforms are thought to meet strong resistance (Castanheira et al. 2006). Moreover, the complementarities between reforms in certain markets as previously discussed (e.g. product and labour markets) could be used in the context of a sequencing strategy, with reforms in markets that are expected to produce positive short-term welfare effects (product markets) preceding reforms in markets where there may be short-term negative effects and therefore increased resistance (labour markets).

Empirical evidence seems to back the idea that certain types of reforms can facilitate reforms in other areas. Thus, for example, empirical studies suggest that product market reforms can facilitate subsequent labour market reforms (e.g. Helbling et al. 2004; Boeri 2005; Høj et al. 2006; Fiori et al. 2007). Likewise, in some cases privatization policies can facilitate subsequent liberalization (Høj et al. 2006). With regard to sequencing within the same markets, empirical results are more diverse. For example, Abiad and Mody (2003) find evidence that even partial initial reforms may induce further future reforms in the financial sector, while Høj et al. (2006) find evidence of spill-over effects from reforms among different product market segments, but fail to do so for different segments of the labour market.

2.4 The external constraint – the role of the IMF

When a country is hit by a crisis, it often needs financial assistance to overcome it. In most cases this effectively means asking the International Monetary Fund (IMF) for a loan. However, funding by the IMF comes at the price of policy conditionality and supervision. These requirements raise additional policy design and political economy issues, which complicate even further the preceding discussion. This section will review the most important of these issues.

2.4.1 Policy design

In terms of substance, policy conditionality under IMF programmes typically takes two forms: (a) quantitative performance criteria and (b) structural benchmarks. Quantitative performance criteria refer to policy measures regarding macroeconomic variables, whereas structural benchmarks effectively refer to structural reforms (structural conditionality). The content of policy conditionality is predominantly determined by the IMF staff. This is due to the expertise that the IMF is supposed to have, but also due to the inherent power asymmetry in a situation where during a crisis, the debtor country depends on the financial resources of the creditor. The degree of this asymmetry is bound to increase when the debtor lacks material resources (e.g. poor or severely fiscally constrained country) and expertise (e.g. due to low institutional capacity). The ability of the IMF to dictate policy in such circumstances raises at least two important issues related to policy design:

(1) Does the IMF have superior information for the economy? There is a substantial amount of empirical evidence which demonstrates that IMF's projections for countries in a programme are biased, typically leaning towards over-optimistic scenarios (e.g. Musso and Phillips 2002; Baqir et al. 2005; Aldenhoff 2007; Atoyan and Conway 2011). Technical factors, such as incomplete information on initial conditions and country-specific differences in projection errors have been found to be significant sources of the observed discrepancies between projections and actual outcomes (Atoyan and Conway 2011). Moreover, political economy factors such as a country's political alliance with IMF's main stakeholders (Dreher et al. 2008), the receipt of funds by the IMF (Aldenhoff 2007), the size of an IMF programme and the willingness to facilitate a programme launch or encourage local ownership (Luna 2014) may lead to biased projections. Whatever the cause, the result is that IMF's projections often miss the target and this can have serious consequences. The most important of these, for the purposes of policy design, is that biased projections will lead to missed targets, which in turn will lead to additional policy measures to correct the deviations, and/or an adjustment of the targets, all of which will increase uncertainty and make macroeconomic management much more difficult (Bird 2005).[20] This situation may also undermine IMF's signalling function with adverse effects on its ability to act as a catalyst for foreign investment into the country.

(2) Is IMF's policy conditionality appropriate for the country, given its particular characteristics? One of the most important criticisms against the IMF is that it employs a one-size-fits-all approach (Easterly 2001; Stiglitz 2002; Gabor 2010; Islam et al. 2012; Ostry et al. 2016). The prescribed recipe is typically associated with the so-called 'Washington Consensus', a term coined by Williamson (1990) to denote a list of measures promoted by International Financial Institutions (IFIs) such as the IMF. The commitment to this recipe can be attributed to the prevalence of the new classical economic paradigm among the IMF's economists (Cwieroth 2007), the adherence to this paradigm by recipient countries' top economic policy makers (Nelson 2014) or the influence of IMF's main stakeholders, primarily the United States, in promoting a policy agenda consistent with this set of beliefs (Bhagwati 1998). However, a number of studies find a substantial variety in IMF's conditionality (e.g. Stone 2008), while there seems to be some evidence of the Fund gradually becoming more open to alternative policy instruments (Chwieroth 2013). While the debate continues, there are more grounds than the one-size-fits-all argument to doubt the appropriateness of IMF's programmes in terms of policy design. From the lack, or misuse of information described in the previous paragraph, to the influence of political considerations when it comes to the number of conditions (Dreher and Jensen 2007; Stone 2008; Dreher et al. 2015), or the size of the loans (Oatley and Yackee 2004; Barro and Lee 2005), it seems that there is enough evidence to doubt that IMF programmes are always designed with the true economic needs and institutional and political idiosyncrasies of the recipient country in mind.

Such doubts become even stronger when one considers structural conditionality; here, factors such as knowledge of local economic realities, but also of political and institutional characteristics are all the more important. This may be true not only because IMF's local knowledge may be limited or incomplete in such areas, which could lead to inappropriate policy proposals, but also because the political and institutional characteristics of a country may limit the effectiveness of IMF's recipes even when these are appropriate and are likely to increase social welfare. In this context, Rodrik's (2016) critique of ambitious 'big-bang' programmes and his proposal for the identification a few significant structural problems, which should be supported by political clout is particularly relevant. From this point of view then, the continued expansion of the scope and depth of conditionality programmes, described below, which often results in the micromanagement of an entire economy or civil service is bound to lead not only to incorrect policy proposals, but also to potential political and institutional backlash which would undermine the effectiveness of the reforms.

2.4.2 Political economy

From a political economy point of view, the involvement of the IMF complicates things in at least two ways:

(1) Constraints on democracy

When a government seeks recourse to the IMF, there two possible outcomes: either it agrees with the reforms proposed by the IMF, or it does not. In both cases, political economy dynamics raise issues of democratic legitimacy. An obvious question comes to mind in the latter case; should a democratically elected government succumb to the IMF's demands when there is disagreement over policy conditionality?[21] A different question, but one which also touches on democratic governance, is raised even when the recipient government agrees with the IMF on policy conditions. In such cases conditionality makes sense on political economy grounds if it empowers the government against domestic interests that oppose the proposed reforms (Drazen 2002). Here the question is whether the IMF is legitimized in taking sides in the struggle over policy between governments and domestic interest groups.

In the case of structural conditionality, which by definition touches upon established institutions and norms in a political economy, these issues become all the more important. This problem seems to be getting worse as the number and scope of conditionality, particularly in politically sensitive areas, seem to be increasing (Dreher 2009; Griffiths and Todoulos 2014), despite repeated critical internal IMF evaluations and efforts to increase programme ownership.[22] Although ownership is deemed crucial for success, it is an analytically difficult concept to operationalize in the context of conditionality (Khan and Sharma 2001) and in most cases remains elusive. This is hardly surprising given the limits on national sovereignty imposed by a policy programme originating externally and the challenges it sets for democratic rule outlined above. If the perception that dominates is that conditionality is externally imposed, a perception often cultivated by incumbent governments themselves using the IMF as a 'scapegoat' (Vreeland 1999), or that the programme serves the interests of particular interest groups, in or even out of the country (e.g. Gould 2003),[23] then opposition to reforms is likely to be high.

(2) Distributional costs of policy conditionality

The perception that policy conditionality is designed to serve the interests of specific interest groups is often strengthened by the unequal distributional effects of IMF programmes. It is obvious that not everybody is equally affected by structural reforms. As argued previously in the discussion on compensation, the restructuring of parts of the economy means that those adversely affected (e.g. employees in reformed sectors) should be catered for, at least until reforms start paying dividends in terms of increased growth and thus employment opportunities. The case for such considerations is even stronger when structural reforms are combined with stabilization policies in the aftermath of a crisis, as is typical in IMF programmes. Research into the distributional effects of IMF programmes has shown that they tend to increase inequality (Pastor 1987; Garuda 2000; Vreeland 2002; Oberdabernig 2013; Lang 2016).[24] More generally recent research has shown that fiscal consolidations tend to lead to a significant and long-lasting increase in inequality (Ball et al. 2013; Woo et al. 2013). The unequal distribution of adjustment costs (typically in favour of upper economic strata) raise significant ethical and democracy issues, but also, to the extent that increased levels of inequality can reduce both the level and durability of growth (Ostry et al. 2014) point to concerns over reform sustainability. In this context, it is obvious that attention to distributional considerations should be an integral part of any reform programme.

2.5 Concluding remarks

The aim of this chapter has been to set the background for the empirical chapters of the volume, by reviewing the theoretical and empirical literature on structural reforms, with an emphasis on the particular difficulties that emerge when reforms are pursued in the aftermath of a crisis. Based on the rationale of the volume the discussion was organized along the lines of policy design and political economy issues; a third category, labelled the external constraint and more specifically the role of the IMF was also considered, as it has been an important player in the handling of the crisis in Europe's south, and its intervention affects both policy design and political economy aspects of structural reform programmes. A number of issues have emerged that seem to be of relevance for the handling of the crisis that engulfed the countries of southern Europe. The empirical chapters will test the validity of the literature findings, contributing to a better understanding of what is a very complex and challenging issue-area.

Notes

1 See the introductory chapter for the definition of structural reforms employed in this volume.
2 The recent, acknowledged failure of the IMF to estimate properly the depth of the economic recession in countries undergoing a crisis, which led to a miscalculation of fiscal multipliers and therefore to inappropriate policy recommendations, is characteristic in this respect (see Blanchard and Leigh 2013).
3 Although there are other institutions which can act as an external constraint (e.g. the World Bank), the IMF is most appropriate for the set of countries examined in this volume and more generally for situations of crisis-induced adjustment programmes. Also, there is a voluminous literature on the IMF and consequently more empirical evidence available.
4 By polity institutions here are meant both political institutions, such as for example political parties, the parliament, the constitution, the structure of the political system and so on, as well as institutions of the public sector, in the sense of the state apparatus that takes care of everyday governing (public administration). Obviously the former determines to a large degree the jurisdiction, mandate and mode of operation of the latter, with significant knock-on effects on the regulation of the market, while they may also exercise a distinct and direct impact on the operation and institutions of the market.
5 Arguably, one of the factors that accounts for the very different paths that Greece and other countries of the European periphery, such as Ireland, followed in recent years, are the significant differences in terms of the institutions in these countries, going into the crisis. For example, the fact that Ireland's labour and product markets were considered quite flexible even before the crisis, may have maximized the benefits from the internal

devaluation policy that was adopted and the resulting improvement in cost competitiveness, by facilitating the movement of factors from the non-tradable to the tradable sector of the economy; in Greece the internal devaluation policy did not yield similar results, not least due to structural rigidities in the product and labour markets (see for example Katsikas and Filinis 2015; Zografakis and Kastelli 2017).

6 The term 'stabilization policy' is used here to describe both fiscal consolidation and other adjustment policies, like for example internal devaluation measures.

7 Such a scenario is consistent with the evolution of the crisis in Greece. The empirical chapters of this volume will shed more light on this hypothesis.

8 A fiscal crisis occurs when large fiscal deficits are thought to have become unsustainable; this raises fears about public debt sustainability, depriving governments of access to market credit and typically results in an abrupt consolidation of public finances.

9 Nonetheless Anderson et al. (2014) find that there is a limit to this effect, which is related to the size of the consolidation; for countries of the Eurozone periphery with substantial consolidations, it will take several years for the positive effects of structural reforms to become evident. For a similar conclusion for the case of Greece, see Katsikas et al. (2017).

10 In addition to the critique that the idea of expansionary fiscal consolidation itself has received (e.g. Baker 2010; IMF 2010), the problem here is that, as was previously discussed, structural reforms' positive effects typically take time to manifest and in the short-term, they may even have recessionary effects.

11 The only exception is the case of reforms in the financial sector (see Helbling et al. 2004, p. 115).

12 Not all areas where consensus has been reached are relevant for the purposes of this volume. For example, there is considerable agreement that trade and financial market liberalization should precede the opening up of the capital account (for related arguments, see McKinnon 1973; Johnston 1998 respectively); these reforms however were implemented in Southern Europe a long time ago; indeed some of them were prerequisites for participation in the EU and/or the Eurozone and are taken for granted when examining the handling of the current crisis.

13 The dual structure of the Japanese economy with a competitive and extrovert industrial sector and inefficient and heavily regulated primary and services' sectors, is an illustrative example in this context (OECD 2010).

14 In the categorization that follows large social groups (e.g. workers in the private economy) are distinguished to interest groups, which are conceived as narrower, purpose specific groups (e.g. a specific profession or industry).

15 The wave of demonstrations and strikes in France against a labour market reform during the spring and summer of 2016 is a typical example of such opposition.

16 Although the paper refers to stabilization policies, the model is well suited for analyzing structural reforms as well.

17 The 'war of attrition' model can also be thought of as an interest group model.

18 Fragmentation refers to the existence of different segments in a market or system, which are governed by different rules, thereby attributing different rights, obligations and therefore benefits and costs, to their participants and/or beneficiaries.

19 The countries under examination in this volume are often characterized by such dynamics (Heinemann and Grigoriadis 2013).

20 IMF's failure to properly assess the effects of austerity policies in crisis-hit countries is a case in point (see note 2 above). For the deviations of IMF's projections from actual outcomes in the case of Greece, see Petralias et al. (2013).

21 Although IMF is an international public organization and could be thought of as representing the interests of the world taxpayers, the legitimacy of imposing a policy programme in a country against the will of its elected leaders remains questionable, as it effectively removes the authority of policy making from the hands of the elected government.

22 According to the IMF, 'National ownership refers to a commitment to a program of policies, by country officials who have the responsibility to formulate and carry out those policies, based on their understanding that the program is achievable and is in the country's best interest', Statement of the IMF Staff Principles Underlying the Guidelines on Conditionality, Revised, January 9, 2006.

23 Gould (2003) argues that IMF conditionality is influenced by supplementary financiers and in particular by private financial institutions.

24 Some of the studies find a correlation only under certain circumstances, such as when pre-programme external imbalances were severe (Garuda 2000), or only for the short-term (Oberdabernig 2013).

Bibliography

Abiad, M. A., and Mody, M. A. (2003) *Financial Reform: What Shakes It? What Shapes It?* IMF. Working Paper No. 03/70.

Acemoglu, D., and Robinson, J. A. (2012) *Why Nations Fail: The Origins of Power, Prosperity and Poverty*, New York, Crown.

Agnello, L., Castro, V., Jalles, J. T., and Sousa, R. M. (2015) What Determines the Likelihood of Structural Reforms? *European Journal of Political Economy*, 37, 129–145.

Aldenhoff, F. O. (2007) Are Economic Forecasts of the International Monetary Fund Politically Biased? A Public Choice Analysis. *Review of International Organizations*, 2, 239–260.

Alesina, A., and Ardagna, S. (2010) Large Changes in Fiscal Policy: Taxes Versus Spending. In: Brown, J. (ed.) *Tax Policy and the Economy*, Chicago, IL, University of Chicago Press, pp. 35–68.

Alesina, A., and Ardagna, S. (2012) *The Design of Fiscal Adjustments*. National Bureau of Economic Research. Working Paper No. 18423.

Alesina, A., Ardagna, S., and Trebbi, F. (2006) *Who Adjusts and When? The Political Economy of Reforms*. IMF. Staff Papers No. 53, pp. 1–49.

Alesina, A., and Drazen, A. (1991) Why Are Stabilizations Delayed? *American Economic Review*, 81(5), 1170–1189.

Alesina, A., and Perotti, R. (1995) Fiscal Expansions and Adjustments in OECD Countries. *Economic Policy*, 21, 207–247.

Anderson, D., Hunt, B., and Snudden, S. (2014) Fiscal Consolidation in the Euro Area: How Much Pain Can Structural Reforms Ease? *Journal of Policy Modeling*, 36(5), 785–799.

Atoyan, R., and Conway, P. (2011) Projecting Macroeconomic Outcomes: Evidence From the IMF. *Review of International Organizations*, 6(3), 415–441.

Baker, D. (2010) *The Myth of Expansionary Fiscal Austerity*. Washington, DC, Center for Economic and Policy Research.

Ball, L., Furceri, D., Leigh, D., and Loungani, P. (2013) *The Distributional Effects of Fiscal Consolidation*. IMF. Working Paper No. 13(151).

Baqir, R., Ramcharan, R., and Sahay, R. (2005) *IMF Programs and Growth: Is Optimism Defensible?* IMF. Staff Paper No. 52, September.

Barro, R. J., and Lee, J. W. (2005) IMF Programs: Who Is Chosen and What Are the Effects? *Journal of Monetary Economics*, 52(7), 1245–1269.

Bassanini, A., and Duval, R. (2009) Unemployment, Institutions and Reform Complementarities: Re-assessing the Aggregate Evidence for OECD Countries. *Oxford Review of Economic Policy*, 25(1), 40–59.

Bernstein, H. (1955) *Regulating Business By Independent Commission*, Princeton, NJ, Princeton University Press.

Bhagwati, J. (1998) The Capital Myth: The Difference Between Trade in Widgets and Dollars. *Foreign Affairs*, 77(3), 7–12.

Bird, G. (2005) Over-optimism and the IMF. *The World Economy*, 28(9), 1355–1373.

Blanchard, O., and Giavazzi, F. (2003) The Macroeconomic Effects of Regulation and Deregulation in Goods and Labor Markets. *Quarterly Journal of Economics*, 118(3), 879–909.

Blanchard, O., and Leigh, D. (2013) Growth Forecast Errors and Fiscal Multipliers. *American Economic Review*, 103(3), 117–120.

Boeri, T. (2005) *Reforming Labor and Product Markets: Some Lessons From Two Decades of Experiments in Europe*. IMF. Working Paper No. 5(97).

Bordon, A. R., Ebeke, C., and Shirono, K. (2016) *When Do Structural Reforms Work? On the Role of the Business Cycle and Macroeconomic Policies*. IMF. Working Paper No. 16/62. Washington: International Monetary Fund.

Bouis, R., Causa, O., Demmou, L., Duval, R., and Zdzienicka, A. (2012) *The Short-Term Effects of Structural Reforms: An Empirical Analysis*. OECD Economics Department. Working Paper No. 949.

Bouis, R., Duval, R., and Eugster, J. (2016) *Product Market Deregulation and Growth: New Country-Industry-Level Evidence*. IMF. Working Paper No. 16/114. Washington, DC: International Monetary Fund.

Cacciatore, M., and Fiori, G. (2016) The Macroeconomic Effects of Goods and Labor Markets Deregulation. *Review of Economic Dynamics*, 20(1), 1–24.

Campos, N. F., Hsiao, C., and Nugent, J. B. (2010) Crises, What Crises? New Evidence on the Relative Roles of Political and Economic Crises in Begetting Reforms. *The Journal of Development Studies*, 46(10), 1670–1691.

Castanheira, M., Galasso, V., Carcillo, S., Nicoletti, G., Perotti, E., and Tsyganok, L. (2006) How to Gain Political Support for Reforms. In: Boeri, T., Castanheira, M., Faini, R. and Galasso, V. (eds.) *Structural Reforms Without Prejudices*, Oxford, Oxford University Press.

Christiano, L., Eichenbaum, M., and Rebelo, S. (2011) When Is the Government Spending Multiplier Large? *Journal of Political Economy*, 119(1), 78–121.

Chwieroth, J. M. (2007) Testing and Measuring the Role of Ideas: The Case of Neoliberalism in the International Monetary Fund. *International Studies Quarterly*, 51(1), 5–30.

Chwieroth, J. M. (2013) Controlling Capital: The International Monetary Fund and Transformative Incremental Change From Within International Organisations. *New Political Economy*, 19(3), 445–469.

Chwieroth, J. M. (2014) Professional Ties That Bind: How Normative Orientations Shape IMF Conditionality. *Review of International Political Economy*, 22(4), 757–787.

Coe, D., and Snower, D. (1997) *Policy Complementarities: The Case for Fundamental Labour Market Reform*. Centre for Economic Policy Research. Discussion Paper No. 1585.

Desai, P. (1995) Beyond Shock Therapy. *Journal of Democracy*, 6(2), 101–111.

Dewatripont, M., and Roland, G. (1992) Economic Reform and Dynamic Political Constraints. *Review of Economic Studies*, 59, 703–730.

Drazen, A. (2002) *Conditionality and Ownership in IMF Lending: A Political Economy Approach*. IMF. Staff Paper No. 9.

Drazen, A., and Easterly, W. (2001) Do Crises Induce Reform? Simple Empirical Tests of Conventional Wisdom. *Economics & Politics*, 13(2), 129–157.

Drazen, A., and Grilli, V. (1993) The Benefits of Crises for Economic Reforms. *The American Economic Review*, 83(3), 598–607.

Dreher, A. (2009) IMF Conditionality: Theory and Evidence. *Public Choice*, 141(1–2), 233–267.

Dreher, A., and Jensen, N. M. (2007) Independent Actor or Agent? An Empirical Analysis of the Impact of U.S. Interests on International Monetary Fund Conditions. *Journal of Law and Economics*, 50(1), 105–124.

Dreher, A., Marchesi, S., and Vreeland, J. R. (2008) The Political Economy of IMF Forecasts. *Public Choice*, 137(1–2), 145–171.

Dreher, A., Sturm, J. E., and Vreeland, J. R. (2015) Politics and IMF Conditionality. *Journal of Conflict Resolution*, 59(1), 120–148.

Easterly, W. (2001) *The Elusive Quest for Growth: Economists' Adventures and Misadventures in the Tropics*, Cambridge, MA, MIT Press.

Edwards, S. (1984) *The Order of Liberalization of the External Sector in Developing Countries*. Essays in International Finance, No. 156. Princeton, NJ, Department of Economics, Princeton University.

Eggertsson, G., Ferrero, A., and Raffo, A. (2014) Can Structural Reforms Help Europe? *Journal of Monetary Economics*, 61(C), 2–22.

Fernández, R., and Rodrik, D. (1991) Resistance to Reform: Status Quo Bias in the Presence of Individual-Specific Uncertainty. *American Economic Review*, 81(5), 1146–1156.

Fiori, G., Nicoletti, G., Scarpetta, S., and Schiantarelli, F. (2007) *Employment Outcomes and the Interaction Between Product and Labor Market Deregulation: Are They Substitutes or Complements?* Bonn, Institute for the Study of Labor, No. 2770.

Funke, N. (1993) Timing and Sequencing of Reforms: Competing Views. *Kyklos*, 46(3), 337–362.

Gabor, D. (2010) The International Monetary Fund and Its New Economics. *Development and Change*, 41(5), 805–830.

Galasso, V. (2014) The Role of Political Partisanship During Economic Crises. *Public Choice*, 158(1–2), 143–165.

Garuda, G. (2000) The Distributional Effects of IMF Programs: A Cross-Country Analysis. *World Development*, 28(6), 1031–1051.

Giavazzi, F., and Pagano, M. (1990) Can Severe Fiscal Contractions Be Expansionary? Tales of Two Small European Countries. In: Blanchard, O. J. and Fischer, S. (eds.) *Macroeconomics Annual 1990*, Cambridge, National Bureau of Economic Research, Cambridge, MA, MIT Press.

Gould, E. R. (2003) Money Talks: Supplementary Financiers and International Monetary Fund Conditionality. *International Organization*, 57, 551–586.

Griffiths, J., and Todoulos, K. (2014) *Conditionally Yours: An Analysis of the Policy Conditions Attached to IMF Loans*. Eurodad, April 2014.

Grüner, H. P. (2013) *The Political Economy of Structural Reform and Fiscal Consolidation Revisited*. European Commission. Economic Papers 487.

Haggard, S., and Webb, S. B. (1994) *Voting for Reform: Democracy, Political Liberalization, and Economic Adjustment*, New York, Oxford University Press.

Heinemann, F., and Grigoriadis, T. (2013) *Origins of Reform Resistance and the Southern European Regime*. wwwforEurope Project. Working Paper No. 20.

Heinemann, F., and Tanz, B. (2008) The impact of trust on reforms. *Journal of Economic Policy Reform*, 11(3), 173–185.

Helbling, T., Hakura, D., and Debrun, X. (2004) *Fostering Structural Reforms in Industrial Countries*. IMF World Economic Outlook, pp. 103–146.

Høj, J., Galasso, V., Nicoletti, G., and Dang, T. T. (2006) *The Political Economy of Structural Reform: Empirical Evidence From OECD Countries*. OECD Economics Department. Working Paper No. 501.

IMF (2010) *Will It Hurt? Macroeconomic Effects of Fiscal Consolidation.* IMF World Economic Outlook, pp. 93–124.

IMF (2015) *Structural Reforms and Macroeconomic Performance: Initial Considerations for the Fund.* IMF. Staff Report, November.

Islam, I., Ahmed, I., Roy, R., and Ramos, R. (2012) *Macroeconomic Policy Advice and the Article IV Consultations: A Development Perspective.* ILO. Research Paper No. 2.

Johnston, R. B. (1998) *Sequencing Capital Account Liberalizations and Financial Sector Reform.* IMF Paper on Policy Analysis and Assessment.

Katsikas, D., Anastasatou, M., Nitsi, E., Petralias, A., and Filinis, K. (2017) *Structural Reforms in Greece During the Crisis (2010–2014)*, Athens, Bank of Greece (forthcoming in Greek).

Katsikas, D., and Filinis, K. (2015) *Crisis and Sustainable Growth: On the Inability to Reform the Production Model of the Greek Economy.* Centre of Planning and Economic Research (KEPE). Greek Economy No. 21 (in Greek).

Katsikas, D., Filinis, K., and Anastasatou, M. (eds.) (2017) *Understanding the Greek Crisis: Answers to Key Questions About the State, the Economy and Europe*, Athens, Papazisis Publications (in Greek).

Khan, M. S., and Sharma, S. (2001) *IMF Conditionality and Country Ownership of Programs.* IMF. Working Paper No. 01(142).

Lang, V. F. (2016) The Democratic Deficit and Its Consequences: The Causal Effect of IMF Programs on Inequality. *9th Annual Conference on The Political Economy of International Organizations*, Salt Lake City, Utah, 7–9 January.

Lian, P., and Wei, S.-J. (1998) To Shock or Not to Shock? Economics and Political Economy of Large-Scale Reform. *Economics & Politics*, 10, 161–183.

Lipton, D., and Sachs, J. (1990) Privatization in Eastern Europe: The Case of Poland. *Brookings Papers on Economic Activity*, 2, 293–341.

Lora, E., and Olivera, M. (2004) What Makes Reforms Likely: Political Economy Determinants of Reforms in Latin America. *Journal of Applied Economics*, 7(1), 99.

Luna, F. (2014) *IMF Forecasts in the Context of Program Countries.* IMF Independent Evaluation Office. Background Paper No. 14(05).

Martinelli, C., and Tommasi, M. (1993) Sequencing of Economic Reforms in the Presence of Political Constraints. *Economics & Politics*, 9(2), 115–131.

McKinnon, R. I. (1973) *Money and Capital in Economic Development.* Washington, Brookings Institution.

Mishkin, F. S. (2007) *Financial instability and monetary policy.* Speech at the Risk USA 2007 Conference, New York, 5 November 2007. BIS Review 127/2007. [Online]. Available from: http://www.bis.org/review/r071108e.pdf.

Musso, A., and Phillips, S. (2002) *Comparing Projections and Outcomes of IMF Supported Programs.* IMF. Staff Paper No. 49.

Nelson, S. C. (2014) Playing Favourites: How Shared Beliefs Shape the IMF's Lending Decisions. *International Organization*, 68(2), 297–328.

Nsouli, M. S. M., Rached, M. M., and Funke, M. N. (2002) *The Speed of Adjustment and the Sequencing of Economic Reforms: Issues and Guidelines for Policymakers.* IMF. Working Paper No. 02/132.

Oatley, T., and Yackee, J. (2004) American Interests and IMF Lending. *International Politics*, 41(3), 41–429.

Oberdabernig, D. A. (2013) Revisiting the Effects of IMF Programs on Poverty and Inequality. *World Development*, 46, 113–142.

OECD (2009) Structural Reform at a Time of Financial Crisis. In: *OECD Economic Policy Reforms: Going for Growth*, Paris, OECD Publishing, pp. 17–25.

OECD (2010) *Regulatory Reform for Recovery: Lessons From Implementation During Crisis.* OECD. Reviews of Regulatory Reform. Paris, OECD Publishing.

OECD (2016) Short-Term Labour Market Effects of Structural Reforms: Pain Before the Gain? In: *OECD Employment Outlook 2016*, Paris, OECD Publishing.

Olson, M. (1965) *The Logic of Collective Action: Public Goods and the Theory of Groups*, Cambridge, MA, Harvard University Press.

Olson, M. (1982) *The Rise and Decline of Nations*: *Economic Growth, Stagflation, and Social Rigidities*, New Haven, CT, Yale University Press.

Ostry, J. D., Berg, A., and Tsangarides, C. (2014) *Redistribution, Inequality, and Growth.* IMF. Staff Discussion Note No. 14/02.

Ostry, J. D., Loungani, P., and Furceri, D. (2016) Neoliberalism: Oversold? *Finance and Development*, June 38–41.

Page, S. E. (2006) Path Dependence. *Quarterly Journal of Political Science*, 1(1), 87–115.

Pastor, M. (1987) The Effects of IMF Programs in the Third World: Debate and Evidence From Latin America. *World Development*, 15(2), 249–262.

Peltzman, S. (1976) Towards a More General Theory of Regulation. *Journal of Law and Economics*, 19, 211–240.

Perotti, R. (2012) The 'Austerity Myth': Gain Without Pain? In: Alesina, A. and Giavazzi, F. (eds.) *Fiscal Policy After the Financial Crisis*, Chicago, IL, University of Chicago Press, pp. 307–354.

Petralias, A., Petros, S., and Prodromídis, P. (2013) *Greece in Recession: Economic Predictions, Mispredictions and Policy Implications.* Hellenic Observatory Papers on Greece and Southeast Europe, London School of Economics and Political Science. GreeSE Paper No. 75.

Pierson, P. (2004) *Politics in Time: History, Institutions, and Social Analysis.* Princeton and Oxford, Princeton University Press.

Pitlik, H., and Wirth, S. (2003) Do Crises Promote the Extent of Economic Liberalization? An Empirical Test. *European Journal of Political Economy*, 19(3), 565–581.

Przeworski, A. (1991) *Democracy and the Market: Political and Economic Reforms in Eastern Europe and Latin America*, Cambridge, Cambridge University Press.

Rodrik, D. (1989) Promises, Promises: Credible Policy Reform via Signalling. *The Economic Journal*, 99, 756–772.

Rodrik, D. (1996) Understanding Economic Policy Reform. *Journal of Economic Literature*, 34(1), 9–41.

Rodrik, D. (2016) The Elusive Promise of Structural Reform. *Milken Institute Review*, 18(2), 26–35.

Romer, C. (2012) *Fiscal Policy in the Crisis: Lessons and Policy Implications.* IMF Fiscal Forum 18.

Romer, C., and Romer, D. (2010) The Macroeconomic Effects of Tax Changes: Estimates Based on a New Measure of Fiscal Shocks. *American Economic Review*, 100(3), 763–801.

Sachs, J. (1994) Life in the Economic Emergency Room. In Williamson, J. (ed.) *The Political Economy of Policy Reform*, Washington, DC, Institute for International Economics.

Stigler, G. J. (1974) The Theory of Economic Regulation. *Bell Journal of Economics and Management*, 2(1), 3–21.

Stiglitz, J. E. (2002) *Globalization and Its Discontents*, New York: Norton.

Stone, R. W. (2008) The Scope of IMF Conditionality. *International Organization*, 62(4), 589–620.

Tanzi, V. (2015) Crises, Initial Conditions and Economic Policies. In: *Structural Reforms and Fiscal Consolidation: Trade-Offs or Complements?* Berlin, German Federal Ministry of Finance & IMF.

Thelen, K. (1999) Historical institutionalism in comparative politics. *Annual Review of Political Science*, 2, 369–404.

Tommasi, M., and Velasco, A. (1996) Where Are We in the Political Economy of Reform? *The Journal of Policy Reform*, 1(2), 187–238.

Tompson, W., and Dang, T. T. (2010) *Advancing Structural Reforms in OECD Countries: Lessons From Twenty Case Studies*. OECD Economics Department, Working Paper No. 757.

Vreeland, J. R. (1999) The IMF: Lender of Last Resort or Scapegoat? *Conference Paper for the Midwest Political Science Association Annual Meeting*, Chicago, IL, 15–17 April.

Vreeland, J. R. (2002) The Effect of IMF Programs on Labor. *World Development*, 30(1), 121–139.

Wei, S. J. (1997) Gradualism versus Big Bang: Speed and Sustainability of Reforms. *The Canadian Journal of Economics*, 30(4b), 1234–1247.

Williamson, J. (1990) What Washington Means By Policy Reform. In: Williamson, J. (ed.) *Latin American Readjustment: How Much Has Happened*, Washington, DC, Institute for International Economics.

Woo, J., Bova, E., Kinda, T., and Zhang, Y. S. (2013) *Distributional Consequences of Fiscal Consolidation and the Role of Fiscal Policy: What Do the Data Say?* IMF. Working Paper No. 13(195).

World Bank (2015) *Doing Business 2015: Going Beyond Efficiency*. Washington, DC.

Zografakis, S., and Kastelli, I. (2017) Is It True that Reducing Labour Costs Is Sufficient to Improve the Competitiveness of the Greek Economy? In Katsikas, D., Filinis, K. and Anastasatou, M. (eds.), *Understanding the Greek Crisis: Answers to Key Questions About the State, the Economy and Europe*. Athens, Papazisis Publications (in Greek).

3 The political conditions for economic reform in Europe's South

Alessio Terzi[1]

3.1 Introduction

In May 2010, Greece entered an International Monetary Fund (IMF)-European Union (EU) macroeconomic adjustment programme, officially marking the beginning of the so-called Euro area crisis. For several European countries, the following years were characterized by a period of financial instability, which has few precedents among developed economies in the post-World War era. Greece, Ireland, Portugal, and Cyprus were pushed into a fully fledged IMF programme, while Spain received a bailout to restructure its banking sector. Italy, while avoiding financial assistance, at the peak of the crisis was refinancing its long-term debt at an unsustainable interest rate of over 7 percent (Pisani-Ferry et al. 2013).

As discussed more in detail in the next country-focused chapters, 10 years of single currency led to the build-up of large macroeconomic imbalances (Darvas 2012; Sapir et al. 2014). Some countries, most of which are located in Europe's south, experienced a significant loss of competitiveness, marked by wage inflation that had not been matched by labour productivity gains (Thimann 2015). At the same time, the bulk of economic activity switched from a more competitive tradable sector, to non-tradables; current account deficits widened and so did, in some instances, budget deficits (see Figure 3.1).

Governments were hence under pressure to quickly reignite growth in the aftermath of the Global Financial Crisis of 2008–09, while keeping public accounts in order. Importantly, being part of a monetary union meant that this sharp loss of competitiveness could not be offset by an exchange rate devaluation. Deep economic reform programmes were hence needed across the board, often marked under the term 'internal adjustment' or 'structural reforms'.

Some countries in Europe's south implemented reforms within the framework of an IMF-EU programme,[2] others under technocratic governments (Italy), while some countries felt the need to call early elections and obtain from voters a fresh mandate for reform (Spain, Greece, Italy). In all instances, the need for change was clear, not only called for by European institutions, foreign institutional creditors and financial markets, but also by voters, who saw (youth) unemployment rates balloon and demanded political action (Terzi 2015b).

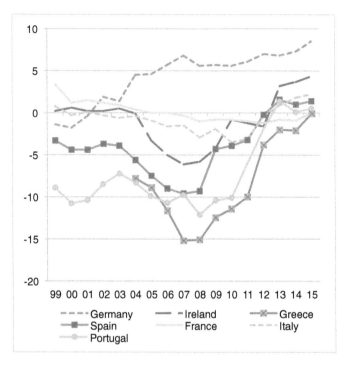

Figure 3.1 Current account balances as % of GDP, selected Euro area countries

Source: Eurostat

Implementing wide-ranging structural reforms is however no walk in the park for any government at any given time, and Europe was no exception. Issues of timing, sequencing, packaging and prioritization remain largely unresolved in the economic literature. On top of this, broad reform programmes usually face obstacles belonging to three general classes:

(1) **Technical knowledge**: this is the case of a reformist government, which is convinced that change is needed, however does not know which reforms would be needed or how to design them. This instance of 'you don't know what to do' might be of relevance in a developing country context, where indeed the IMF is often involved in regular work of technical assistance, but is unlikely to have played a major role as an obstacle to reforming Europe's South after the inception of the Euro crisis.

Even conceding that the quality of the bureaucratic apparatus was far from stellar in some European capitals (Terzi 2015a), programme countries were advised by top-notch technical experts of the EU Commission,

IMF, and the European Central Bank (ECB). Greece also benefited from the assistance of a purposely made facility: the Task Force for Greece, consisting of experts and consultants from other EU national administrations. Spain's government was advised by high-profile private sector consultants such as Oliver Wyman and BlackRock, on top of the Troika (the European Commission, the ECB and the IMF), in its restructuring of the banking sector. From 2011, Italy had a technocratic government led by Bocconi University President and economist Mario Monti. Moreover, its economic problems were widely known and had been debated for years in the run up to the crisis, as evidenced, for example, in successive editions of the IMF's Article IV report.[3]

(2) **Political will**: this is the case of a government that does not see the need to implement significant reforms, as the status quo is perceived as broadly sustainable. At a time of economic crisis, it could be that a head of state or government misjudges the size and urgency of the challenges facing his/her country and believes a mild cure will be sufficient.

> While this cavalier behaviour might have played a role in the initial phases of the crisis, it quickly became evident, as discussed above, that there was no real alternative to adopting wide-reaching reform programmes. Aside from the financial pressure mounting, large capital flights, and the rising probability of a banking system meltdown, most Southern governments saw unemployment rates soar (Figure 3.2). Moreover, pressure from European institutions and other member states providing urgent reform reminders was sizable. As such, in principle, the status quo bias argument should not have played a crucial role in determining the extent of reform implementation in Europe's south: governments were well aware that wide-ranging reform programmes were needed, and urgently.

(3) **The Juncker dilemma**: This class of obstacles can be exemplified best by the famous quote from the then Luxembourgish Prime Minister Jean-Claude Juncker who, speaking of economic reforms, stated in 2007: '*We all know what to do, we just don't know how to get re-elected after we've done it*'. Some governments might have all the technical expertise and political goodwill to put in place a wide-ranging economic reform programme, but simply do not know how to garner and sustain political support for it. This can be due to the presence of strong interest groups, to wobbly majorities in parliament or to the composition of the electorate, just to mention a few, and the political economy literature is wide on this topic (see Katsikas, this volume). This element is likely to have played a major role in determining reform adoption in Europe's south throughout the crisis.

The Juncker dilemma constitutes therefore the starting point for this chapter, which looks at the political conditions that enabled policy reform in Europe's south.

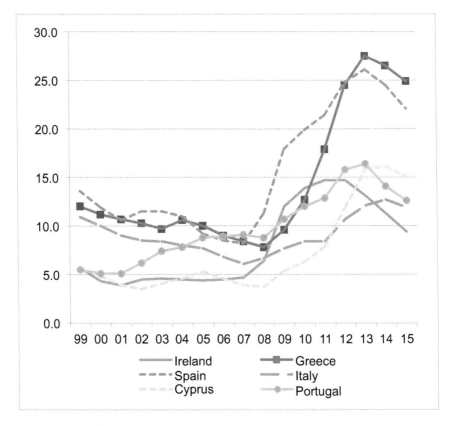

Figure 3.2 Unemployment rates, selected Euro area countries
Source: Eurostat

Some policy pundits during the crisis were effectively pushing governments to adopt a 'kamikaze-mode' and ram reform bills through parliament without having first garnered clear support for them. This make-or-break approach might have worked in a few instances, but at a very high risk, and is definitely not an example of good politics. This chapter is hence written as a handbook for reformist governments, and is largely inspired by an editorial effort carried out in 1994 by John Williamson for the Institute of International Economics.

Williamson (1994) gathered evidence from 13 case studies in order to identify necessary and/or sufficient political conditions that would enable 'technopols'[4] to implement policy reform. To this purpose, he asked high-level policy makers from Europe, Asia, Australasia, and Latin America to comment on their country's experience with radical reform programmes: successes, failures and lessons learnt. Interestingly, of the 13 countries considered, two were not successful in their reform efforts – namely Brazil in 1987 and Peru in 1980. Lessons can obviously be drawn also from these cases.

The focus on political conditions was due to the fact that, at the time, reform programmes were not perceived to be held back by lack of technical knowledge, but rather political will and feasibility. This is because a consensus had been reached among 'all serious economists' regarding the set of standard policies that 'were expected to yield good results in due course', especially regarding the stabilization phase of a crisis (Williamson 1994, p. 18). The so-called 'Washington Consensus' can be summarized as:

- fiscal discipline;
- public expenditure rationalization;
- tax reforms, aimed at broadening the tax base and lowering the marginal tax rate;
- financial liberalization;
- low nominal exchange rates, aimed at kick-starting the economy;
- trade liberalization;
- abolition of barriers to foreign direct investment;
- privatization of state enterprises;
- deregulation, aimed at promoting domestic competition; and
- protection of property rights.

Although later research partially modified this mantra, introducing the concept of so-called 'second generation reforms' and stressing the importance of institutional quality (Krueger 2000), in the early 1990s the pressing issue was to identify the political economy conditions that would allow the Washington Consensus measures to be successfully implemented.

By virtue of the fact that most radical economic reform programmes had taken place in emerging and developing countries, Williamson's book was not very much focused on developed economies. However, the inclusion of the likes of Australia and New Zealand was part of an attempt to produce results that could be as generalizable as possible and of use to any technopol. In spite of this, one can still wonder how much of the Williamson (1994) findings are of relevance for a developed southern European context over 20 years down the road.

The European context is definitely different from several standpoints:

(1) Type of crisis: first of all, evidently the kind of crisis that hit Europe from 2010 onwards is different in nature from the standard sovereign debt, currency or banking crisis that affected the countries considered by Williamson (1994). Though some of them were in a fixed exchange rate regime, none of them was in a monetary union like the euro. Moreover, as stressed by Darvas (2012), 10 years of EMU had led to the build-up of unprecedented imbalances. These two facts combined meant that the toolkit available to European policy makers did not include exchange rate devaluations, and their to-do list was at least partially different from previous crisis episodes.

(2) Type of countries: while some countries analyzed by Williamson (1994) can be considered developed (Australia in 1983, New Zealand in 1984) or Western European (Spain in 1982, Portugal in 1985), we can generally say that his sample is broadly different in nature from Europe nowadays. Though with large heterogeneity, Europe's southern countries are very well placed in worldwide rankings in terms of quality of institutions, of respect of the rule of law, of political and media freedom, of levels of education. This clearly could have potential repercussions on the acceptability of reform programmes by the population, or on the capacity of a government to implement complex policy packages under time pressure, among other things. Finally, many of the 'Washington Consensus' policies would not apply to EU countries, where financial liberalization is not an issue any more, nor is trade liberalization, being part of the Single Market.

(3) Different period: although only a few decades separate the Euro area crisis from the bulk of the Williamson (1994) episodes, the historic and economic context today is definitely different from back then. Aside from general considerations about globalization, the ICT revolution, the rise of China, the fall of communism as an ideology, the ballooning of global debt, it must be noted that the Euro area crisis happened simultaneously, or in the immediate aftermath, of the worst global depression since 1929. This, inevitably, influenced the overall macroeconomic context and credibly hampered the effect of reform programmes. An obvious example, mentioned also in Terzi (2015a), is fiscal consolidation in Greece (broadly points 1 and 2 of the Washington Consensus outlined above) and how this has proved highly detrimental at a time when the country's major trade partners (in the rest of Europe) were engaging in qualitatively similar policies. This, in turn, has alimented a deepening of the recession and political instability, which has weighed on the government's capacity to implement further reforms.

That being said, it is also true that past crisis episodes should not be wholly disregarded, as several patterns seem to repeat themselves across time and countries: a point convincingly stressed by Reinhart and Rogoff (2009). In this particular instance, it is noteworthy that the Euro area crisis displayed several elements in common with past crises and macroeconomic adjustment episodes around the world. In particular, (a) heavy financial market pressure on domestic banks and sovereign bonds, which sparked the call for (b) sharp fiscal consolidation and far-reaching (yet unpopular) (c) structural reforms. Before the ECB enacted its Outright Monetary Transactions (OMT), Euro area governments were effectively (d) borrowing in a foreign currency – another popular trait of past crisis episodes (De Grauwe and Ji 2013). Moreover, at least for some countries this whole process was accompanied by (e) the presence of international financial institutions and strict conditional lending, as in many emerging markets over the past decades.

Perhaps the single largest overarching mistake made during the crisis, which applies also by-and-large to the days when the euro was designed, was an act of hubris by policy makers, convinced that 'Europe was different' and some macroeconomic events happened only in emerging economies. Many lessons from the past were hence completely disregarded.

The rest of this chapter will be dedicated to reading the Euro area crisis through the lenses of Williamson (1994), identifying the political elements that hampered or enabled reform in Europe's south. Comparing this with past crisis experiences from the rest of the world will allow light to be shed on how much the European act of hubris was justified.

3.2 Williamson's conditions for reform

In order to structure the discussion of policy experts about their country experience, Williamson formulated some hypotheses about the circumstances under which policy reform is possible. The findings, which were based both on past political economy literature and on the accepted wisdom at the time, are briefly mentioned here below.

The (a) *authoritarian regime* hypothesis postulated that reforms were easier to undertake in a non-democratic context, whereas the (b) *rightist government* hypothesis wondered whether right-wing governments had an upper hand at implementing a Washington Consensus-type of reform agenda.

The (c) *crisis* hypothesis built on the wide perception that crisis situations help to accelerate the reform process (Drazen and Grilli 1993). The (d) *honeymoon* hypothesis stated that governments are more likely to act in the immediate aftermath of an election, especially if they campaigned on a pro-reform agenda (e) *political base* hypothesis).

This, contrasts sharply with the (f) *Voodoo politics* view that politicians should pretend they don't believe in reforms, only to then renege on their promises after they get elected. Williamson (1994) also wondered whether a (g) *demoralized* (or fragmented) *opposition* contributed to reform implementation, or whether a (h) *visionary leader* was needed, also with the aim of building a (i) *social consensus* around reforms.

For what concerns the internal organization of the government team, Williamson explored whether it mattered to have a (j) *coherent team* in charge of economic policy, better if led by a (k) *technocrat*.

The final hypotheses put to the test of policy experts were whether having a broad (l) *comprehensive programme* helped push reforms forward, and whether the presence of international financial institutions (like the IMF or World Bank) providing (m) *external aid* and conditionality contributed to a positive reform outcome.

Williamson drew important conclusions from the 13 (countries) by 13 (hypotheses) matrix. First of all, it is interesting to note that there is no necessary and sufficient condition for reform. However, some patterns do emerge. The authoritarian and rightist government hypotheses were rejected in full, with several cases of left-wing democracies pushing through important policies. The presence of a visionary leader and of a coherent team found very strong support, though partially disproved by the case of New Zealand in 1984. Having a strong political base in favour of reform was obviously important throughout the spectrum of countries considered, although in post-soviet Poland popular support quickly eroded and, while this made the government's life more complicated, it did not stall the reform process.

Crises, which are widely acknowledged to play a crucial role in destabilizing interest groups and forcing a government's hand into reforms, did indeed characterize most episodes analyzed. However, while playing a critical role, a sudden sharp crisis situation was neither a necessary nor a sufficient condition for reform. Countries from across the geographical spectrum (Australia, Colombia, and Portugal) showed it is possible to go down the route of far-reaching reforms even without the presence of this push factor.

Another push factor that is widely acknowledged to be true, the honeymoon hypothesis, was confirmed in several cases. However, there was also a surprising number of counterexamples: both Felipe Gonzales in Spain and Hawke in Australia did not push through reforms in their first months in office. Nor did Barco in Columbia, who actually waited until his last months in office. As such Williamson concluded that no firm generalizations could be made on this topic.

Regarding the effectiveness of external aid, policy makers stressed that the presence of the IMF strengthened the hand of reformers, while enhancing the credibility of the overall reform strategy. On the other hand, if a government was not committed to reform, even the strictest conditionality would not yield results. Again, however, the presence of the IMF was not perceived as neither necessary nor sufficient, as many countries (in particular the more developed ones, like Australia and New Zealand, Portugal, and Spain) had put in place large reform programmes with very limited or no external support.

One hypothesis that was almost unequivocally confirmed was the fact that the presence of a weak, fragmented or demoralized opposition made the implementation of reforms easier. Similarly, the presence of a leader with a vision of where the country was going (though not necessarily how to get there) was a common trait in broadly all cases analyzed.[5]

The importance of building a social consensus for reform was left instead open to debate. In particular, Williamson came to the conclusion that while intellectual persuasion might not be needed to implement reforms, particularly at a time of deep crisis, having built it will ensure that measures are not reversed as soon as the emergency situation alleviates.

In terms of the characteristics of the leadership, all cases analyzed displayed a coherent team of economic advisors. However, it must be noted that this condition was satisfied also in Brazil and Peru, the two countries considered where policy reform did not succeed. As such, it is definitely not a sufficient condition for success. Having a technocratic leader, on the other hand, was not really found to be fundamental, though with some qualifiers.[6]

No clear-cut conclusions were reached regarding the need for a comprehensive reform programme, also because the definition of the latter required an exact evaluation of what was needed in a country. Voodoo politics was instead legitimized by Williamson, who noted that several reform packages were implemented in such a way. While this kind of U-turn was not essential in order to win the elections, it is also true that a clear reform mandate was not a *sine qua non* for successful implementation.

3.3 Political economy of reform in Europe's South

When looking at a Euro area crisis setting, we must realize that only a subset of the original Williamson propositions can be put to test. Hypotheses such as whether we are in presence of an authoritarian regime clearly do not apply. At the same time, all the Southern European countries considered were in a situation of high financial market pressure, and edging towards the potential of a sovereign debt default. As such, the crisis hypothesis, at least in the formulation originally developed by Williamson, does not seem to be possibly testable, even just qualitatively, within our setting.[7] This notwithstanding, the other hypotheses are worth at least some reflection.

Table 3.1 offers an overview of how the Williamson hypotheses played out in the Euro area south. In order to display a deeper level of granularity, rather than identifying a single year of inception of the reform effort as was done in the original Williamson cross-country table, countries are further divided according to the various governments in charge over the period 2010–15.[8] Clearly, at least some of these propositions cannot be objectively tested, as is the case for example for the presence of a visionary leader. However, inasmuch as possible, evaluations were made based on Troika reports, press material and in consultation with country-specific experts.

As was the case in Williamson (1994), Table 3.1 also largely contains instances of governments that went through with reform approval during their mandate, and can hence be considered 'successful reformers'.[9] Over the course of 5 years, although with ups and downs, Greece implemented a total of over 160 reform measures (as identified in the IMF's MONA database), overhauling the labour market, collective wage bargaining, restructuring the public sector, intervening on pensions and much more (see Terzi 2015a). A crosscheck with all major objective indicators of structural reform confirm this pattern. For example, while discussing Product Market Regulation, OECD remarks that (2014, p. 66):

> even though there was little progress on average in the OECD, several countries implemented important reforms over the past five years [. . .]. The country with the largest improvement overall is Greece, followed by Poland, Portugal and the Slovak Republic.

When looking at World Bank Doing Business indicators, by 2014 Greece had made significant progress, climbing almost 50 positions over 5 years, from its 109th place in 2008–09.[10] As stressed in Terzi (2015c), this fact should not be mixed with the country's unequivocally dismal economic performance, which is likely to rest on factors related to fiscal austerity, deep uncertainty and a still very fragile financial system.

Table 3.1 Assessment of reform conditions in 11 southern European governments

	Greece				Portugal	Spain	Italy				Cyprus
HoSoG	Papandreou	Samaras	Tsipras 1	Tsipras 2	Coelho	Rajoy	Berlusconi	Monti	Letta	Renzi	Anastasiades
Rightist government	N(L)	Y	N(L)	N(L)	Y	Y	Y	N(GC)	N(L)	N(L)	Y
Honeymoon	N	Y	N	Y	N	Y	N	Y	N	Y	Y
Political base	N	Y	N	Y	Y	Y	N	N	N	N	Y
Demoralized opposition	Y	Y	Y	Y	Y	(Y)	N	N	N	Y	N
Social consensus	N	N	N	N	N	(Y)	N	N	N	(Y)	Y
Visionary leader	N	Y	N	Y	N	Y	Y	Y	N	(Y)	N
Coherent economic team	Y	Y	Y	Y	Y	Y	N	Y	Y	Y	Y
Led by a technocrat	N	N	N	N	N	N	N	Y	N	N	N
Voodoo politics	(Y)	(Y)	Y	N	N	(N)	N	N	N	N	N
Comprehensive programme	Y	N	N	N	Y	Y	N	N	N	–	Y
External aid	Y	Y	Y	Y	Y	(Y)	N	N	N	N	Y

Source: author's elaboration based on the framework of Williamson (1994)

Note: Y = yes, hypothesis satisfied; (Y) = hypothesis satisfied with qualifications; N = no, hypothesis not satisfied; (N) = hypothesis not satisfied with qualifications; (L), (GC) = left of centre and grand coalition respectively. Shaded identifies non-successful reform experiences.

Similarly, Portugal under the oversight of PM Coelho, successfully implemented a full IMF/EU adjustment programme, passing wide-ranging reforms of the labour market, education, housing market, network industries and more broadly improving the business environment (European Commission 2014; Turrini, this volume). Under Mariano Rajoy, Spain implemented two far-reaching reform packages in terms of labour market liberalization in February 2012 and banking sector reforms (Carlos Cuerpo, Federico Geli and Carlos Herrero; Miguel Otero-Iglesias and Federico Steinberg, this volume). While Mario Monti in Italy implemented among other things a large pension reform (Riforma Fornero), according to the IMF (2016, p. 7), 'the list of reform initiatives [taken by Prime Minister Matteo Renzi] has been impressive, and included institutional, public administration, fiscal, labour market, and banking sector reforms'. Finally, Cyprus under the lead of President Anastasiades, requested a bailout programme and managed to bring it to successful completion after having significantly overhauled its banking sector.

In line with Williamson (1994), Table 3.1 contains however also two instances of governments that were largely unsuccessful at pushing forward a wide-ranging reform agenda: Berlusconi in the early crisis phase (late 2010–11) and Letta. While the failings of the former on the reform side are highlighted by the letter sent to the Italian government by the President of the ECB Trichet,[11] the latter lasted only 300 days and failed to bring to completion any major economic breakthrough. The inclusion of these two cases can nonetheless be of interest in shedding light on the political determinants of reform. While some could argue that also Tsipras's first government (January–September 2015) failed to implement reforms, it must be noted that towards its end, it did manage to adopt all the prior actions required for the negotiations of a Third Greek Programme to start. These included VAT and pension reform measures, the transposition of the EU Bank Recovery and Resolution Directive (BRRD), the statutory independence of the Greek statistical office (ELSTAT), and the adoption of a Code of Civil Procedure. For the purpose of our analysis, it will hence not be classified as a failure.

As clarified in the previous session, the Washington Consensus does not fully apply to a European context. However, as discussed by Mussa and Savastano (1999), its main elements can be summarized under a three-pronged reform strategy consisting of (a) macroeconomic (and in particular fiscal) stabilization, (b) privatization, and (c) deregulation. During the Euro area crisis, the Troika adopted a similar strategy when formulating its Memoranda of Understanding (MoU). As such, these three elements guided the identification and discussion of reform efforts below.

Table 3.2 summarizes the general assessment on the validity of the various hypotheses in a European context. In line with Williamson (1994), it is fair to conclude that also in Europe's south no clear pattern can be detected with respect to right-wing governments being systematically more successful at implementing reforms. Actually, the *rightist government* hypothesis seems to be entirely disproved in Italy, especially on topics like labour market liberalization. This could be a case of what Dani Rodrik calls the 'Nixon-in-China syndrome': centre-left governments being more trusted by labour unions and hence managing to implement reforms that would never be accepted under a right-wing government.

Table 3.2 Hypotheses validity

	Y-share	General assessment	Counterexamples
Rightist government	44%	little support	Samaras (GR), Coelho (PT), Rajoy (ES)
Honeymoon	75%	strong support	Tsipras 1 (GR), Coelho (PT)
Political base	56%	(partially supported)	Tsipras 1 (GR)
Demoralized opposition	78%	strong support	Anastasiades (CY)
Social consensus	33%	little support	Rajoy (ES), Renzi (IT)
Visionary leader	33%	little support	Tsipras 2 (GR), Coelho (PT), Anastasiades (CY)
Coherent economic team	89%	strong support	–
Led by a technocrat	11%	little support	Monti (IT)
Voodoo politics	33%	little support	Tsipras (GR)
Comprehensive programme	50%	partially supported	Tsipras (GR), Monti (IT)
External aid	78%	strong support	Monti (IT), Renzi (IT)

Source: author's elaborations

Note: Generally, a score < 50% indicates little support, between 50–65% partial support, > 65% strong support. Parentheses indicate qualifications mentioned in the text.

In line with the widespread feeling of its importance, in Europe's case the *honeymoon* hypothesis found a rather strong validation. Most reformers tried to front-load harsh reforms, like Samaras in 2012 or Monti's 'Salva Italia' decree in 2011. There were however also a few counterexamples, as was the case for Coelho's Portugal, where the harshest reforms were not front-loaded.

In terms of having a *political base* for reform, Europe confirms the earlier finding by Williamson that having campaigned on a pro-reform platform was indeed important. In particular, once you exclude the few governments that either found themselves in the crisis (Papandreou, Berlusconi), or were not the result of fresh elections, most episodes considered confirm the political base hypothesis (bringing the Y-score from 56 percent, as expressed in Table 3.2, to 83 percent). Nonetheless, it must be noted that consensus for reform eroded quickly in most countries, as was the case in the Williamson episodes. At this point, Southern European governments by and large did not make an active effort to persuade the electorate of the quality and need of the reforms taken, preferring to blame them on the markets, on the Troika, or 'Europe'. It is hence difficult to find a confirmation of the *social consensus* hypothesis in the Euro area south.[12]

Another hypothesis that was strongly confirmed throughout the Euro area south was the fact that a weak and *demoralized opposition* gave the upper hand to reformist governments. This factor was present in almost all successful reform instances, with the exception of Anastasiades in Cyprus and the Monti government, which was however the result of a grand coalition.[13] The presence of a demoralized opposition was not a sufficient condition however, given that for example Letta's government did not manage to leverage this push factor fully.

Moving on to the characteristics of the leadership, the picture becomes blurrier. Having a *visionary leader* – meaning with a clear and organic view of what the country should look like in the medium term – was neither a necessary nor sufficient condition for reform success. This element somewhat clashes with the Williamson findings. However, it must be noted that many leaders were pushed into implementing reforms by external forces (either market pressure or conditionality), rather than inspired by an organic view of the country's future.

On the other hand, Europe's south confirmed the importance of having a *coherent team* of economic advisors. Few are the instances where this was not the case, most notably under Tsipras's first government, which indeed did not implement reforms until this heterogeneity was solved (in July 2015). Similarly, to Williamson, having a technocratic government was not seen as a *sine qua non* for reform in Europe which, to the contrary, displayed few of these instances (Monti, Papademos).

Voodoo politics, or the proposition according to which governments should campaign on an anti-reform agenda, only to renege on their promises once elected, deserves a broader reflection in the European context. One can widely deny this has been a determining element in Europe's south, with the Tsipras government as the sole real instance of such a behaviour. However, it must be noted that in all crisis countries that went to the ballots after the peak of the crisis, reformist governments were ousted (Samaras, Coelho and Renzi – following a referendum on constitutional reform). As such, in the future reformist leaders might be forced to consider Voodoo politics more carefully than this historical analysis would suggest.

As was the case for Williamson, drawing conclusions on the comprehensive nature of the reform programme is all but trivial. This not only because such an assessment would require an exact knowledge of the challenges the country faced, which is problematic in the absence of a counterfactual, but also as there are instances of short-lived governments. Focusing on Italy for instance, in the case of Monti, Letta and Renzi, it is hard to judge whether the programme was planned to be comprehensive, but then not fully implemented because of time constraints. Moreover, in the case of Coelho, Samaras, Tsipras and Anastasiades, the question is ultimately two-fold: whether the Troika's Memoranda of Understanding were comprehensive enough, and whether the government implemented them fully or only partially.[14]

Before moving to the conclusions, a final word should be devoted to the role of external assistance which, in the case of Europe, came under the presence of the Troika. In line with Williamson (1994), the Troika was definitely not a necessary condition for reform, though it is open to debate whether it was sufficient. In the end, although to a varying degree, all countries under a programme implemented more reforms than their (OECD/EU) peers, and significantly accelerated their own reform pace with respect to the previous years. This is shown in Figure 3.3, which makes use of a biannual reform effort index produced by the OECD. However, as discussed above, the presence of external actors and strict conditionality might

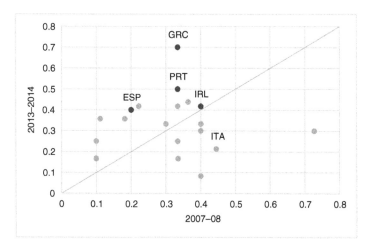

Figure 3.3 Reform responsiveness rate for OECD EU countries, 2007–08 and 2013–14[16]

Source: OECD, author's calculations

Note: Countries in dark underwent a Troika adjustment programme. For a detailed explanation of the construction of the Reform Responsiveness Indicator, refer to OECD (2015).

have weighed on the government's incentive to sell their reform programme at home. Moreover, some leaders have implemented reforms without being fully persuaded by them, but rather just as a means to prevent a sovereign default and Euro expulsion.[15] This might in turn weigh on the durability of reform as the crisis pressure abates, an issue I return to in the conclusions.

3.4 Conclusions

While broadly agreeing with (an updated version of) the Washington Consensus, most economists nowadays are ready to acknowledge that structural reforms are very country-specific and that there is no one-size-fits-all approach to foster growth successfully (see Rodrik 2007; IMF 2015). However, this chapter shows that political requirements for reform are also very country-specific, with no real silver bullets available. Nonetheless, a set of conditions and decisions do seem to facilitate implementation.

In the idea of Williamson, his book was supposed to be a manual for reformist policy makers, granting them key lessons that would enhance their effectiveness going forward. When reading it through these lenses, the modern day European reformer would distil the following findings from this chapter:

(1) Moments of crisis, of which the Euro area one was a master example, do indeed accelerate the reform process. However, deep reform actions are possible also in peace times.

(2) The first months in office are indeed a good time to secure the approval of harsh reforms.
(3) Being faced by a demoralized and divided opposition enhances significantly the chances of successfully implementing a reform programme. However, this factor alone is not sufficient to guarantee a government ample leeway for action.
(4) A coherent team of economic advisors, inspired by a comprehensive vision of where the country is heading, tends to be associated with more successful reform programmes, with respect to piece-meal approaches facing contingent crises.
(5) Requesting the intervention of the Troika seems to be a sufficient condition for far-reaching reforms to be adopted.

This latter point would seem to vindicate the national and European policy makers that have spent the last 5 years setting up the Euro area's crisis management mechanisms, composed of the European Stability Mechanism, conditionality and the OMT. Related to this point, Italy clearly stands out as the only southern country that managed to implement reforms (either under the technocratic Monti government, or under Renzi) without formally falling under international financial supervision. This Italian peculiarity can surely be an interesting venue for further research.

More broadly, it is worth reflecting on whether an external intervention is truly successful at pushing through reforms, especially given that, at least in Europe's south, it seemed to come at the expense of mustering a social consensus for reform and, often, of a broader economic vision. As discussed above, policy makers who implement reforms not out of conviction but rather out of market – or institutional pressure are more likely to revert to bad old habits as soon as the incentive disappears. Moreover, reforms are more likely to be implemented only *de jure*, rather than *de facto*. This in turn is likely to limit their beneficial impact on the economy.

Interestingly, this discussion connects neatly to the never-ending debate, both in the IMF literature and among policy makers, on whether countries are better off to pursue a 'reform shock' or a step-by-step approach. While Jeffrey Sachs (Williamson 1994, p. 501) is right in arguing that at crisis times governments are more likely to be successful at swiftly implementing reform packages all at once, Dani Rodrik's defence of a phasing-in for reform (Williamson 1994, p. 212) seems convincing. He argues that, as reforms start bearing fruit, the reform programme will build its own consensus, making the measures more durable.

Bringing this discussion back to southern Europe, it is true that Troika programme and strict conditionality ensured the parliamentary adoption of wide-reaching reform packages – lending some evidence to the Sachs argument. However, only time will tell whether the measures adopted under duress will last. And indeed, we already start seeing preliminary signs of a backtracking of reforms in many of those countries that were reform leaders until less than a year ago. Portugal's new left-wing government is currently discussing whether to increase public sector wages, pensions, shift taxation back towards labour and reduce indirect taxes, just to mention one. At the same time, in Italy the opposition parties are calling for a repeal of the 'Fornero' pension reform and of the liberalization of hours of opening in the retail sector. Interestingly, both these measures were taken by Monti's technocratic government as part of the shock approach, and are still attracting a starker opposition than more recent measures, such as the labour market liberalization or the education reform, implemented more progressively.

While making use of this 'political manual', policy makers should not forget that the success of economic reforms is not only measured on the speed and depth of implementation. Reforms that make it into (economic) history books are those that have a strong positive impact on the economy by tackling the country-specific bottlenecks and, for this, rigorous prior analysis must always be warranted.

Notes

1 The author would like to thank Dani Rodrik, André Sapir, Paolo Manasse, Dimitris Katsikas, and all the participants of the Athens Workshop for their comments and suggestions. All errors and omissions remain the sole responsibility of the author.
2 For a detailed discussion of reforms implemented under the Greek programme, see Terzi (2015a).
3 IMF (2007, p. 1), before the eruption of the financial crisis, concluded that the challenges for the Italian economy were 'insufficient domestic competition, still-rigid labour markets, a discouraging business environment, relatively undeveloped capital markets, and unsustainable fiscal accounts'. Arguably, these are precisely the problems that successive governments have tried to tackle since 2010 in a crisis environment.
4 Defined as 'economic technocrats who assume positions of political responsibility' (p. 11). The idea of focusing on technocrats was based on the desire to clear out barriers to reform (1) and (2) identified above, namely technical knowledge and political will.
5 Given most of the interviewees writing the case studies in Williamson (1994) had been in government at the time of the reform programme implementation, and given how subjective the assessment of this specific hypothesis is, this is perhaps a finding that should be taken with a pinch of salt.
6 Especially in democracies, it is difficult to evaluate whether the finance minister, the president or the prime minister should be from an economic/technocratic background.
7 This discussion connects to a wider debate in the empirical literature and within European policy circles as to whether financial market pressure contributes to reform implementation, keeping tension high on governments or makes reforms harder to implement by reducing the fiscal space (see Terzi 2015b).
8 The Lucas Papademos government was excluded from the analysis given its short duration (6 months) and very narrow mandate to negotiate the second MoU for Greece and the Private Sector Involvement (PSI).
9 The keen reader will note that throughout the chapter, reference is never made to economic outcomes of reforms but rather to the implementation of reforms per se. While identifying the right reforms that target a country's specific bottlenecks is clearly crucial, this chapter is written as a guide to policy makers who have already developed a growth strategy, and are looking for political economy advice on how to implement it.

10 As discussed in Terzi (2015c), in its 2014 Report, the World Bank itself using slightly more sophisticated metrics, identifies Greece as one of the top broad reformers worldwide (8th to be precise).
11 Available from: www.voltairenet.org/article171574.html.
12 Both Rajoy and Renzi by and large attempted to present reforms as needed for the sake of the country, rather than being imposed from the outside.
13 In the case of Spain, the opposition was not fragmented but rather weak as a result of the electoral results.
14 Particularly in the case of Greece, there is evidence to suggest that MoUs were only partially implemented (Katsikas et al. 2017).
15 'We chose a compromise that forces us to implement a program we don't believe in and we will implement it' – Alexis Tsipras, 22 July 2015.
16 Interestingly, the other outlier as an outperforming reformer in the year 2007–08 is Hungary which, at the time, was under financial assistance.

Bibliography

Darvas, Z. (2012) *Intra-Euro Rebalancing Is Inevitable, But Insufficient.* Bruegel. Policy Contribution 2012/15.

De Grauwe, P., and Ji, Y. (2013) From Panic-Driven Austerity to Symmetric Macroeconomic Policies in the Eurozone. *Journal of Common Market Studies*, 51(S1), 31–41.

Drazen, A., and Grilli, V. (1993) The Benefit of Crises for Economic Reforms. *The American Economic Review*, 83(3), 598–607.

European Commission (2014) *The Economic Adjustment Programme for Portugal 2011– 2014.* European Commission. European Economy Occasional Paper No. 202.

IMF (2007) *Italy: 2006 Article IV Consultation–Staff Report.* IMF Country Report No. 07/64, February.

IMF (2015) *Structural Reforms and Macroeconomic Performance: Initial Considerations for the Fund.* IMF. Staff Report, November.

IMF (2016) *Italy Staff Report for the 2016 Article IV Consultation.* IMF. Country Report No. 16/222.

Katsikas, D., Anastasatou, M., Nitsi, E., Petralias, A., and Filinis, K. (2017) *Structural Reforms in Greece During the Crisis (2010–2014).* Athens, Bank of Greece (forthcoming in Greek).

Krueger, A. (2000) *Economic Policy Reform: The Second Stage*, Chicago, IL, and London, University of Chicago Press.

Mussa, M., and Savastano, M. (1999) The IMF Approach to Economic Stabilization. In: Bernanke, B. S. and Rotemberg, J. J. (eds.) *NBER Macroeconomics Annual 1999*, Volume 14, Cambridge, MA, MIT Press, pp. 79–128.

OECD (2014) *Going for Growth Interim Report*, Chapter 2, Paris, OECD Publishing.

OECD (2015) *Going for Growth*, Paris, OECD Publishing.

Pisani-Ferry, J., Sapir, A., and Wolff, G. (2013) *EU-IMF Assistance to Euro-Zone Countries: An Early Assessment.* Bruegel Blueprint No. 19.

Reinhart, C. M., and Rogoff, K. S. (2009) *This Time Is Different: Eight Centuries of Financial Folly*, Princeton, NJ, Princeton University Press.

Rodrik, D. (2007) *One Economics, Many Recipes: Globalization, Institutions, and Economic Growth*, Princeton, NJ, Princeton University Press.

Sapir, A., Wolff, G., De Sousa, C., and Terzi, A. (2014) *The Troika and Financial Assistance in the Euro Area: Successes and Failures.* ECON Committee Study, Brussels.

Terzi, A. (2015a) *Reform Momentum and Its Impact on Greek Growth*. Bruegel. Policy Contribution 2015/12.

Terzi, A. (2015b) *Is the ECB Sacrificing Reforms on the Altar of Inflation?* Bruegel Blog. [Online]. Available from: http://bruegel.org/2015/03/is-the-ecb-sacrificing-reforms-on-the-altar-of-inflation/.

Terzi, A. (2015c) *Can Greece Become Competitive Overnight?* Bruegel Blog. [Online]. Available from: http://bruegel.org/2015/02/can-greece-become-competitive-overnight/.

Thimann, C. (2015) The Microeconomic Dimensions of the Eurozone Crisis and Why European Politics Cannot Solve Them. *Journal of Economic Perspectives*, 29(3), 141–164.

Williamson, J. (ed.) (1994) *The Political Economy of Policy Reform*, Washington, DC, Peterson Institute Press.

Part II

Policy design

Getting structural reforms right

4 The persistence-resilience trade-off in unemployment

The role of labour and product market institutions

Tolga Aksoy and Paolo Manasse

4.1 Introduction

The financial crisis that started in 2008 hit all Eurozone economies and resulted in a very sharp recession and soaring unemployment rates in the area as a whole. The size of the decline in output and jobs, however, was markedly different across countries. Southern Europe, Ireland and the Baltic Republics were dramatically hit, while other Central and Northern European countries were only mildly touched. Figure 4.1 shows the impressive divergence in unemployment rates between Southern European countries and Ireland, on the one hand, and Germany, on the other, where unemployment actually declined. The reasons that made the former group more vulnerable are well known. Before the crisis, large capital inflows financed very large current account imbalances, between 10 to 15 percent of GDP, in Spain, Portugal and Greece (see Figure 4.2). Foreign borrowing translated into excessive domestic lending, and led to a real estate bubble (in Spain and Ireland), to excessive risk taking and bank exposure to private and public debt, and to large explicit and implicit fiscal liabilities for sovereigns. In Greece, Italy and Portugal, sluggish productivity growth, fiscal proclivity and political instability were crucial sources of vulnerability. A sudden stop in capital flows and a simultaneous segmentation of the European inter-bank market gave rise to a run on banks (Ireland, Spain and later Greece) and on sovereign debts (Greece, Ireland, Portugal, Italy). The credit crunch and the austerity measures that followed pushed these countries into their worst recession of the post-war period. International Financial Institutions, in exchange for support, pushed these countries to adopt 'structural reforms' while implementing the fiscal consolidation measures.

In fact, these reforms programmes covered a large variety of measures, broadly aimed at improving the supply-side of the economy and the efficiency of the public sector: for example, reducing entry barriers and de-regulating product and services markets, reducing firing and hiring cost for firms, de-centralizing wage bargaining, reducing public employment, fighting tax evasion/elusion, reforming the judiciary, eliminating red tape, privatizing state assets and companies. The idea behind the new structural reforms 'consensus', pioneered by the OECD and later shared by the 'Troika', the European Commission, the ECB and the IMF, was that many of

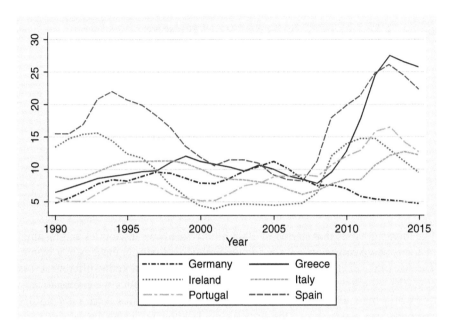

Figure 4.1 Unemployment rate

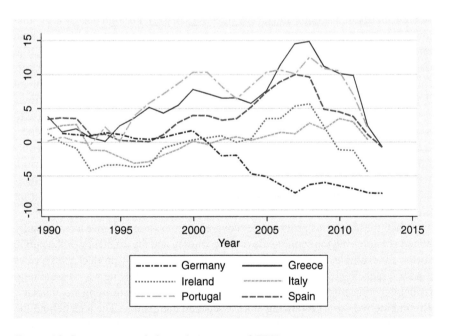

Figure 4.2 Current account balance (percentage of GDP)

the problem-countries were characterized by decades of stagnant productivity growth. A 'supply-side' boost would contrast the recessionary impact of the fiscal squeeze. Many critics of this approach (see for example Rodrik 2016), objected that: (a) these reforms work only in the long run by raising potential output, so that they are ineffective, if not costly, in the short run; and (b) reforms should be targeted at removing few, well-specified constraints to growth, rather than being applied across the board, where they are less likely to be effective and more likely to undermine political support.

In this paper, we focus on labour and product markets. First, we document that unemployment rates in the Eurozone countries have responded very differently to the 'great recession'. We focus on two dimensions of this response: the *impact* of output shocks on the rate of unemployment (resilience), and the *speed of recovery* (persistence) of unemployment following a shock. By estimating a 'dynamic' Okun regression relating output to unemployment gaps, we show that the Eurozone countries lie on a trade-off between resilience and persistence. Countries that are characterized by more resilience typically show more unemployment persistence. Furthermore, we show that a country's position along the trade-off is related to the characteristics of its labour and product markets institutions. We find that more regulated product and labour markets (less 'flexible') tend to cushion employment in the short run (more resilience) but lead to slower recovery (more persistence) in the medium term. Among Southern European countries, Spain and Italy exemplify two extreme cases, Italy representing an example of high short-run resilience and high medium-run persistence ('rigid' labour and 'regulated' product markets), and Spain representing the opposite case of 'flexible' markets, with large impact but fast recovery.

This finding is important in the general discussion of the effects of reforms on society's welfare, since with 'flexible' markets, consumers, workers and firms may suffer from large employment and output volatility, but may benefit from faster recovery. It has also strong implications for the debate on structural reforms: have the labour and product market reforms hastily implemented during the crisis in Southern European countries aggravated the employment consequences of their fiscal consolidation? Our estimates suggest that they did, but we find that the effect is small and short-lived. On impact, structural reforms account for about one extra percentage point rise in the unemployment gap in Greece, and for even less in other Southern European countries. However, we find that the reforms have contributed to a faster recovery from unemployment with positive effects materializing after 2 years.

The plan of the paper is the following. In Section 2 we review the relevant literature. In Sections 3 and 4 we present some stylized facts on the unemployment and output dynamics as well on the structural reforms implemented in the Eurozone countries, focusing on the labour and product markets. In Section 5 we report the estimation results, and in Section 6 we use them in order to measure the consequences of structural reforms on the unemployment rate. Section 7 concludes the chapter.

4.2 A brief literature review

This paper brings together three different strands of literature. The first is the literature on the 'causes and persistence' of high unemployment rates in Europe, dating back from the early 1980s, when Europe, unlike the United States, suffered from a prolonged period of high unemployment, and when the term 'Euro-sclerosis' became fashionable. The early contributions highlighted the role of macroeconomic shocks, such as the oil crises (see Bruno and Sachs 1985); the literature that followed focused on features of the labour market such as the wage-bargaining process, the role of unions and 'insiders', and 'hysteresis', e.g. the persistence of high unemployment following transitory shocks. Labour market institutions that are associated to high firing and hiring costs, are discussed for example in Bentolila and Bertola (1990): they may cushion employment from negative shocks in the short run, but may also slow down the employment recovery, as firms are less willing to hire in good times if they cannot shed labour in bad times. Similarly, a wage-bargaining system where insiders play an important role in determining the wage rate, and where the wage rate is largely independent of firms' productivity and of unemployment, may be associated to real wage rigidity and to high and persistent unemployment rates (see the 'hysteresis' effect discussed in Blanchard and Summers 1986). A centralized wage bargaining may have ambiguous effect on labour market outcomes: either a very centralized or a very decentralized system may in principle achieve wage moderation and deliver lower/less persistent unemployment, either via coordination or via competition (see Calmfors and Driffill 1988). More recently, the role of labour market institutions such as employment protection legislation has come to the fore (see Blanchard and Portugal 2001, 2006 for a discussion). An impulse to this literature has come from the OECD, who has provided new indicators and new evidence for the importance of the institutions of the labour and product market in developed economies (see OECD Employment Outlook 2004, 2015, and Conway and Nicoletti 2006). Blanchard and Giavazzi (2003) argue that the interaction of the product and labour markets play an important role. Lower barriers to entry may raise the equilibrium number of firms, reduce their market power and lead to more employment in the long run; product market deregulation may also reduce the rents that are shared by firms and unions, so that the latter may have a weaker incentive to bargain for a higher wage.

The second strand of relevant literature concerns the effects of 'structural reforms' in developing and developed countries. Early contributions discuss episodes of liberalizations in Asia, Africa, Latin America and in the ex-Soviet Republics. Eicher and Schreiber (2010) suggest that pro-market reforms introduced in the 1990s in transition countries, such as deregulation in the product market, privatization of state assets and services, removal of state-fixed pricing, the creation of a private financial sector, the introduction of competition in the banking sector and of an effective system of prudential supervision were positively associated to growth. Eslava et al. (2004) find that social security, labour and financial markets reform introduced in Colombia in the 1990s had a positive effect on Total Factor Productivity. Schiffbauer and Ospina (2010), suggest that product market reforms in emerging markets have substantially raised productivity growth, as much as 12 percent in some countries. For industrialized countries, Alesina et al. (2005) argue that product market reforms such as the reduction of entry barriers and privatization tend to raise investment; Griffith et al. (2006) find positive effects on employment. Di Tella and MacCulloch (2005) find that reducing the Employment Protection Legislation (EPL) in the labour market stimulates employment and labour force participation.

Some studies find evidence that structural reforms may involve short-run costs in terms of negative growth rate or unemployment. For example, pro-market reforms have short-terms costs with regard to lower growth during the initial year, but promote growth from the second year onwards in transition countries (see Staehr 2005). Similarly, Cacciatore et al. (2015), for developed countries, find that lower firing costs and lower entry barriers reduce initially the entry of firms in the product market and lead to large lay-offs of the least productive workers in the short run. A number of studies find that labour market liberalizations have negative effects on employment, when they are introduced during unfavourable economic conditions. This holds for cuts in unemployment benefit (see Bouis et al. 2012; IMF WEO 2015) and for reforms in the employment protection legislation, EPL (see IMF WEO 2015).

The third strand of literature that is relevant for our paper concerns the relationship between unemployment and output changes, the so-called Okun Law. The Okun Law is a simple reduced-form equation which posits an empirical relationship between the change in unemployment and the change in output. For the United States, the typical rule-of-thumb is that a 1 percent fall of GDP relative to potential output is associated to 0.5 percent rise in the unemployment rate (see Mankiw 2013). Many authors have questioned the stability of this relationship over time, claiming for example that the recent recovery in the United States was a 'job-less recovery' (see Gordon 2011; Cazes et al. 2011; IMF 2010). However, recent evidence finds that this relationship is remarkably stable over the past decades, and holds significantly in many countries (see Ball et al. 2013). Interestingly, this latter study finds that the Okun Law's parameters appear quite different across countries, but admittedly fail in providing a convincing explanation of these differences in terms of different labour market institutions.

Our analysis brings these strands of research together, and focuses on the role of labour and product market institutions in explaining the cross-country heterogeneity described in the preceding section. We frame the discussion of structural reforms in the Okun 'tradition', and we add an element of dynamics in order to describe the impact *and* the persistence of output shocks on the rate of unemployment in different countries. Our results give a rationale for the finding that labour and product market reforms may be associated to employment losses and may involve short-run costs. Moreover, we give an explanation for the different response of unemployment in the Eurozone, during the recent crisis. We find that the characteristics of the labour and product markets such as the centralization of wage bargaining, employment protection and the degree of product market competition affect the resilience of labour markets to output shocks: more 'protected' labour and product markets tend to shelter employment from these shocks; however, these same features are associated to a slower 'speed of adjustment', so that the employment recovery from a recession is slower the more protected are labour and product markets.

4.3 Stylized facts on unemployment and output in the Eurozone

This section presents some stylized facts on the labour market response of Eurozone countries to the crisis. Figure 4.3 shows the evolution of the unemployment gap, the deviation of the unemployment rate from the equilibrium 'non – accelerating (wage) – inflation unemployment rate (NAWRU)', and the GDP gap, the difference between the actual and 'potential' GDP, for Eurozone countries between 1965 and 2014. The NAWRU is defined as the rate of unemployment that is consistent with stable wages and with an economy that is working at its potential level of output. A positive gap implies that the unemployment rate is above equilibrium level. Regarding the output gap, a negative number denotes an economy operating below potential GDP, which is the level of output consistent with projected productivity growth and historical factor utilization. The two definitions are consistent, so that in principle when output is at potential, e.g. the output gap is zero, the unemployment rate should be at the NAWRU level, so that also the unemployment gap should be zero. The methodology adopted for the gaps' calculations is somewhat controversial. The problem is that potential output is pro-cyclical, e.g. it tends

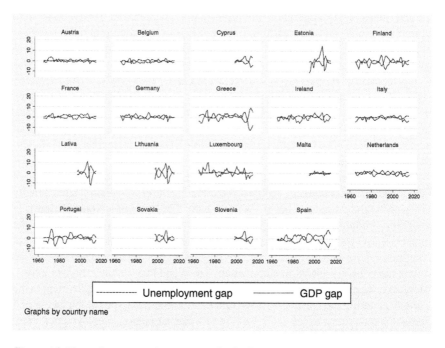

Figure 4.3 Unemployment and output gaps in the Eurozone

to fall in a downturn: low investment leads to low capital and reduces estimates of potential output. Thus, when real GDP falls, potential output also falls and the output gap underestimates the size of the recession. Our results are not affected, however, if this error of measurement affects in a comparable way both the output and the unemployment gaps. In the empirical section, we will use both the gaps' measures as well as the changes in the unemployment rate and in (the log of) GDP, with similar results. Here we focus on the output and unemployment gaps mainly for two reasons: first, because we want to compare our results with those in the literature, where they are commonly used (see for example Gordon 2011); second, we are interested in the speed of adjustment to some long-run equilibrium in the labour market, and output and unemployment gaps lend themselves to this interpretation.

Figure 4.3 shows these gaps for Eurozone countries between 1965 and 2014. A few things emerge quite clearly. First, *the changes in unemployment (gaps) largely reflect output (gaps) movements*: the unemployment gap unsurprisingly rises by more in countries that experience larger drops in the output gap. Second, over time the two gaps move symmetrically, so that they seem to imply, over time, a stable 'Okun Law'.

Countries differ markedly as to the size and in the persistence of shocks. Columns 1 and 2 of Table 4.1 show the peak-to-trough change in the unemployment

Table 4.1 GDP and unemployment losses in Eurozone countries, 2008–14

Country	Unemployment Change, peak-trough (1)	GDP Change, peak-trough (2)	-Unemployment Change/GDP Change (−1/2)
Austria	1.50	−5.92	0.25
Belgium	1.50	−5.77	0.26
Cyprus	12.40	−10.79	1.15
Estonia	11.20	−17.48	0.64
Finland	2.30	−8.27	0.28
France	2.90	−4.90	0.59
Germany	2.60	−9.41	0.28
Greece	19.70	−26.24	0.75
Ireland	8.30	−9.15	0.91
Italy	6.00	−8.08	0.74
Latvia	11.80	−17.59	0.67
Lithuania	12.00	−16.25	0.74
Luxembourg	1.40	−14.31	0.10
Malta	1.00	−15.00	0.07
Netherlands	3.70	−3.77	0.98
Portugal	7.60	−7.90	0.96
Slovakia	4.90	−12.35	0.40
Slovenia	5.70	−9.57	0.60
Spain	14.80	−8.58	1.72

Source: AMECO database

rate and in GDP respectively during the crisis. The numbers confirm the visual impression of the previous picture, with unemployment peaks largely reflecting GDP losses. In particular Greece, the Baltic Republics, Luxembourg and Malta stand out as the countries that suffered the largest GDP losses, about 26 percent in Greece, 17 percent in Baltic countries and 13 percent in Luxembourg and Malta; the rise in unemployment rate was particularly severe in Greece, Spain and in the Baltic Republics. It was surprisingly muted in Luxembourg and Malta.

The last column of the table shows another interesting measure of the labour markets response to the recent crisis: the average elasticity of the rate of unemployment to output. This is calculated by simply dividing column 1 by column 2 (with the minus sign).

The largest elasticity of unemployment to GDP is found in Spain, 1.72, followed by Cyprus, the Netherlands, Portugal and Ireland which are close to unity; the lowest unemployment elasticity to GDP is found in Malta and Luxembourg (0.07, and 0.10 respectively). In the following section, we will refer to 'resilience' to indicate that unemployment in a particular country shows a relatively small elasticity to GDP changes. In the next section, we will discuss another feature of national labour markets, unemployment 'persistence'. By this we mean a country's relatively slow adjustment of unemployment following a shock.

4.4 Resilience and persistence: econometric analysis

Our aim here is to measure the speed of recovery of the unemployment rate following a shock in different countries of the Euro area, and to relate this to 'resilience'. We will show that typically labour markets that are more 'resilient' following a shock are also slower to recover. In order to do so, we estimate an Okun-type relationship separately for 19 countries in the Eurozone, using OECD annual data from 1965 to 2014. We focus on the cross-country differences in the parameters. The next step will be to relate these parameters to country-specific labour and product market characteristics.

Unlike previous studies that only consider the 'short run' impact of output on unemployment in the standard Okun relationship, we add a minimum amount of dynamics so as to evaluate speed of adjustment towards the long-run equilibrium (the parameter α below). For each country, separately we estimate the following model:

$$u_{it} - u_{it}^p = \beta_i \left(y_{it} - y_{it}^p \right) + \alpha_i \left(u_{it-1} - u_{it-1}^p \right) + v_{it} \qquad i = 1..C, \qquad t = 1,..T \qquad (1)$$

where u_{it} is unemployment rate at time $t = 1,..T$ in country $i = 1..C$, Y_{it} is the logarithm of real GDP of country i at time t, u_{it}^p is the NAWRU, y_{it}^p the log of potential real GDP, and v_{it} denotes a stochastic disturbance term at time t for country i. Equation (1) says that the deviation of the unemployment rate from the 'equilibrium' level, the unemployment gap, depends on the 'cyclical' deviation of output from potential, the output gap, $y_{it} - y_{it}^p$, and on the lagged unemployment gap. A long-run equilibrium in this model occurs when $u_{it} = u_{it}^p$, $y_t = y_{it}^p$ for all t. In order to check the robustness of our result we also estimate a different specification where the first difference in the unemployment rate and the rate of growth of output replaces the corresponding gaps (see Appendix). The coefficient β_i, which is negative *a priori*, measures the impact of deviations of output from potential on unemployment gaps in each country: the smaller this parameter is, the more *resilient* is the country's unemployment rate to output shocks; parameter α_i, which should be less than 1 in absolute value for stability reasons, measures the persistence of the unemployment response. The closer this parameter is to 1 in absolute value, the more *persistent* is the unemployment deviation from the equilibrium, i.e. the slowest the return to the equilibrium following a shock. In the limit where $|\alpha_i| = 1$, a temporary shock has permanent consequences on unemployment ('hysteresis'). This specification allows us to calculate statistics such as the time required for unemployment to adjust, say, half-way, back to its long-run equilibrium. This is simply given by the expression $T*(i) = -\dfrac{\ln(2)}{\ln(\alpha_i)}$.[1] This statistic considers a purely temporary and idiosyncratic unemployment shock, e.g. one that lasts only one period and does not affect output directly. Thus, it clearly underestimates the actual persistence of unemployment in a country, since typically shocks, e.g. fiscal ones, are long lasting and affect output and the labour market at the same time. Nevertheless, this is a useful indicator for assessing how national labour markets respond to the same hypothetical shock. The indicator is increasing in α_i, the persistence parameter, and tends to infinity as α_i tends to 1.

Table 4.2 shows the estimates for the impact (β_i) and the persistence (α_i) parameters, obtained by country-by-country regression using OLS, over the period 1965–2015. These parameters are significantly different from zero, and have the expected sign in all countries (the parameter α_i is not statistically different from zero only in Malta). We have checked that the parameters are stable through the decades, and we can reject the presence of structural breaks when we consider subsamples starting in 1975, 1985, 1995 and 2005 for all countries. The table illustrates the heterogeneity of 'Okun Laws' across the Eurozone.

Consistently with the peak-to-trough elasticities previously reported, the estimated impact effect of the cyclical output gap on the unemployment gap is large in Spain, Cyprus and in the 'new' Euro members such as Latvia, Lithuania and Slovakia. In these countries, a 1 percent output fall relative to potential is associated, within a year, to about half of a percent rise in the unemployment gap, similarly to the 'standard' estimates obtained for the United States; conversely, the unemployment response is very small in Malta, Luxembourg and Austria, as well as in the other Mediterranean countries such as Italy, Portugal and Greece.

Interestingly, many of the countries in the first group, the least 'resilient', show a relatively fast rebound of unemployment (a small estimate in absolute value for α_i). This is true for Spain, Cyprus, Estonia and Slovakia, where it takes a year or less to halve the initial effect. At the other extreme are Greece, France, Germany and Slovenia, where the persistence of unemployment is very large. Italy has the most sluggish recovery of all, taking more than five and a half years to revert half-way to the initial equilibrium following a hypothetical temporary shock. Figure 4.4

Table 4.2 Okun coefficients in the Eurozone (Gap regression)

Country	beta	alpha	Half-way time
Austria	0.132***	0.479***	0.942
Belgium	0.286***	0.523***	1.069
Cyprus	0.454***	0.409***	0.775
Estonia	0.233***	0.426***	0.812
Finland	0.348***	0.555***	1.177
France	0.24***	0.682***	1.811
Germany	0.233***	0.582***	1.281
Greece	0.246***	0.702***	1.959
Ireland	0.228***	0.524***	1.073
Italy	0.126***	0.885***	5.674
Latvia	0.474***	0.247***	0.496
Lithuania	0.498***	0.255**	0.507
Luxembourg	0.033**	0.619***	1.445
Malta	0.107**	0.101	0.302
Netherlands	0.332***	0.48***	0.944
Portugal	0.134***	0.542***	1.132
Slovakia	0.49***	0.36***	0.678
Slovenia	0.184***	0.663***	1.687
Spain	0.493***	0.515***	1.045

Source: Authors' calculations

Notes: Alpha in absolute value. *** significant at 1 percent; ** significant at 5 percent; * significant at 10 percent.

illustrates the relationship between 'resilience' and 'persistence'. Each country is represented by a dot: the coordinates are, on the vertical axis, the estimated β coefficient (in absolute value) representing the size of the impact response of unemployment to output; on the horizontal axis, the estimated α coefficient, in absolute value, measuring the persistence of the shock. *The evidence suggests a trade-off: where the impact effect of output on unemployment is smaller (low beta, i.e. high resilience), unemployment is more persistent (high alpha).* Malta appears to be an outlier (but remember that the persistence parameter is very imprecisely estimated). The correlation and rank correlation between the alpha and the beta (in absolute value) coefficients, omitting Malta, are respectively 0.69 (significant at 0.1 percent) and 0.62 (significant at 0.06 percent). Southern Mediterranean countries appear either in the upper-right region of large resilience and persistence (Italy, Portugal and Greece), which is typically associated with 'rigid' markets, or in the lower-left region of low resilience and persistence (Cyprus and Spain) which is typically associated with 'flexible' markets.

The evidence suggests that on average labour markets which are more effective in cushioning employment from output shocks, 'pay' this in terms of more persistent unemployment.

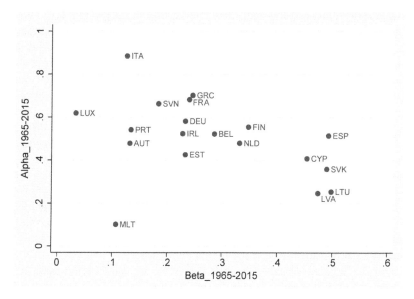

Figure 4.4 Trade-off between resilience (low beta) and persistence (high alpha)

In order to assess the robustness of these results, in the Appendix we run an equation which is similar to (1) but where unemployment and output gaps have been replaced with the first-time difference of the unemployment rate and of log GDP (Table 4.A1). The results are very similar to those described here. As mentioned above, we prefer the 'gap' specification since it allows an interpretation of in terms of convergence to a long-run equilibrium and it is largely used in the literature.

4.5 Product and labour market institutions

Our next aim is to understand the role that product and labour market institutions play in this trade-off. We want to test the hypothesis that 'more regulated' labour and product markets may, on the one hand, cushion employment from output shocks, for example preventing lay-offs, insuring labour income and limiting entry/exit, but may also lead to more 'hysteresis', as wage and price rigidities slow down the employment recovery. This section describes the indexes of labour and product market institutions that we use in the following econometric analysis.

For the labour market, we consider the OECD employment protection legislation index (EPL) and the centralization in wage bargaining index, CWB. The EPL is a synthetic measure of the strictness of regulation on dismissals and of the diffusion of temporary contracts. In particular, it covers the dismissal notification procedures, the delay and length of the notice period, the size of severance payments, the compensation after unfair dismissal and the possibility of reinstatement for employees on regular/indefinite contracts (see OECD Employment Outlook 2004, 2015). EPL indicators are generally available since 1985.

The CWB indicator is obtained from the Database on Institutional Characteristics of Trade Unions, Wage Setting, State Intervention and Social Pacts (ICTWSS), see Visser (2015). It describes the predominant level at which wage bargaining takes place, and takes into account the frequency of contracts, the importance of the clauses of collective agreements and the extent to which local agreement can derogate from them. This indicator is a measure of the degree to which wages respond to local conditions (e.g. productivity) or are determined by collective bargaining; it is generally available since 1960.

For product market institutions, we employ the OECD index of regulation (see Conway and Nicoletti 2006). The index measures the pervasiveness of regulation in seven non-manufacturing industries: electricity and gas supply, road freight, air passenger transport, rail transport, post and telecommunications. The index is calculated as the arithmetic average of the following sub-indexes: barriers to entry, public ownership, market share of new entrants and price controls. All the indicators, in product and labour markets, take values between 0 and 6, with higher values corresponding to more regulation. They capture similar features of the respective markets and are typically highly correlated.

Figure 4.5 in panel (a) shows the evolution of the average EPL indicator for the Euro area (dark line) together with the coefficient of variation (scv), defined as the ratio of the cross-country standard deviation and the average, at a point in time (light line). European labour protection legislations were reformed in two large waves: the first occurred in the early 1990s, when the average EPL shows a marked decline, and the second in the early years of the crisis, starting in 2008. Interestingly, in both episodes the move towards a more competitive model implied a

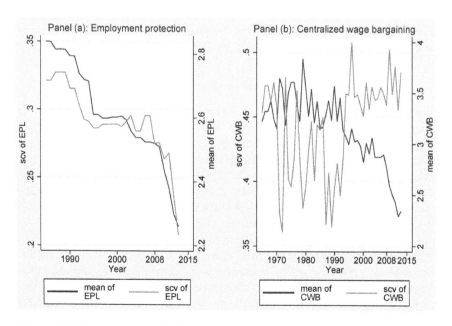

Figure 4.5 Labour markets in the Euro area

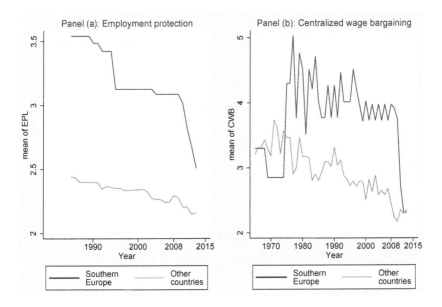

Figure 4.6 Labour markets in the southern Europe and Euro area

significant convergence of European labour market institutions, as shown by the fall in the coefficient of variation. Figure 4.6, panel (a), shows that in both episodes this dynamic was mainly due to the convergence of southern European countries' legislations to that of the other countries. The dismantling of employment protection legislation was particularly rapid and sizable during the recent crisis, possibly as a counterpart to the financial assistance obtained from the European and International Institutions. Similarly, the process of decentralization of wage bargaining started in the 1990s, see Figure 4.5 (b). Following the first wave of reforms of the 1990s the reform effort of Southern European countries stalled until the crisis, so that the cross-country differences in the degree of centralization in wage bargaining remained quite high, see the dark line in Figure 4.6 (b). Reforms and convergence re-appeared only in the most recent period.

Product market deregulation also accelerated in the 1990s, following the adoption of the Maastricht treaty, the European Single Market Programme, and the European Monetary Union (see Boeri 2005). Figure 4.7 shows that, unlike in the employment protection legislation, there was little convergence in the Eurozone until 2008. As product markets were liberalized over time, cross-countries differences, captured by the cross-country *standard deviation* (not shown) were stable until 2007: the rise in the coefficient of variation simply reflects the fall in the mean product market index (in the denominator). In fact, unlike labour markets, product markets in Southern Europe in the wake of the crisis were already quite similar to those of the rest of the Eurozone, see Figure 4.8.

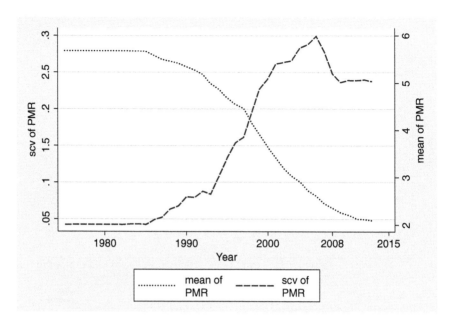

Figure 4.7 Product markets in the Euro area

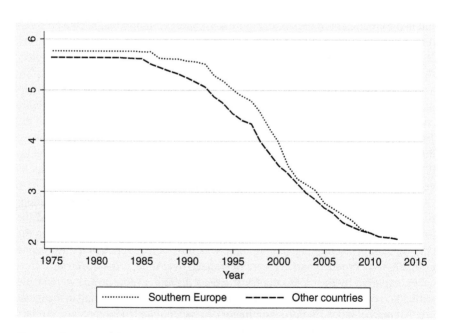

Figure 4.8 Product markets in the southern Europe and Euro area

4.5.1 Measuring the role of labour and product
market institutions

In this section, we want to evaluate the role of labour and product market institutions in explaining the persistence/resilience trade-off. We adopt the following
empirical strategy. We assume that the country-specific resilience and persistence
coefficients β_{it} and α_{it} depend on 'country-specific' characteristics of the labour and
product market that may change over time when reforms are implemented. These
include the indexes of employment protection, centralized wage bargaining and
product market regulation. These characteristics are summarized by the generic
indicator(s), IND_{it}. In addition, the parameters may depend on some common factors, summarized by β_0 and α_0 below:

$$\beta_{it} = \beta_0 + \beta_1 IND_{it} \quad \alpha_{it-1} = \alpha_0 + \alpha_1 IND_{it-1} \tag{2}$$

We also allow for the possibility that our labour and product market indicator(s)
may exert a direct effect on the unemployment gap, over and above that on the
resilience and persistence parameters. Therefore, we include them in the model of
equation (1). Substituting (2) into (1) and adding a direct effect of labour indicator
IND we obtain:

$$u_{it} - u_{it}^p = \left(\beta_0 + \beta_1 IND_{it}\right)\left(y_{it} - y_{it}^p\right) + \left(\alpha_0 + \alpha_1 IND_{it-1}\right)$$
$$\left(u_{it-1} - u_{it-1}^p\right) + \left(c_0 + c_1 IND_{it}\right) + v_{it} \tag{3}$$

As before, our labour and product market indicators take the value of zero for the
'most competitive' case and increase when markets become more heavily regulated.
We expect some persistence in unemployment, i.e. $0 \le \alpha_0 < 1$ and that positive
output gaps should negatively affect unemployment gaps, $\beta_0 < 0$. Also, *a priori*
the values of both interaction parameters β_1 and α_1 should be positive. This would
imply for example that a more 'rigid' labour market (higher value for IND) is associated with more resilience, e.g. a lower impact of output on the unemployment gap
(in absolute terms) and with higher persistence/slower recovery of the unemployment rate. We estimate equation (3) using generalized least squares (GLS) with
random effects. We include time (year)-fixed effects but not country-fixed effects,
since the latter are already captured by the structural indicators. The results obtained
with country-fixed effects are very similar and available upon request.

Table 4.3 presents the results. We start by including in the model one indicator
at a time, in order to avoid collinearity problems and to preserve the sample size.
Collinearity stems from the fact that when reforms occur, they tend to apply to
many markets. Later on, we will include more indicators simultaneously. Column 1
presents the baseline regression of the simple unemployment gap on a lag and on
the output gap. The estimated coefficients for the GDP gap and the lagged unemployment gap are statistically significant with the expected signs. A 1 percent rise
in the GDP gap is associated with a 0.24 percent decline in unemployment gap.
This value is similar to the average of the individual coefficients estimated previously, country by country. In addition, a 1 percent increase in the lagged unemployment gap carries over to a 0.63 percent rise after one period.

Table 4.3 Modified Okun Law regressions (dependent variable: unemployment gap)

	(1)	(2)	(3)	(4)	(5)
GDP gap	−0.241***	−0.587***	−0.467***	−0.352***	−0.596***
	(0.043)	(0.063)	(0.107)	(0.076)	(0.075)
Unemployment gap (*t*−1)	0.627***	0.540***	0.384***	0.341***	0.434***
	(0.061)	(0.058)	(0.144)	(0.086)	(0.097)
PMR		0.041			0.050
		(0.050)			(0.052)
GDP gap × PMR		0.078***			0.078***
		(0.014)			(0.020)
Unemployment gap (*t*−1) × PMR		0.034***			0.018
		(0.010)			(0.011)
EPL			−0.009		
			(0.032)		
GDP gap × EPL			0.050		
			(0.030)		
Unemployment gap (*t*−1) × EPL			0.107*		
			(0.060)		
CWB				−0.060***	−0.036*
				(0.023)	(0.019)
GDP gap × CWB				0.035*	0.001
				(0.018)	(0.020)
Unemployment gap (*t*−1) × CWB				0.100***	0.045*
				(0.021)	(0.023)
Constant	−0.422***	−0.495**	−0.158	−0.190	−0.355*
	(0.139)	(0.209)	(0.144)	(0.131)	(0.213)
Observations	728	499	347	677	494
within R^2	0.81	0.86	0.87	0.83	0.86

Source: Authors' calculations

Note: All regressions are estimated with Random Effects with year fixed effects. *significant at 10 percent; ** significant at 5 percent; *** significant at 1 percent.

The second column adds the product market regulation index (PMR) and its interactions with the output and lagged unemployment gaps to the explanatory variables. Relative to the first regression, the output gap coefficient becomes larger (−0.587 against −0.241) in absolute value, while the persistence coefficient is somewhat reduced. The first effect is due to the fact that introducing the PMR index allows for the heterogeneity among countries. The 'total' impact effect of the output gap on the unemployment gap now equals −0.587 + 0.078*PMR, which takes the largest value (−0.587) for the least regulated (PMR = 0) market, and the smallest value (= −0.12) for the most regulated one (PMR = 6), confirming our *a priori* that a more regulated market is associated to a more 'resilient' labour market. The PMR interaction with the lagged unemployment gap shows that a more regulated market is characterized by higher unemployment persistence (the α parameters now can take values in the range of $0.54 + 0.034*6 = 0.74$ for the theoretically most regulated product market, corresponding to a half-time adjustment $T*(i) = 2.3$ years, to $\alpha = 0.54$ for the least regulated, implying $T*(i) = 1.1$ years). Conversely, the PMR has no significant independent effect on the level of the unemployment gap.

The third column shows the results for the employment protection legislation (EPL) indicator. This index is not available for many years so that the number of observations shrinks from 728 in the first regression to only 347. The table shows that the EPL interaction term with the lagged unemployment gap is large and statistically significant (at 10 percent confidence), implying that employment protection has a potentially very large effect on persistence. A country with the smallest possible degree of labour regulation (EPL = 0) would take $T*(i) = 0.72$ years to revert half-way to equilibrium following a unit temporary shock to unemployment, compared to $T*(i) = 32$ years (!) for the (theoretically) most regulated country (EPL = 6). The estimates do not show any significant effect of EPL on either the resilience parameter, the β_1 coefficient in equation (3), nor a significant EPL level effect on the dependent variable. Thus, this result implies that a labour legislation more oriented to employment protection is associated with a higher duration of unemployment but does not significantly 'protect' the labour market from demand shocks in the short run.

In column 4 we report the results for the index of centralized wage bargaining, CWB. A more centralized system is associated with a lower impact of the output on the unemployment gap. In fact, the impact effect is lowest (-0.14 percent $= -0.352 + 0.035*6$) for the most centralized bargaining system, and largest for the most decentralized one (-0.352). On the other hand, consistently with the previous results, a more centralized bargaining system is associated with larger persistence of the unemployment gap. The coefficient of the CWB-unemployment-gap interaction is positive and sizable (0.1), and implies that the half-time adjustment ranges from 0.64 years for theoretically least centralized system (CWB = 0) to 11 years for the most centralized one (CWB = 6). Unlike other indicators, the level of CWB is significantly and negatively associated with the unemployment gap.

Finally, column 5 shows the estimates obtained when we add the product market indicator PMR together with the centralized bargaining indicator CWB (we do not include EPL indicator because of collinearity problems and lack of observations). We find that higher regulation of the product market, PMR, increases resilience by reducing the output effect on unemployment exactly by the same amount found in the previous regression in column (2), while the CWB index raises again the persistence effect, although by less than previously estimated, compare columns (4) and (5).

In the Appendix, we repeat the analysis using a specification that replaces unemployment and output gaps with their first/log-differences respectively (see Table 4.A2). We obtain coefficients of the same sign as those discussed, but the estimates of the lagged unemployment interactions, measuring the persistence effect, are less precise (have *p*-values higher than 10 percent). In the case of the last model of column 5, this alternative specification has 'wrong', e.g. negative, sign for the CWB-lagged unemployment interaction.

Summarizing, we find that the persistence-resilience trade-off in unemployment that we have documented in the previous section can be meaningfully explained by the different national labour and product market institutions of the Euro area's countries. More regulated markets tend to display higher resilience, e.g. a lower response of unemployment to output shocks, and higher persistence of unemployment.

4.6 The estimated effects of structural reforms on unemployment in southern Europe

Given the book's focus on structural reforms in Southern European countries, one important question is whether the structural reforms hastily introduced by these countries during the crisis have affected, over and above the austerity measures, the size and persistence of the unemployment rate. In order to answer this question, we adopt the following methodology. We calculate the predicted unemployment gap (estimated from the regression in column 5, in Table 4.3), assuming that both the output gap and the structural indicators take their actual realizations, the latter reflecting the effects of structural reform; we compare these values with those obtained calculating a 'counterfactual' unemployment gap, that is obtained for the same values of the output gaps, when the structural indicators are frozen at their 2007 values, in a 'no reform' scenario. The difference between the predicted and counterfactual unemployment gap gives an imperfect measure of the impact of structural reforms on unemployment gaps that is not affected by other policy measures, such as fiscal policy, that mostly affect the labour market through output (note that these calculations assume that structural reforms do not directly affect actual and potential output).

Greece

Some of the reforms recently implemented in Greece are described in this book's Chapter 8. Figure 4.9 shows the results of our counterfactual analysis. The indexes of product market regulation and wage centralization are shown in panel a, while panel b shows the difference between the predicted ('with reforms') and the counterfactual ('no-reforms') unemployment gap. We see that the product market reforms that occurred since the crisis are not as substantial as those of the labour market (see Manasse 2015 for a discussion). Conversely, the large wave of labour market deregulation occurring in 2010 is associated with a large increase in the actual unemployment relative to the counterfactual, with a differential reaching 1.1 percentage points in 2011. According to our previous results, this reflects the fact that the reforms reduced the resilience of the labour market by raising the impact of output shocks on unemployment. However, we also see that as soon as 2013 the differential turns negative, suggesting that a 'positive' effect of the reforms eventually kicks in, by reducing the unemployment persistence. While

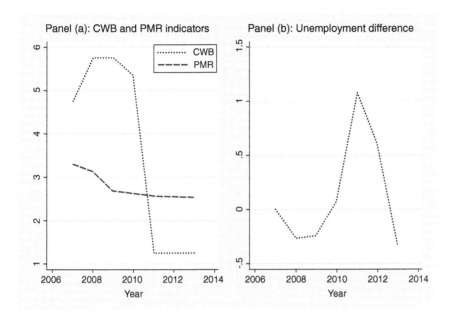

Figure 4.9 Reforms and unemployment: Greece

these effects are not large, the actual and counterfactual unemployment gaps are found significantly different in mean.

Italy

Figure 4.10 shows that the labour market reforms that were introduced in 2009 were quite timid and gradual and some liberalization of product markets occurred in the same years, although far less effective than in the other countries considered here. The effect was to raise the actual level of unemployment by a tenth of a percentage point (these estimates do not include the 'jobs act' labour reform introduced in Italy only in 2014–15). At the same time, there is no 'catching-up' so that there appears to be little positive effects in terms of gained speed of recovery.

Portugal

The main labour market reforms implemented in Portugal are described in Chapter 6 of this book. Figure 4.11 shows the evolution of market regulation indicators as well as the actual and counterfactual unemployment gap in Portugal. The index of product market regulation declines steadily since 2008, while only in 2012, as a consequence of reforms, we observe a sharp decline of the wage centralization index, CWB. The estimated effects are relatively small: for 2012, we estimate an increase of the actual relative to the counterfactual unemployment rate of about a tenth of a percentage point. The difference is short lasting and almost disappears one year later.

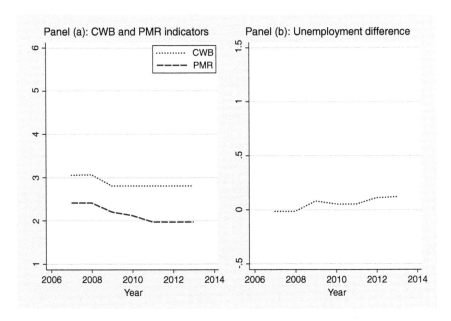

Figure 4.10 Reforms and unemployment: Italy

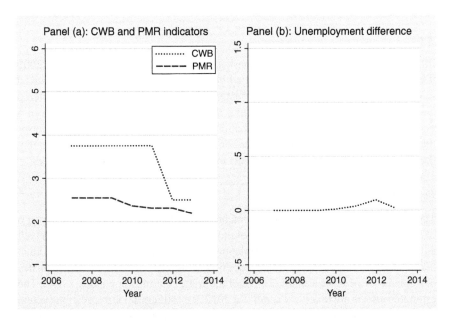

Figure 4.11 Reforms and unemployment: Portugal

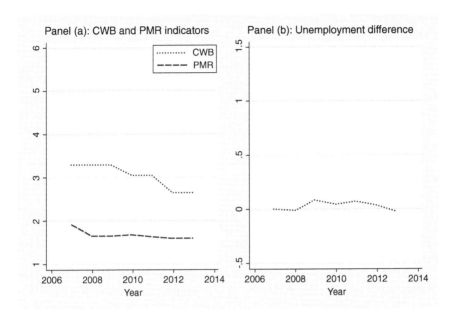

Figure 4.12 Reforms and unemployment: Spain

Spain

The main labour reforms implemented in Spain are described in Chapter 7. These reforms show up in a significant reduction on the index of centralization of wage bargaining, first in 2008 and later in 2011, while product market reforms result in a more gradual decline in the index of regulation since 2007 (see Figure 4.12, left panel). The right panel of the figure shows that in correspondence with the reforms the unemployment gap slightly rises above that of the no-reform scenario, by about a tenth of a percentage point, but already in 2013, the effect is reversed and the unemployment rate falls below that of the no-reform scenario.

4.7 Conclusion

Southern European countries went through a very painful process of fiscal consolidation, debt and bank restructuring, credit squeeze and recession, and, under pressure from creditors, started an ambitious and politically sensitive programme of reforms stretching from the public sector to credit, labour and product markets. These countries experienced their worst recession since World War II, with unemployment soaring to unprecedented levels. The jury is still out on the role of austerity. Opinions differ also on the role of structural reforms (see the discussion in the introductory chapter of this book). Some observers for example, consider that the reforms were insufficient, not fully implemented or were not fully credible, while other critics blame them for being too radical, unfocused, wrongly sequenced or counter-productive in terms of the short-run effects on the economy. Given that many adverse shocks were affecting these economies at the same time, it not easy to isolate the role, if any, of the reforms.

And yet while unemployment soared in all Southern European countries during the crisis, the impact of the output squeeze on the labour market as well as the persistence of high unemployment rates differed sharply among countries, with Spain and Cyprus displaying the largest short-run elasticity of unemployment to output, but also the fastest speed of adjustment, and the opposite in Greece, Italy and Portugal.

In this paper, we analyze the response of the labour markets in the Eurozone. First, we document two important aspects of this response: the resilience of unemployment to output shocks, and the persistence of shocks to unemployment. We find that most countries of the Eurozone lie on a trade-off between resilience and persistence: countries where the rate of unemployment is less affected on impact, displaying thus higher resilience, typically also show higher unemployment persistence.

In order to isolate the effects of structural reforms on the working of the labour market, we investigate empirically the role of employment protection, centralization of wage bargaining and of product market institutions, in affecting unemployment as well as its dynamic response to shocks. We find evidence that more protected labour and product markets are characterized by more resilience at the expense of greater persistence, while more competitive markets make employment more vulnerable to output shocks but also experience a faster recovery.

We estimate how much product and labour market reforms may have contributed to the rise of unemployment in Southern Europe, and/or to the faster/slower recovery, by comparing projection of unemployment gaps with an artificial counterfactual of no-reform, obtained by freezing labour and product markets to their pre-2008 situation. For Greece, we find that the front-loaded labour market reforms introduced since 2010 account for one (extra) percentage point rise in the unemployment gap. The effect for other Southern European countries is smaller, also in the light of the less pronounced reforms implemented since 2008. The case for Greece is interesting because we also find that the reforms significantly entail a faster recovery relative to the counterfactual scenario, so that after only two years the rate of unemployment becomes lower and more rapidly falling than in the absence of reforms. This is true, although to a lesser extent, also for the other South European countries.

To some extent these results should not come as a surprise: the crisis that hit Southern European countries was unprecedented, summing the effects of harsh fiscal consolidations, sudden stops and current account reversals, wage deflation, sovereign and banks' defaults leading to credit crunches and ending in the worst recession of the post-war era. Employment and unemployment changes were, to a first degree, driven by these factors. Our analysis has shown that degree of product and labour market competition can significantly affect the short-run resilience and the medium-run persistence of unemployment in these economies.

Note

1 This formula can be derived as follows: consider an initial situation where the unemployment rate and output are at their equilibrium values, and a temporary shock at time 0, v_0, raises the unemployment rate. After T periods, the unemployment rate will deviate from its natural level by $\alpha^T v_0$. Provided $|\alpha| < 1$, the rate of unemployment will have converged half-way back to the equilibrium at time T^*, where T^* satisfies $\alpha^{T^*} v_0 = \frac{1}{2} v_0$. Simplifying and taking logs gives the expression in the text.

Bibliography

Alesina, A., Ardagna, S., Nicoletti, G., and Schiantarelli, F. (2005) Regulation and Investment. *Journal of the European Economic Association*, 3(4), 791–825.

Ball, L. M., Leigh, D., and Loungani, P. (2013) *Okun's Law: Fit at Fifty?* National Bureau of Economic Research. Working Paper No. 18668.

Bentolila, S., and Bertola, G. (1990) Firing Costs and Labour Demand: How Bad Is Eurosclerosis? *The Review of Economic Studies*, 57(3), 381–402.

Blanchard, O. J. (2006) European Unemployment: The Evolution of Facts and Ideas. *Economic Policy*, 21(45), 6–59.

Blanchard, O. J., and Giavazzi, F. (2003) Macroeconomic Effects of Regulation and Deregulation in Goods and Labour Markets. *The Quarterly Journal of Economics*, 118(3), 879–907.

Blanchard, O. J., and Portugal, P. (2001) What Hides Behind an Unemployment Rate: Comparing Portuguese and US Labor Markets. *American Economic Review*, 91(1), 187–207.

Blanchard, O. J., and Summers, L. H. (1986) Hysteresis and the European Unemployment Problem. In: Fisher, S. (ed.) *NBER Macroeconomics Annual 1986*, Volume 1, Cambridge, MA, MIT Press, pp. 15–90.

Boeri, T. (2005) *Reforming Labor and Product Markets: Some Lessons From Two Decades of Experiments in Europe*. IMF. Working Paper No. 05/97.

Bouis, R., Causa, O., Demmou, L., and Duval, R. (2012) How Quickly Does Structural Reform Pay Off? An Empirical Analysis of the Short-Term Effects of Unemployment Benefit Reform. *IZA Journal of Labor Policy*, 1(1), 1–12.

Bruno, M., and Sachs, J. (1985): *Economics of Worldwide Stagflation*, Cambridge, MA, Harvard University Press.

Cacciatore, M., Duval, R., Fiori, G., and Ghironi, F. (2015) *Short-Term Pain for Long-Term Gain: Market Deregulation and Monetary Policy in Small Open Economies*. National Bureau of Economic Research. Working Paper No. 21784.

Calmfors, L., and Driffill, J. (1988) Bargaining Structure, Corporatism and Macroeconomic Performance. *Economic Policy*, 3(6), 13–61.

Cazes, S., Heuer, C., and Verick, S. (2011) Labour Market Policies in Times of Crisis. In: Islam, I. and Verick, S. (eds.) *From the Great Recession to Labour Market Recovery*, London, UK, Palgrave Macmillan, pp. 196–226.

Conway, P., and Nicoletti, G. (2006) *Product Market Regulation in the Non-Manufacturing Sectors of OECD Countries*. OECD Economics Department. Working Paper No. 419.

Di Tella, R., and MacCulloch, R. (2005) The Consequences of Labor Market Flexibility: Panel Evidence Based on Survey Data. *European Economic Review*, 49(5), 1225–1259.

Ebell, M., and Haefke, C. (2009) Product Market Deregulation and the U.S. Employment Miracle. *Review of Economic Dynamics*, 12(3), 479–504.

Eicher, T. S., and Schreiber, T. (2010) Structural Policies and Growth: Time Series Evidence From a Natural Experiment. *Journal of Development Economics*, 91(1), 169–179.

Eslava, M., Haltiwanger, J., Kugler, A., and Kugler, M. (2004) The Effects of Structural Reforms on Productivity and Profitability Enhancing Reallocation: Evidence From Colombia. *Journal of Development Economics*, 75(2), 333–371.

Fiori, G., Nicoletti, G., Scarpetta, S., and Schiantarelli, F. (2012) Employment Effects of Product and Labour Market Reforms: Are There Synergies? *The Economic Journal*, 122(558), F79–F104.

Gordon, R. J. (2011) The Evolution of Okun's Law and of Cyclical Productivity Fluctuations in the United States and in the EU-15. *Presentation at EES/IAB Workshop, Labour Market Institutions and the Macroeconomy*, Nuremberg, June.

Griffith, R., Harrison, R., and Simpson, H. (2006) *The Link Between Product Market Reform, Innovation and EU Macroeconomic Performance*. European Commission Directorate General for Economic and Monetary Affairs. Economic Paper No. 243.

IMF (2010) *World Economic Outlook*. October 2010. Available from: https://www.imf.org/external/pubs/ft/weo/2010/01/.

Kugler, A. D. (1999) The Impact of Firing Costs on Turnover and Unemployment: Evidence From the Colombian Labour Market Reform. *International Tax and Public Finance*, 6(3), 389–410.

Manasse, P. (2015) *What Went Wrong in Greece and How to Fix It*. VoxEU. [Online]. Available from: http://voxeu.org/article/what-went-wrong-greece-and-how-fix-it.

Mankiw, N. G. (2013) Defending the One Percent. *The Journal of Economic Perspectives*, 27(3), 21–34.

OECD (2004) *Employment Outlook*. OECD. Available from: http://www.oecd.org/els/emp/oecdemploymentoutlook2004.htm.

OECD (2015) *Employment Outlook*. OECD. Available from: http://www.oecd-ilibrary.org/employment/oecd-employment-outlook-2015_empl_outlook-2015-en.

Rodrik, D. (2016) The Elusive Promise of Structural Reform: The Trillion-Euro Misunderstanding. *Milken Institute Review*, 18(2), 26–35.

Schiffbauer, M., and Ospina, S. (2010) *Competition and Firm Productivity: Evidence From Firm-level Data*. IMF. Working Paper No. 10/67.

Staehr, K. (2005) Reforms and Economic Growth in Transition Economies: Complementarity, Sequencing and Speed. *The European Journal of Comparative Economics*, 2(2), 177–202.

Visser, J. (2015) *ICTWSS Data Base*. Version 5.0. Amsterdam: Amsterdam Institute for Advanced Labour Studies AIAS.

Appendix
An alternative specification

In order to check for the robustness of our results we estimate an alternative specification for our model, summarized by equation (1). This replaces the unemployment gap and the (log) output gap with their respective first differences:

$$u_{it} - u_{it-1} = \beta_i\left(y_{it} - y_{it-1}\right) + \alpha_i\left(u_{it-1} - u_{it-2}\right) + v_{it} \qquad i = 1..C, \qquad t = 1,..T \qquad (1a)$$

Table 4.A1 shows the impact and persistence parameters based on estimating equation (1a) country by country.

Table 4.A1 Okun coefficients in the Eurozone (difference regression)

Country	beta	alpha	Half-way time
Austria	0.12***	0.08	0.28
Belgium	0.24***	0.43***	0.81
Cyprus	0.35***	0.36***	0.67
Estonia	0.38***	0.29***	0.56
Finland	0.31***	0.49***	0.97
France	0.26***	0.28***	0.54
Germany	0.23***	0.44***	0.85
Greece	0.11***	0.61***	1.39
Ireland	0.24***	0.21	0.44
Italy	0.15***	0.50***	1.00
Latvia	0.20***	0.27	0.54
Lithuania	0.14***	0.16	0.38
Luxembourg	0.03***	0.20	0.43
Malta	0.12***	0.00	
Netherlands	0.28***	0.19*	0.42
Portugal	0.15***	0.40***	0.76
Slovakia	0.40***	0.20	0.43
Slovenia	0.16***	0.46***	0.89
Spain	0.47***	0.18*	0.40

Source: Authors' calculations

Notes: Alpha in absolute value. *** significant at 1 percent; ** significant at 5 percent; * significant
at 10 percent.

In this specification, countries differences in the impact and persistence parameters are less pronounced than before, but still exhibit a trade-off. According to Table 4.A1, the impact of output change on unemployment change is highest in Spain, Slovakia, Estonia and Cyprus where a 1 percent output fall relative to previous period is associated, within a year, to about 0.40 of a percent rise in the unemployment difference. The response of unemployment is lowest in Luxembourg, Greece, Austria and Italy. It is also interesting to see that Greece and Italy are also the countries where unemployment rebounds relatively slowly (high α_i). In Greece, it takes more than a year to halve the unemployment shock, whereas in Italy it takes exactly one year.

The 'trade-off' picture corresponding to these new estimates is shown in Figure 4.A1.

In the new specification, the countries are less heterogeneous in terms of their impact and persistence coefficients. Some countries (Austria, Lithuania and Luxembourg in addition to Malta) seem to lie off the trade-off curve. However, countries like Spain, Slovakia, Cyprus and Finland still appear as displaying among the largest impact and the smallest persistence coefficients, as with our previous model; similarly, Italy, Slovenia, Portugal and Greece continue to be characterized by very large persistence and very low impact effects. After removing the countries which have insignificant alpha coefficient, we obtain a correlation and rank correlation between the new estimated parameters which are similar to the previous ones respectively 0.65 (significant at 4 percent) and 0.61 (significant at 6 percent).

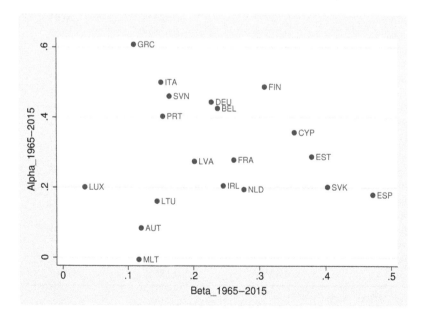

Figure 4.A1 Trade-off between impact and persistence (difference regression)

Table 4.A2 Okun analysis with market indicators (dependent variable: unemployment change)

	(1)	(2)	(3)	(4)	(5)
GDP growth	−0.136***	−0.342***	−0.236***	−0.252***	−0.310**
	(0.022)	(0.090)	(0.087)	(0.056)	(0.137)
Unemployment change (t−1)	0.391***	0.516***	0.284*	0.263***	0.619***
	(0.039)	(0.106)	(0.157)	(0.089)	(0.151)
PMR		0.028			0.015
		(0.078)			(0.082)
GDP growth × PMR		0.044**			0.047**
		(0.019)			(0.020)
Unemployment change (t−1) × PMR		−0.022			−0.010
		(0.026)			(0.030)
EPL			−0.012		
			(0.081)		
GDP growth × EPL			−0.005		
			(0.019)		
Unemployment change (t−1) × EPL			0.061		
			(0.066)		
CWB				−0.156**	0.035
				(0.065)	(0.074)
GDP growth × CWB				0.026*	−0.014
				(0.014)	(0.025)
Unemployment change (t−1) × CWB				0.040	−0.049**
				(0.026)	(0.019)
Constant	0.078	−0.120	−0.004	0.500*	−0.220
	(0.219)	(0.301)	(0.221)	(0.296)	(0.270)
Observations	736	500	347	689	495
R^2	0.52	0.61	0.68	0.54	0.62

Source: Authors' calculations

Note: All regressions are estimated with Random Effects with year fixed effects. *significant at 10 percent; ** significant at 5 percent; *** significant at 1 percent.

Table 4.A2 contains the estimation results of the second step, where we consider all countries jointly, and allow the coefficients to depend on labour and product market indicators. In practice, here we use the specification with first differences, equation (1a) above, together with equation (2) and estimate the following equation:

$$u_{it} - u_{it-1} = \left(\beta_0 + \beta_1 IND_{it}\right)\left(y_{it} - y_{it-1}\right) + \left(\alpha_0 + \alpha_1 IND_{it-1}\right)\left(u_{it-1} - u_{it-2}\right) \\ + \left(c_0 + c_1 IND_{it}\right) + v_{it} \tag{1b}$$

As in the previous analysis, we start without any market indicator in column 1. The result is that GDP growth and lag unemployment change have respectively significant negative and positive impacts on unemployment change. We introduce

PMR indicator in column 2. It appears that greater rigidity in the product market decreases the impact of economic growth on the unemployment change. However, there is no significant relationship between PMR and unemployment persistence. Column 3 shows that the coefficients of EPL become insignificant at the standard confidence levels. Regarding the CWB, we find in column 4 that CWB rigidity tends to reduce the impact effect of output growth on unemployment. The interaction of CWB with lagged unemployment is of the expected positive sign, so that rigidity raises persistence, but it is only marginally significant (0.12 *p*-value). Also, we find a negative level effect of CWB on the unemployment change. We introduce both CWB and PMR in column 5. Here we have that the coefficients of the interaction of PMR with GDP growth is positive and significant, suggesting that, as before, a more regulated product market alleviates the negative impact of negative GDP shocks. However, the parameter estimate of the interaction of the lagged unemployment change-CWB changes sign relative to column (4), now suggesting that a more centralized system reduces the unemployment persistence. In general, the new specification with first differences has lower *p*-values relative to 'gap' specification.

5 Reforms and external balances in Southern Europe and Ireland

Luís A. V. Catão[1]

2.1 Introduction

A key macroeconomic development leading to the financial crises of 2009–12 in Europe was the emergence of very large deficits in the external current accounts (CAs) of Greece, Ireland, Portugal and Spain. In particular, the three southern countries posted CA deficits that exceeded 10 percent of GDP in the run-up to the crises. Not only were such deficits rather sizeable relative to those countries' own historical record since World War II, but also large relative to those typically observed in external financial crises in emerging markets – where 'sudden stops' in capital inflows hit when the CA deficit rises above 4 to 5 percent of GDP (Catão and Milesi-Ferretti 2014).

To be sure, crisis-free countries with CA deficits of the order of 10 percent or so of GDP are not unheard of historically. Some of today's advanced economies such as Australia, Canada and some of the Scandinavian economies, experienced deficits approaching such magnitudes between the late 19th century and early 20th century, as swift growth of labour and capital inputs together with rising total factor productivity (TFP henceforth) and persistent improvement in the price of their exports relative to the domestic cost of producing them, assured investors that those deficits would be eventually reversed and the large accumulation of external liabilities be fully repaid.

Those conditions were not apparent in some of Eurozone by the eve of the 2009–12 financial crises. Table 5.1 shows that despite higher real GDP growth than the median of other non-crisis EU countries (3.9 percent vs. 2.2 percent) since the onset of the euro, key macroeconomic fundamentals were generally weaker – and some of them significantly so – in the four crisis countries. In particular, TFP growth was negative in three of the four countries; unit labour costs (measured as the ratio of the average wage to labour productivity) were also rising relative to the EU average in all four countries, implying that domestic production was getting costlier; and so was consumer goods' price inflation, implying an appreciation of the real exchange rate (the price of domestic vs. foreign goods expressed in a common currency) again pointing to a loss of external competitiveness. Finally and no less importantly, net foreign assets (NFA) – which is equal to the

Table 5.1 Real GDP growth and relative country fundamentals in the EU, 1999–2007

	Real GDP growth	TFP growth	CPI Inflation	Unit Labour Cost Growth	Real Exchange Rate Growth	Exports/ GDP	Net Foreign Assets/ GDP
			Selected Fundamental Indicators				
	(1999– 2007)	(1999– 2007)	(1999– 2007)	(1999– 2007)	(1999– 2007)	(1999– 2007)	2007
Austria	2.37	0.63	1.90	−0.96	0.25	47.11	−21.55
Belgium	2.24	0.11	2.09	1.62	0.63	72.50	29.73
Finland	3.48	1.51	1.59	−1.54	0.02	40.52	−30.51
France	2.11	0.18	1.93	−0.29	0.33	26.90	−4.30
Germany	1.65	−0.29	1.68	−1.81	0.02	35.70	25.70
Greece	4.09	0.66	3.28	2.35	1.08	21.39	−102.42
Ireland	6.05	−1.03	3.50	−0.73	3.09	84.58	−20.94
Italy	1.49	−0.61	2.38	2.05	0.75	25.19	−29.43
Netherlands	2.27	0.64	2.46	0.55	0.82	65.39	−8.60
Portugal	1.52	−0.60	3.03	1.00	1.20	28.03	−99.90
Spain	3.74	−0.79	3.30	1.80	1.62	26.10	−84.44
Crisis Countries' Median	**3.92**	**−0.70**	**3.29**	**1.40**	**1.41**	**27.07**	**−92.17**
Non-Crisis Countries' Median	**2.24**	**0.18**	**1.93**	**−0.29**	**0.33**	**40.52**	**−8.60**

Sources: International Financial Statistics and IMF/WEO databases, and Penn World (Table 9.0).

accumulation of current account balances plus valuation effects – were highly negative in Greece, Portugal and Spain at close to 100% of GDP. Furthermore, because openness to international trade (as measured by the ratio of exports of goods and services to GDP) was lower than the EU average – with the exception of Ireland, the ratio of net foreign assets to exports was even higher. This is an important indicator of the sustainability of external balances because, in the absence of valuation effects, the present value of net external liabilities has to be ultimately paid with net exports.

The upshot is that weaker macroeconomic fundamentals made those four countries externally more 'fragile' relative to other Eurozone peers. In those circumstances, as observed many times in macroeconomic crises in emerging markets in the past, a large external shock – such as that triggered by the financial panic in the United States in the summer of 2008, can rapidly unravel high external deficits.[2] Figure 5.1 shows that the turnaround of current account balances was massive in all four countries from 2008 onwards.[3]

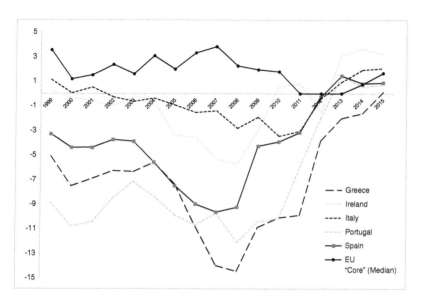

Figure 5.1 Current account balances in the Eurozone, 1999–2015 (percentage of GDP)

Data source: IMF World Economic Outlook database, April 2016

The fact that this was so notwithstanding the large injection of external multi-lateral financing by the European Central Bank, the International Monetary Fund (through adjustment programmes in Greece, Ireland and Portugal) and (from 2012) by the European Financial Stability Facility (EFSF) and European Stability Mechanism (ESM), gives an idea of the exceptional nature of the external adjustment that southern Europe and Ireland underwent between 2009 and 2015. Figure 5.1 also indicates that swings in current account surpluses in the north of the Eurozone (here defined as Austria, Belgium, Finland, France, Germany and the Netherlands) have been the flip side of the external adjustment in the South.

Against this background, this chapter seeks to answer three related questions:

(1) To what extent have the current account adjustments since 2008 in Greece, Ireland, Portugal and Spain responded to macroeconomic adjustments?
(2) To what extent have structural reforms helped current account adjustment and in making these economies more 'competitive' going forward?
(3) In light of recent developments in relative competitiveness and reforms, what could one expect regarding the path of their external balances going forward?

5.2 Current account determinants in the Eurozone

The view that the size of the current account should matter for macroeconomic performance is controversial among macroeconomists (see Obstfeld 2012, for a broad discussion and references). After all, the current account is the net balance between gross financial flows in and out of a country, and international financial integration implies that both inflows and outflows can (and arguably should) be very large as a share of GDP. Thus, it is natural that non-trivial gaps between such inflows and outflows may sometime arise in the course of the economic cycle; hence the CA may experience temporary large deficits. Such imbalances should be even more expected and possibly longer lasting in a currency union where non-trivial differences in economic structures across member countries remain and exchange rate flexibility is no longer present to speed up the adjustment in the relative price of domestic- vs. foreign-produced goods to macroeconomic shocks.

Yet, even in a currency union where exchange rate risk is removed and common central bank policies may greatly help reduce country-specific risk, large CA deficits lasting several years may also be problematic. For instance, such deficits may call into question a member country's incentive to restore fiscal discipline and repay the accumulated net foreign liabilities when they grow large, thereby raising investors' concerns about what economists call the 'inter-temporal solvency constraint'. Since outright default and/or 'hair-cuts' of the contractual value of those liabilities is one way to satisfy that constraint, investors may seek to limit the country's indebtedness relative to its income (i.e. the ratio of external liabilities to GDP). A market mechanism through which this is accomplished is the rise in a positive interest 'premium' charged by investors to lend to indebted governments.[4] Once this financing constraint begins to hit, external borrowing can become very expensive to the point that net foreign borrowing cannot remain large, i.e. the country's current account balance has to adjust to that reality. A well-known gauge of this situation is the spread in the interest rate of government bonds denominated in the same currency – in this case the euro – between countries. Such an interest spread began to widen rapidly for South European government bonds starting in the summer of 2008. While the spike in government bond spread was far from homogeneous across countries (in Spain for instance it started only in 2011–12), they do suggest that debt sustainability was becoming a growing cause of investors' concern under a less favourable global economic outlook. Since a non-trivial portion of those bonds were sold to foreigners, they were a clear counterpart of CA flows and thus a manifestation of concerns about the sustainability of these countries' own CA deficits which persisted and grew even larger for several years (as illustrated in Figure 5.2). As often witnessed in history, large current account deficits and sovereign debt crises go hand in hand.

The key question is then what makes a CA deficit 'sustainable' in the sense that such a constraint on further external indebtedness does not emerge. Learning about which variables make CA position 'sustainable' is clearly important for policy makers to design a system of measures – of both a conjectural and a structural nature – to mitigate the risk of abrupt reversals in the flow of external financing which can take a long-lasting toll on output and employment.

Theoretical and empirical research over the past two decades has highlighted a number of critical variables in this connection. These are listed in Table 5.2.[5] Since basic national income accounting says that the CA is what a country's residents

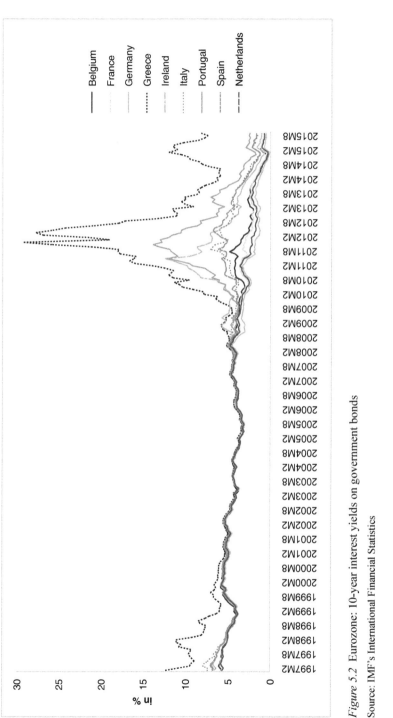

Figure 5.2 Eurozone: 10-year interest yields on government bonds

Source: IMF's International Financial Statistics

Table 5.2 Theoretical determinants of current account balances

Domestic Saving shifters	Domestic Investment Shifters	External Financing Shifters
Initial NFA	TFP growth	Global Risk Aversion (VIX)
Per capita income	Output Gap	Cross-Border Capital Controls
Age dependency ratio	Domestic credit growth	
Population growth		
Domestic credit growth		
Fiscal balance		
Commodity TOT growth		

save minus what they invest, it is useful to break down CA determinants between drivers of domestic saving and investment, in addition to external influences that are not directly under the country's control (what is called in the table 'External Financing Shifters'), but which may nevertheless affect both domestic saving and investment, and hence the CA.

Table 5.3 shows how these variables affect CAs across the Eurozone. It does that by regressing the ratio of the overall current account to GDP (CA/GDP) of each of the original twelve members (Austria, Belgium, Finland, France, Germany, Greece, Ireland, Italy, Luxembourg, the Netherlands, Portugal and Spain) on the variables above starting in the year following the introduction of the Exchange Rate mechanism (i.e. 1980) through 2015.[6] As standard in the analysis of cross-country CA regressions, fixed effects are omitted and all right-hand side variables are measured relative to the foreign country counterparts, in this case the EU12 (GDP weighted) average.[7] To corroborate the robustness of the estimates to the potential reversed causality from the CA to variables like the output gap, the fiscal balance and credit growth, an instrumental variable (IV) estimator is also reported, with very similar results.[8]

Table 5.3 shows that a relatively parsimonious model can explain about 60 percent of intra Eurozone imbalances. This is respectful explanatory power given how difficult it is to explain CA variations over time and across countries. Scrolling down the list of explanatory variables from the top, the positive effect on NFA reflects the counter-point of two effects at play. On the one hand, a very negative net foreign asset position (like those in Southern Europe) creates a negative wealth effect and calls for a positive trade balance so that net liabilities are eventually paid off and the inter-temporal budget constraint is satisfied. On the other hand, more negative NFA implies greater flow of interest payments abroad which depresses the CA. On balance, the latter effect typically dominates in broad cross-country regressions spanning advanced and emerging market economies (see Phillips et al. 2013). Table 5.3 shows that this is also the case for the Eurozone. The effect is economically large: a country that has a net foreign liability of 60–80 percentage points above the EU12 average (which is roughly what Greece, Portugal and Spain had before the 2008–12 financial crisis), should be expected to run a CA deficit of 1.5 to 2% of GDP, all else constant.

Table 5.3 Determinants of CA balances in EU 12 countries

	Pooled OLS	*IV Method*
Net Foreign Assets/GDP, lag	0.0255*	0.0263*
	(0.0138)	(0.0136)
Per Capita GDP, lag	2.61e-06**	2.55e-06**
	(9.60e-07)	(9.26e-07)
Population Growth	−1.714***	−1.690***
	(0.453)	(0.457)
Old Dependency Ratio	−0.247*	−0.254*
	(0.121)	(0.120)
Ageing Speed	0.144**	0.143**
	(0.0536)	(0.0541)
Capital Controls	−0.0455*	−0.0476*
	(0.0241)	(0.0232)
Primary Fiscal Balance	0.270**	0.278**
	(0.0888)	(0.0915)
Output Gap	−0.534***	−0.545***
	(0.145)	(0.144)
VIX * EU core	−0.00535	−0.00519
	(0.00356)	(0.00342)
Terms of Trade Growth	−0.0427	−0.0444
	(0.0656)	(0.0694)
TFP Growth	0.274**	0.259**
	(0.0977)	(0.0999)
Change in Credit/GDP	−0.145**	−0.146**
	(0.0590)	(0.0588)
Constant	−0.00171	−0.00175
	(0.00349)	(0.00341)
Observations	437	432
R^2	0.599	0.601

Source: Author's calculations

Robust standard errors in parentheses *** $p < 0.01$, ** $p < 0.05$, * $p < 0.1$

As the general empirical literature on current account determinants has also found (see Phillips et al. 2013), differences in per capita income are also significant determinants of intra Eurozone CA imbalances. The sign of the estimates coefficient accords with a central prediction of the neo-classical model that richer countries (which are typically more capital abundant) should export capital and hence run current account surpluses on average. The attendant point estimate in Table 5.3 indicates that every US$5,000 increase in per capita income relative to the EU12 weighted average improves the CA by 1 percentage point of GDP. So, the fact that Southern Eurozone members are a few thousand euros poorer (in per capita income terms) than Northern Eurozone members, together with having a 60–80% more negative NFA/GDP ratio, already puts their current accounts into substantively negative territory, of the order of 3 to

4 GDP percentage points, holding all other (particularly cyclical) considerations constant.

The following triplet of demographic variables (population growth, current dependency ratios and the speed of its future evolution) have the expected signs and also hold significant explanatory power together, though the net effect is smaller than those of the above two variables and more disparate across countries.[9] This is both because intra Eurozone differences in those variables are smaller and also because some of the crisis-hit countries (notably Ireland) have higher population growth and dependency ratios well below the EU12 average, whereas some of them (like Greece) have dependency ratios which are non-trivially above the EU12 average. In particular, the much lower dependency ratio of Ireland (about 11% below EU12 average) coupled with an estimated coefficient of about –0.25 does help account by nearly half (2.5 percentage points) of its CA/GDP gap *vis-à-vis* the Southern peers on the eve of Eurozone financial crisis.

The above results also reject changes in the countries' Terms of Trade growth and in global risk aversion – as measured by an index of implied stock market volatility (the so-called VIX index) as drivers of intra-European imbalances. This lack of significance is not surprising: terms of trade changes tend to be correlated with the output variables included in the regression and risk aversion (as captured by the VIX) only matters if it affects countries differently (so that its effect on exports and imports are different).[10] In the case of capital controls (measured as in Phillips et al. 2013), the coefficient is statistically significant only at a 10% level and is economically small. This is not surprising since the bulk of capital account restrictions in Europe have been lifted in the 1990s and, in the sample of countries considered, were re-introduced only in Greece in 2015.

Yet, the regression results point to three remaining variables as key to explain both how pre-crisis 'excess' imbalances arose and how the post-2008 reforms may impact future external balances in the four crisis-hit countries.[11]

The first is the general government balance – here entered net of interest expenses to capture the component of fiscal policy that is more closely under control of national governments and which is more exogenous to the current account. As mentioned above and widely documented elsewhere, fiscal imbalances (on both the positive and negative side) have been an important driver of external imbalances in the Eurozone. The highly significant – both statistically and economically – coefficient of 0.27 on the primary fiscal balance shown in Table 5.3 suggests that saving-investment decisions are not neutral to fiscal policy, implying that the so-called 'Ricardian equivalence' does not hold: the attendant point estimate says a 10-percentage point improvement in the general government primary balance (a magnitude which is not too much off the mark for crisis-hit countries between 2009 and 2015) translates into a nearly 3-percentage point improvement in the CA/GDP ratio. So, these regression results clearly indicate that reform efforts which impart a significant and sustained improvement in fiscal balances should have far-reaching effects on Southern Europe's external positions.

The second key variable is the gap between real GDP and its 'potential' or trend level (measured as in Phillips et al. 2013 by the HP filter), i.e., the so-called 'output gap'. The significant negative sign of that variable indicates that when demand outpaces domestic supply (i.e. the economy is 'overheated' in popular parlance), such an excess is met by a rise in imports relative to exports, thus implying that the CA balance declines.

The high-demand effect associated with a positive output gap may be counterbalanced by what happens to total factor productivity (TFP). As shown in Table 5.3, higher TFP growth relative to EU partners tends to improve the CA. This positive effect is not obvious in theory because higher TFP can boost investment (insofar as it raises firms' profits) and lower savings (insofar as households anticipate higher income growth resulting from higher TFP, and increase their consumption relative to present income). Yet, a positive effect of higher TFP on the CA can also be rationalized. For one thing, a higher TFP (implying a more productive use of domestic production factors) also reduces inefficient capital, thus lowering actual investment for a given unit of output. In addition, to the extent that a higher TFP signals greater investment opportunities in the future that firms may choose to finance out of current earnings, firms may choose to distribute fewer dividends, thereby raising corporate savings. More generally, a higher TFP implies that the country can produce at lower cost and hence at lower prices than abroad. Hence, the trade balance and the CA will tend to improve with TFP growth. This interpretation is supported by the fact that TOT growth is not significant in the regression as some of its effects are already captured by TFP growth. It follows from this that structural reforms that boost TFP should also help improve the CA. The links between structural reforms and TFP will be discussed below.

Last but not least, faster growth of domestic bank credit relative to GDP shows up as major negative influence on the CA: a 10-percent rise in the ratio of credit to GDP (relative to Eurozone-wide averages) leads to a CA deterioration of about 1.5% of GDP. Since the regressions in Table 5.3 already control for the output gap (and through it for the effects of lower real interest rates in the home country), such a strong effect of credit growth on the CA accords well with both modern theories of financial amplification, according to which credit expansion fuels aggregate demand (and often by more than it effects aggregate supply). Such a strong effect of changes in credit/GDP ratios on the CA also accords well with widespread commentary on 'excessive' private sector leveraging and the importance of the bank credit channel in driving capital flows across the Eurozone (see, e.g. Lane and McQuade 2013). As will be discussed as follows, since credit growth in excess of GDP is highly correlated with increases in bank sector leverage, the econometric evidence of Table 5.3 does provide a case for an important role of regulatory frameworks in affecting intra-EU imbalances.

Overall, what does this econometric model tell us about seemingly 'excessive' external imbalances? Figures 5.3a–d plot the gaps between actual CA/GDP ratios and those predicted (in-sample) by the model. Two 'model-fit' lines are plotted: one that does not correct for the size of the cyclical expansions/contractions, and the other that does. Neither should be seen as 'desirable' CA/GDP levels, but rather those that are broadly consistent with typical historical responses of the CA to its macroeconomic determinants listed in Table 5.2. Moreover, because shifts in

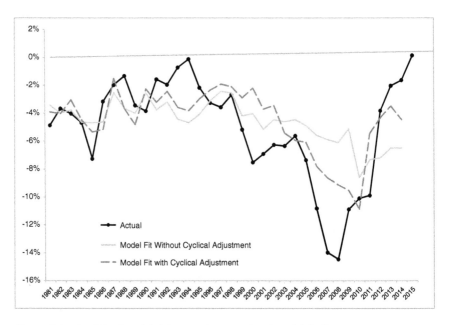

Figure 5.3a CA/GDP in crisis-hit countries: actual and model fit Greece

Sources: IMF World Economic Outlook database, April 2016 and author's calculations

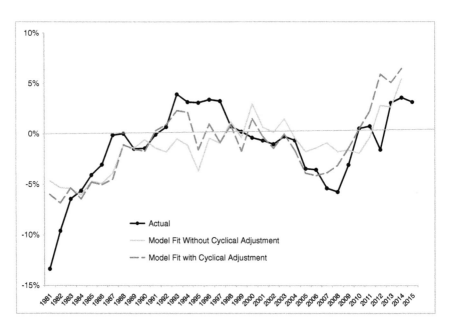

Figure 5.3b Ireland

Sources: IMF World Economic Outlook database, April 2016 and author's calculations

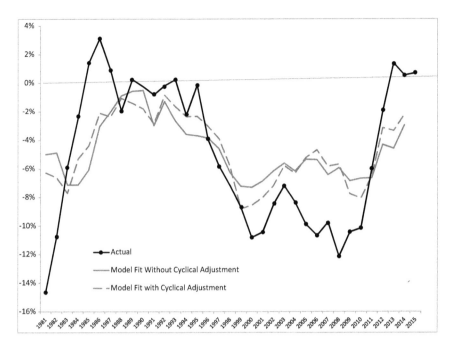

Figure 5.3c Portugal

Sources: IMF World Economic Outlook database, April 2016 and author's calculation

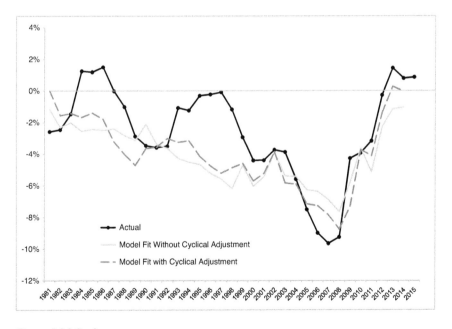

Figure 5.3d Spain

Sources: IMF World Economic Outlook database, April 2016 and author's calculation

private sector expectations (in the direction of either excessive 'pessimism' or over-optimism over the repayment capacity of borrowers) are hard to measure and are deemed to have been important particularly in Ireland and Spain, this is another source of residual discrepancy between model prediction and actual CA values.[12]

These charts highlight four developments. One is that prior to the crises, all four countries had current accounts more negative than what the model would predict. In fact, even adjusting for the large cyclical booms (which only in Portugal was muted), the actual CA/GDP (plotted in black line) was below the model fit adjusted for the cycle (dashed line). In other words, on the basis of *average* model elasticities and even correcting for state of the business cycle (as measured by the output gap), the CA deficit appears to have been 'excessive' by the eve of the crises. Second, these charts also indicate that imbalances grew especially large in Greece and Portugal in the 2000s. Third, the off-shooting in the direction of larger deficits during crisis turned into an overshooting in the surplus direction since 2009 in Greece, Portugal and Spain – but not in Ireland. That is, even controlling for the harshness of the post-2008 output contraction and fiscal adjustment (as done in the regressions of Table 5.3 via the output gap and the primary fiscal balance), the CAs in Greece and Portugal, (and to a much lesser extent also in Spain) have improved by more than anticipated on the basis of the model and much more so than in past recessions in Greece and Portugal – including the harsh downturns of the early 1980s and early 1990s. This suggests that developments specific of those two countries (and to a lesser extent to Spain) played a role. The next section elaborates on this point and discusses what effects structural reforms may have had in this connection.

5.3 Macroeconomic adjustment and external pay-offs of reforms

In terms of their effects on external balances, the structural reforms that Southern Europe and Ireland embarked upon and which are documented in this book can be divided into four broad categories:

(1) Product market deregulation;
(2) Reforms to increase labour market flexibility;
(3) Fiscal sector streamlining aimed at promoting a path of fiscal spending consistent with economy's long-term growth potential;[13]
(4) Tighter financial sector regulation and bank capitalization.

Regarding (1) and (2), their effects on the current account are more easily seen by focusing on developments in the consumer price index (CPI) – based real exchange rate (the ratio of the domestic to the trade-weighted average of foreign CPIs expressed in the same currency) and unit labour costs (the wage cost of producing one unit of a good in the country vs. abroad, i.e. the wage adjusted for differences in labour productivity).[14] Specifically, one should expect product market deregulation to improve the allocation of resources across sectors, reduce rents and raise TFP. As discussed in the previous sections, higher TFP tends to *depreciate* the real exchange rate and hence improve the CA. Put it differently, to the extent that structural reforms reduce the degrees of product and labour market 'frictions' that get in the way of the efficient allocation of economic resources in any given economy, they should be expected to allow such economies to deliver quality-equivalent output at lower prices in world markets – in short, to be more 'competitive', thereby strengthening their current accounts.

Taking the so-called Eurozone 'core' (Austria, Belgium, Finland, France, Germany and the Netherlands) as benchmark, Figure 5.4 plots the respective ratio of consumer price indices (CPIs). The figure shows that all four crisis countries had CPI inflation running lower than in the core Eurozone since 2009, implying that the average consumer basket got cheaper in the reform countries. Such a deflation partly reflects the depth of the recession, i.e. the widening output gap pushing down the price of non-tradable consumer goods. An indication of this demand-based effect is that, the reductions in relative producer price index (PPI) have been more modest, with the exception of Ireland, which experienced a 9% deflation relative to the Eurozone core between 2009 and 2014. But the fact that PPI inflation has also been held back in other reform countries too, suggests that some supply-factor effects may be at play, beyond the slack in the demand for domestic non-tradable goods.

Because Eurozone countries differ considerably in terms of their external exposure to non-Eurozone countries, it is important to consider a real exchange rate index that reflects this effective exposure by individual countries. Figure 5.5 plots the IMF's CPI-based index of the real effective exchange rate (REER) which weighs relative price indices (denominated in the same currency) by the share of

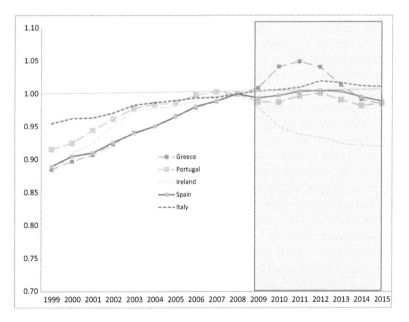

Figure 5.4 Consumer price index relative to Eurozone 'Core' (2008 = 1.00)

Data Source: IMF, International Financial Statistics

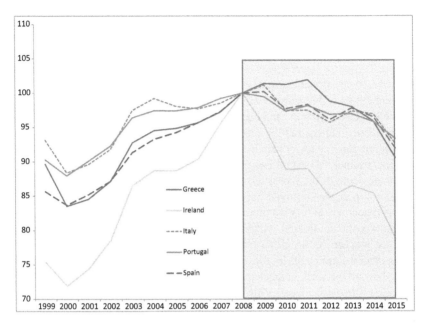

Figure 5.5 Real effective exchange rates based on consumer prices (2008 = 100)
Data Source: IMF, International Financial Statistics

trade with distinct partners. When this is done, it is clear that the crisis-hit countries benefited from the weakness of the euro through a real depreciation relative to non-euro trading partners, particularly from 2014, implying that gains in external competitiveness have been a lot more sizeable than implied solely by intra Euro-zone relative prices.

Such indices based on prices to the final consumer can however underestimate – or only reflect with a long lag – the effects of reforms on production costs, notably those of labour reforms, on external balances.[15] This is not only because changes in taxation – such as higher VAT rates – affect consumer prices, but also because reforms in the retail/distribution sector have not been as far-reaching as labour reforms. In addition, as shown in Cacciatore et al. (2016), the effects of some labour market reforms on costs are typically more immediate than reforms in product markets, insofar as the latter works mainly through firm entry/exit, which is typically slower. That said, even labour market reforms themselves may take some time to have a fuller impact on final product prices and hence on the trade balance. This may not only be due to the slower erosion of monopolistic competition in some sectors (with labour costs reductions being compensated by a higher mark-up), but also to other offsetting (conjectural) factors discussed elsewhere in this volume (financial sector disruptions being one). Because these factors are hard to quantify, they are bound to show up in the regression residual – which during the adjustment period are mostly negative, consistent with this conjecture.

A closer cost-based gauge of the effects of such reforms is the evolution of unit labour costs. Comparing the post-2008 path of unit labour costs in Figure 5.6 with that of CPI in Figure 5.4, it is clear that producers' costs fell by far more than is apparent from trends in consumer prices between the crisis-hit countries and the so-called 'core' countries in the Eurozone.[16] Once again the fall was steepest for Ireland – the country which, as we have seen, experienced the largest turnaround in the current account. A comparison with Italy, where the size of imbalances to be corrected were much smaller and where some reforms were introduced but only more recently (implying that the effects of which cannot be yet been seen in the data), is also suggestive of how structural reforms can help lower production costs and fuel a large turnaround in the current account. Broadening the coverage of the index to reflect changes in unit labour costs (ULC) relative to a broad set of trading partners – as can be seen from the so-called ULC-based real exchange rate index plotted in Figure 5.7 – reinforces the point.

The bottom-line is that structural reforms in product and particularly labour markets since 2009–10 have been associated with non-trivial reductions in unit labour costs, but only with modest gains so far, on the international relative price of final goods. Thus, much of the very sizeable adjustments in the CAs documented above should be mostly ascribed to variables other than a depreciation of the CPI-based real effective exchange rate, as we highlight below.

Such meagre gains in the CPI-based real exchange rate correlate with likewise modest gains in relative TFP except in the case of Greece where TFP dropped sharply during the large output contraction of 2010–12 (Figure 5.8). On the plus

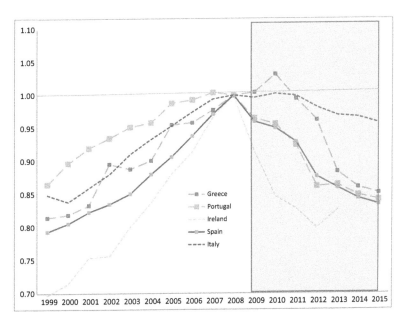

Figure 5.6 Unit labour cost relative to Eurozone 'Core' (index 2008 = 1.00)

Data Source: IMF, World Economic Outlook Database, April 2016

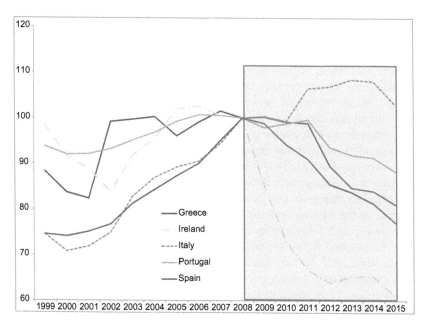

Figure 5.7 Real effective exchange rates based on unit labour costs (index 2008 = 100)
Data Source: IMF, World Economic Outlook Database, April 2016

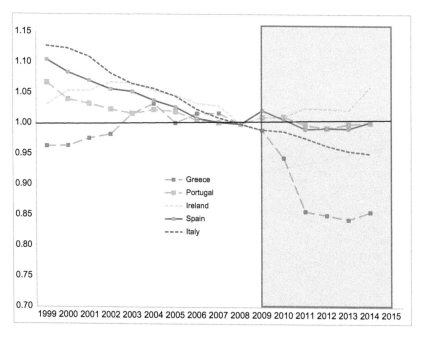

Figure 5.8 Total factor productivity relative to Eurozone 'Core' (index 2008 = 1.0)
Data Source: Penn World Table, version 9.0

side, Portugal and Spain managed to bring to a halt the declining path of TFP relative to the Eurozone peers between 1999 and 2007 (see also Table 5.1). In light of the positive coefficient on TFP in the CA regressions of Table 5.3 relative TFP growth no longer came to have a negative impact on CAs, but the contribution has been relatively small, at least up to 2014 (last observation available). The contribution has been more significantly positive for Ireland, as TFP rose (both in absolute terms and relative to core Eurozone peers) between 2008 and 2014, but also significantly negative for Greece. While such TFP estimates – even though coming from a classical source – must be viewed with some care, due to measurement difficulties that do not plague other macroeconomic indicators, they do paint a picture that is consistent with relative price developments in Ireland, Portugal and Spain.[17] In the case of Greece, they show, however, far less benign developments in external competitiveness than suggested by real exchange rates and unit labour cost indices (Figure 5.8).

On the fiscal side, as also documented elsewhere in this volume, an important segment of structural reforms in southern countries and Ireland has taken the form of public sector streamlining. To the extent that the effects on general government balances are expected to be long-lasting and the so-called Ricardian equivalence does not hold, one might expect that effects on savings and hence on the current account be readily felt. Figure 5.9 shows that the upward trend in general government primary spending (deflated by CPI inflation) since the onset of the euro has been clearly reversed in the crisis-hit countries since 2009. While some of this reversal in public

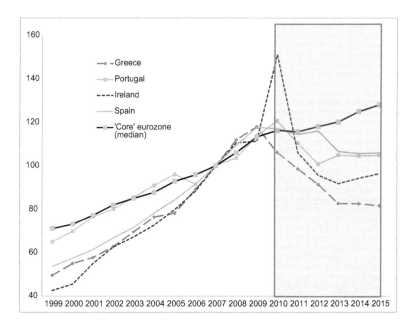

Figure 5.9 Real general government primary expenditure (CPI deflated, index 2007 = 100)

Data Source: IMF, World Economic Outlook Database, April 2016 spending trends have been dictated by cyclical adjustments to falling external financing (and to an extent that is still much debated in policy circles), longer term considerations of attaining fiscal sustainability and increasing the productivity of public sector have also been present. To the extent that the latter are not reversed once cyclical adjustment is over and the supply of external financing returns to 'normal', these countries' CAs should **not** be expected to return to the large deficits of the pre-2008 period.

Turning to the financial sector side, Table 5.3 has established that credit growth in excess of GDP growth has gone hand-in-hand with CA imbalances in the Eurozone in general (i.e. during 'good' and 'bad' times and on average across countries). Figure 5.10 further indicates that much of the CA adjustment in 2010–15 reflects the dramatic contraction of bank credit to the private sector in all four countries. The magnitude of decline was far larger than that of real income in Ireland, Portugal and Spain and about *pari passu* with income in Greece – where output contraction has been the most severe of all.

This sharp curtailment in credit to households and business exacerbated the downward adjustment in consumption, hence inducing a rise in household saving ratios. Insofar as it also contributed to the decline in business investment, the gap between aggregate saving and investment thus fell. Hence, the contraction in bank credit was one main factor in the elimination of large CA deficits.

While the sharp declining in bank credit during 2010–13 reflects the drying up of external financing and the negative effect of falling prices of sovereign bonds

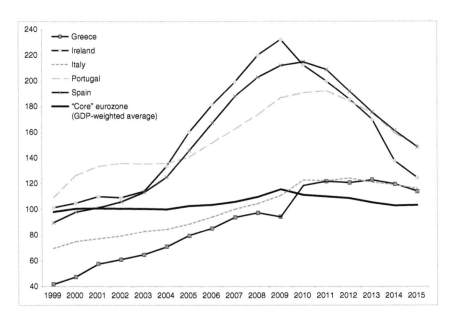

Figure 5.10 Bank credit to the private sector (percentage of GDP)

Data Source: World Bank and Bank for International Settlements on banks' balance sheets (as public bonds were widely held on banks' balance sheets – see, e.g. Popov and Van Horen 2015), it also reflected reform efforts to strengthen domestic bank systems through the closing of insolvent banks, a reduction in leverage and equity building in the surviving institutions, as well as tighter prudential regulations. To the extent that these efforts continue at the distinct national levels as well as under the transnational umbrella of the European banking union going forward, they should help cap CA imbalances and mitigate the risk of a return to the high imbalances of the 2000–07 period.

5.4 Concluding remarks

The dramatic current account reversals in Greece, Ireland, Portugal and Spain after 2008 reflect a mix of retrenchment of external private financing, major fiscal adjustments and bank sector distress associated with highly leverage positions on the eve of the Eurozone sovereign debt crises of 2010–13. However, they also appear to reflect – even if more subtly – some of the reform effort in recent years through a reduction in unit labour costs relative to trading partners and some growth of total factor productivity – even if quite uneven across those four countries.

There are distinct reasons for some opacity in seeing through the effects of reforms on external balances. One is that the pay-off of important reforms in labour and product markets, as well in public sector, may take time, for the reasons already discussed in other chapters of this book. A second, and important reason, is that macroeconomic performance reflects a combination of the supply-side reform effects and current demand conditions; the latter can obfuscate the positive effects of the former on growth and external competitiveness. For instance, export growth may not respond to concomitant improvements in TFP and unit labour costs because credit to exporters has not fully recovered from its crisis set-backs; conversely, the CA balance may look more positive than warranted by the reforms just because aggregate demand is yet to return to its potential growth. Moreover, as also documented in Gerali et al. (2015) and Bassanini and Cingano (2016), labour market reforms can exacerbate the contractionary effects of credit crunches and fiscal consolidations in the short run, before their positive pay-offs on competitiveness and output growth kick in. Third, structural reforms by their own nature create some uncertainty about their own success and duration. Thus, insofar as agents are forward-looking, the effects of reforms on the CA include not only actual developments and policies but also effects associated with uncertainty about the future. Classic manifestations of those include higher private saving for precautionary reasons, a slower-than-warranted recovery of business investment and efforts to reduce corporate leverage via higher corporate savings (see European Commission 2013 for a discussion of the latter) – all of which lead to a higher CA. Because those 'second-order' effects may take long to dissipate, CA balances may overshoot the new post-reform 'normal'. At the same time, one cannot discard the possibility that consumers and business learn from major crisis experiences and become more prudent or 'risk-averse'. This possibility is certainly consistent (but not necessarily the only cause) of the persistent nature of CA turnaround in many countries that experience major financial crises in the 1990s and early 2000s, such as Malaysia, Korea, Mexico, Thailand and Sweden.

On balance, the weight of the evidence suggests that high the CA deficits of the 2000–07 period are unlikely to return. It remains open to discussion, however, how much of the recent improvements in CA balances reflect permanent competitiveness gains due to reform efforts and more prudent macroeconomic management. As discussed in this chapter, this discussion is all the more complicated because some different indicators of external competitiveness do not paint a congruent picture. For instance, data on international relative prices suggest very limited progress in lowering the price of domestic goods relative to that of trading partners, but a far greater effect on relative costs which may, eventually, percolate through lower prices. Yet, more in line with relative final price indicators, TFP data point to modest gains in three of the four countries and non-trivial losses in aggregate productivity in Greece. In light of the econometric results presented in section 2, recent TFP gains in Ireland, Portugal and Spain, should warrant some improvements in their CAs, but likely of modest magnitudes by themselves. Focusing on a broader definition of 'competitiveness', the well-known World Economic Forum index of global competitiveness – which in turn summarizes a wide range of indicators pertaining to product and labour market efficiency, governance, fiscal discipline and the strength of the domestic financial sector – indicates that reforms have generally contributed to CA strengthening, particularly so in the case of Ireland and Portugal (see Figure 5.11).

Altogether, these elements suggest a generally positive gradient running from structural reforms to improved external balances; yet, finer measures of the "pure"

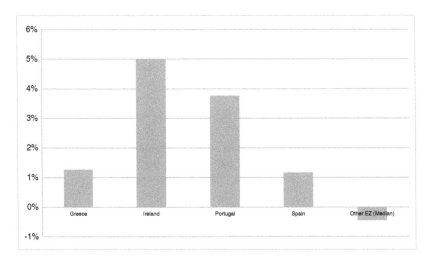

Figure 5.11 Changes in the overall competitiveness between 2010 and 2015

Data Source: World Economic Forum, Global Competitiveness Index.

effect of structural reforms on the CAs of those countries will require further research and reliance on forthcoming data. Be that as it may, some general practical implications seem warranted on the basis of the evidence presented in this chapter – namely:

(1) Fiscal adjustment (some of it stemming from reforms aiming at enhancing public sector efficiency and sustainability of public finances), financial sector de-leveraging and generally tighter credit market conditions played key roles in the massive CA rebalancing within the Eurozone between 2008 and 2015. Thus, smaller fiscal deficits and a more capitalized and less leveraged banking sector appear to be clearly important in mitigating the risk of a return to large imbalances of the past, when output returns to potential.

(2) Reforms tend to improve external balances to the extent that they improve the growth of total factor productivity (TFP) relative to that of trading partners. So, if reducing external vulnerability is one of the main goals of structural reforms and if the positive supply-side effect of higher TFP on current account dominates (as in the above econometric analysis), policy makers should give some prominence to reforms that are likely to have tangible effects on TFP.

(3) CA improvements have been more associated with a reduction of unit labour costs than with improvements in consumer prices relative to trading partners. *Prima facie*, such a decoupling not only suggests that reforms in product markets have lagged behind those in labour markets, but possibly also that the effects of the latter on the prices of final goods are still working themselves out. Given that estimates of the elasticity of exports to changes in unit labour costs appear to be substantial (IMF 2017), even the modest reduction in those costs can have a non-trivial effect, so they appear to be accounting for some of the improvement in the trade balance and the CA.

(4) It thus follows that, to the extent that adjustment programmes under the ESM and IMF stimulated reforms as part of their conditionality, those adjustment programmes facilitated a reduction of external imbalances and improved 'competitiveness', broadly defined.

(5) It must be acknowledged, however, that even correcting for the harshness of the recession, a non-trivial part of the CA adjustment remains unexplained on the basis of historical relationships between macro fundamentals and the CA. This suggests that expectational factors and difficulties in measuring current and prospective effects of the reforms on aggregate savings and investment are at play. Thus, to minimize the risk of a repeat of large imbalances of the past, policy should err, if anything, on the side of caution in assessing the effects of stronger macroeconomic fundamentals on the evolution of external positions. This in turn suggests that further strengthening of macroeconomic fundamentals and a consolidation of the reform agenda are important to minimize the risk of large external imbalances of the past. Such a cautionary stance may be all the more appropriate once the economic recovery gathers momentum and private sector's confidence returns to pre-crisis levels.

Notes

1 Research Department, International Monetary Fund. The opinions expressed here are those of the author and do not necessarily represent those of the IMF, its board of directors or management. I thank, without implicating, Antonio Bassanetti, John Bluedorn, Oya Celasun, Enrique Flores, Alessandro Giustiniani, Daniela Enriquez, Alvar Kangur, Dimitri Katsikas, Subir Lall, Inês Lopes, Paolo Manasse, Michalis Psalidopoulos, Natalia Novikova, Jorge Salas, Johannes Wiegang and Aleksandra Zdzienicka for detailed comments on an earlier draft.

2 This unravelling may not be immediate, however, and one might arguably expect it to be lengthier in advanced countries than in emerging markets. One reason is that the deeper international financial integration of advanced countries grants them access to a wider range of financing instruments. Another reason is greater policy credibility. Knowing that policy authorities can credibly commit to do 'whatever it takes' to save a currency or a monetary regime, helps rule out extreme risk scenarios and thus aid the effectiveness of policy interventions. These factors help explain some of the lag between the financial crisis in the United States and those in the Eurozone.

3 In many external crises of the past, the turnaround in the trade balance (which is typically the main component of the current account, equalling the latter minus net income from abroad and net current transfers) has been even larger of that of the current account. However, a current account reversal in major macroeconomic crises can be larger than that of the trade balance. This happens, for instance, if residents cut down their payments to foreigners (as in defaults or debt re-scheduling arrangements that reduce current interest payments, or if domestic investors buy back national debt held by foreigners reducing the overall stock of foreign debt). In the four countries analyzed in this chapter, only Greece renegotiated its debt. Yet, a slightly larger turnaround of the current account relative to the trade balance was also observed in Portugal and Spain between 2007 and 2015. This chapter focuses on the current account since it is a broader indicator of external balances and a direct measure of the difference between two key macroeconomic variables (domestic saving and domestic investment). Yet, much of the analysis carries over to the trade balance. Sharp turnarounds in trade or current account balances, triggered by the pull-out of foreign investors from a country's assets, are usually dubbed in the literature on international macroeconomics as 'sudden stops'.

4 In the limit, there is a point where no additional lending is forthcoming at any interest rate, so the borrowing limit becomes strict rationing as in many models of sovereign debt (see Eaton and Fernandez 1995, for a classical survey). The reason for such a 'rationing' is that, as interest rates keep rising, the attendant rise in repayment costs increases the borrower's incentive to default, up to the point where no further rise in interest rates compensates investors for the extra risk of additional lending. At this point, investors will stop lending altogether at *any* level of interest rate.

5 See Obstfeld and Rogoff (1996) for the foundations of the inter-temporal CA model and Chinn and Prasad (2003), Lee et al. (2008), Ca'Zorzi et al. (2012), Phillips et al. (2013), Catão and Milesi-Ferretti (2014) for empirical applications and extensions of that workhorse model.

6 Other CA models featuring in the recent literature, which include some vintages of the IMF external balance assessment (EBA) methodology, contain a number of extra variables, such as the oil trade balance, GDP growth forecasting, public health expenditure to GDP and institutional quality indicators. None of them, however, proved to be statistically significant in the intra Eurozone regression and so do not feature in the present discussion. Such a lack of significance is not surprising since most of the explanatory power of those variables comes from cross-sectional differences in a broader panel of countries, which include emerging markets and large commodity exporters. Such cross-sectional differences are relatively unimportant in the Eurozone. One advantage of restricting the country sample to the Eurozone is to keep the specification reasonably

parsimonious while allowing for the possibility of Eurozone-specific coefficients. Since the bulk of the CA imbalances at stake are intra-EU imbalances, such a cross-sectional truncation sample is appropriate for the task at hand. Also, limiting the estimation to the second half of the sample, i.e. from 1996 to 2015, does not change the thrust of the results, nor does the introduction of fixed country effects.

7   See Phillips et al. (2013) for a discussion of the underlying model and various estimation issues. In particular, not including country-fixed effects ensure that the global adding-up constraint, i.e. the worldwide sum of CAs is zero, is met (short of the usual global measurement discrepancies). In the case of the Eurozone, because its CA imbalance with the rest of the world has been small, imposing such a quasi-zero adding-up constraint is also broadly warranted. Unlike in Phillips et al. (2013), growth expectations were not a significant variable in the regression in the presence of the output gap indicator owing to strong collinearity.

8   As often in the literature, the selection of instruments relies on one- and two-period lags of real GDP growth, and one-period lags of the primary fiscal balance and credit growth. In an alternative specification, lagged credit growth was also replaced with the lag ratio of bank credit to bank capital with very similar results and a slightly higher R^2 (0.62). A discussion of the relationship between credit growth and that bank leverage indicator is provided in section 3.

9   The sign of old dependency ratio (the ratio of population outside the working age to total population) is negative, because a lower share of individuals in the employment age lowers savings and hence reduces the CA. Conversely, a higher rate of population ageing means that the share of working-age population will need to save more today to finance the retirement of a higher number of individuals in the future; hence higher values for the "ageing speed" have a positive effect on the CA. While governments can have only a modest control over deeper demographic trends that shape the evolution of those variables, other policies (including reforms in pension systems and the overall fiscal stance) can help offset the effects of demographic trends on a country's external sustainability.

10 The level of the terms of trade does not show up as significant either.

11 Also insignificant is the effect of stock price growth and 5-year ahead expected growth – the latter variable found to be significant in prior cross-country work (Phillips et al. 2013). Both were dropped from the regressions reported in Table 5.3.

12 Another potential source of discrepancy are heterogeneous output composition (for instance, the higher weight of the ICT service in Ireland) and tax policies which in turn can make the 'elasticity' of the current account to output and relative prices to differ. Accurately modelling and estimating those effects is, however, hard and remain an open field for future research on current account modelling.

13 Here, as elsewhere in this volume, short- to medium-term fiscal contraction dictated by an adjustment to meagre external financing is not considered to be a reform. Yet, any potential effect of structural reforms on the long-term path of public expenditure is relevant for the CA going forward, insofar as it lowers the cyclically adjusted fiscal balance on a permanent basis, facilitating CA sustainability.

14 Indeed, in the inter-temporal canonical model of the current account, looking at the quantity flows is theoretically isomorphic to looking at the relevant relative price – the real exchange rate (see Phillips et al. 2013; Catão and Milesi-Ferretti 2014, appendix 1).

15 In general, the literature finds that there is no single universally superior price deflator to gauge changes in export performance or external 'competitiveness' broadly speaking (see Chinn 2006; Giordano and Zollino 2016). Hence, it is standard practice to look at alternative price indicator, as in the analysis that follows.

16 One caveat about the index is that it covers the manufacturing sector only.

17 Such difficulties in measuring TFP growth accurately may be greater for some countries. In the case of Ireland, for instance, those difficulties are exacerbated by the extensive presence of multinationals with offshoring trade activity, which distorts productivity measurement.

Bibliography

Bassanini, A., and Cingano, F. (2016) Short-term Labour Market Effects of Structural Reforms: Pain Before the Gain? In: *OECD Employment Outlook 2016*, Chapter 2, Paris, OECD Publishing.

Cacciatore, M., Duval, R., Fiori, G., and Ghironi, F. (2016) Short-Term Pain for Long-term Gains: Market Deregulation and Monetary Policy in Small Open Economies. *Journal of International Money and Finance*, 68, 358–385.

Catão, L. A. V., Fostel, A., and Rancière, R. (2017) Fiscal Surprises and Yield Decouplings. *IMF Economic Review*, Forthcoming.

Catão, L. A. V., and Milesi-Ferretti, G. M. (2014) External Liabilities and Crises. *Journal of International Economics*, 94(1), 18–32.

Ca'Zorzi, M., Chudik, A., and Dieppe, A. (2012) *Thousands of Models, One Story: Current Account Imbalances in the Global Economy*. Working paper 1441, European Central Bank.

Chinn, M. (2006) A Primer on Real Effective Exchange Rates: Determinants, Overvaluation, Trade Flows and Competitive Devaluation. *Open Economies Review*, 17(1), 115–142.

Chinn, M., and Prasad, E. (2003) Medium-term Determinants of Current Accounts in Industrial and Developing Countries: An Empirical Exploration. *Journal of International Economics*, 59(1), 47–76.

Eaton, J., and Fernandez, R. (1995) Sovereign Debt. In Grossman, G. and Rogoff, K. (eds.) *Handbook of International Economics* vol. 3., Amsterdam, The Netherlands, North Holland.

European Commission. (2013) Assessing the Impact of Uncertainty on Consumption and Investment. *Quarterly Report on the Euro Area*, 12(2), 7–16.

Gerali, A., Notarpietro, A., and Pisani, M. (2016) Macroeconomic Effects of Simultaneous Implementation of Reforms. *International Finance*, 19(1), 42–65.

Giordano, C., and Zollino, F. (2016) Shedding Light on Price- and Non-price-competitiveness Determinants of Foreign Trade in the Four Largest Euro-area Countries. *Review of International Economics*, 24(3), 604–634.

International Monetary Fund (2017) *Spain: Selected Issues*. IMF. Country Report, 17/24.

Lane, P. (2011) *The Dynamics of Ireland's Net External Position*. Trinity College, Mimeo.

Lane, P., and McQuade, P. (2013) Domestic Credit Growth and International Capital Flows. *Scandinavian Journal of Economics*, 116, 218–252.

Lee, J., Ostry, J. D., Prati, A., Ricci, A. L., and Milesi-Ferretti, G. M. (2008) *Exchange Rate Assessments: CEGR Methodologies*, Washington, DC, International Monetary Fund.

Manasse, P. (2015) *What Went Wrong in Greece and How to Fix It: Lessons for Europe From the Greek Crisis*. VoxEU, June 12. Available from: http://voxeu.org/article/what-went-wrong-greece-and-how-fix-it.

Obstfeld, M. (2012) Does the Current Account Still Matter? *American Economic Review*, 102(3), 1–23.

Obstfeld, M., and Rogoff, K. (1996) *Foundations of International Macroeconomics*, Cambridge, MA, MIT Press.

Phillips, S., Catão, L., Ricci, L. A., Bems, R., Das, M., Di Giovanni, J., Unsal, F., Castillo, M., Lee, J., Rodriguez, J., and Vargas, M. (2013) *The External Balance Assessment (EBA) Methodology*. IMF. Working Papers No. 13/272.

Popov, A., and Van Horen, N. (2015) Exporting Sovereign Stress: Evidence From Syndicated Bank Lending During the Euro Area Sovereign Debt Crisis. *Review of Finance*, 19(5), 1825–1866.

6 Labour market reform in Portugal under the adjustment programme

Lessons for policy design

Alessandro Turrini[1]

6.1 Introduction

This chapter discusses labour market reforms in Portugal during the crisis. Following a dramatic current account adjustment and a sovereign debt crisis, Portugal received financial assistance in the framework of an adjustment programme between 2011 and 2014. Because of the structural origin of many of the macro-economic challenges faced by Portugal, the financial assistance was conditioned on a wide set of measures aimed at increasing the resilience and flexibility of the economy and at raising the growth potential.

Labour market measures were given particular emphasis in the Portuguese programme. As compared with the experience of reforms under adjustment programmes carried out over the same period in other EU countries, notably Greece, labour market reforms had been discussed extensively among policy authorities and experts in the years preceding the crisis. A number of measures already agreed with social partners before the start of the programme were carried out in a short time span. In particular, the Labour Code underwent a number of important changes, and the framework for unemployment benefits and active labour market policies was reformed in such a way as to address the post-crisis challenges facing the labour market. Conversely, reforms in other areas, notably the wage-setting framework, despite being included among the objectives of the programme, were implemented to a more limited extent.

The focus of the chapter is on the design and execution of the programme's measures concerning the regulation, the policies and the institutions of the labour market, while a thorough assessment of the impact of the measures is beyond its scope. The aim will be that of distilling the lessons for the design of labour market reforms that we can draw from the Portuguese experience under the adjustment programme.

The first section of this chapter highlights the main challenges faced by the Portuguese labour market during the crisis. The second section reviews the priorities of the programme regarding labour market reforms, and discusses their rationale in the framework of the overall objectives of the programme. The third section focuses on the execution of the programme, discussing its main shortfalls in implementation and/or in effectiveness. The final section draws the main lessons for policy design.

6.2 Labour market challenges at the time of the crisis

6.2.1 Labour market developments

Portugal entered the crisis following two decades of protracted stagnation in productivity and per capita income. Bottlenecks hampering the transition from traditional industries to high value-added sectors were due to the scarcity of high-skilled labour, an oversized government sector and a number of policies and regulatory settings hampering the adjustment of prices and quantities and economic efficiency (e.g. OECD 2006).

The creation of the Economic and Monetary Union resulted in a long cycle of low growth and growing external imbalances for Portugal (e.g. Blanchard 2006). The fall in interest rates supported domestic demand but led to growing current account deficits as domestic supply did not catch up. The large and persistent external deficits resulted in the accumulation of a large stock of net private and public foreign debt. When the financial crisis hit Portugal, the re-appreciation of risk for debt instruments issued by Euro area periphery countries led to a major current account reversal. The ensuing recession and the associated loss in government revenues put government debt on an unsustainable path, which in turn further reduced the appetite for Portuguese sovereign bonds, and made financial assistance necessary.

Buoyant domestic demand during the late 1990s resulted in a steady fall in unemployment (from 7 percent in 1995 to 4 percent in 2001, see Figure 6.1), to a large extent associated with the creation of temporary employment (Figure 6.2) and an increasingly dual labour market, characterized by little transition between

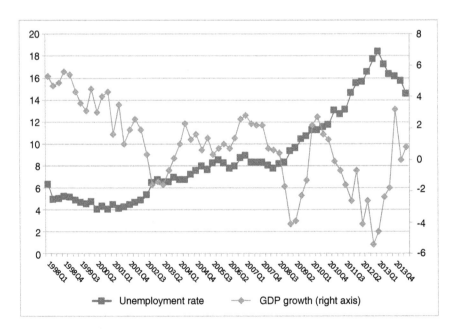

Figure 6.1 GDP growth and unemployment rates, quarterly figures

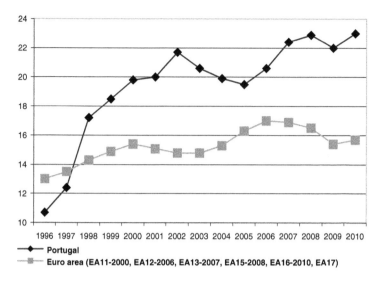

Figure 6.2 Share of temporary labour contracts, Portugal vs. Euro area

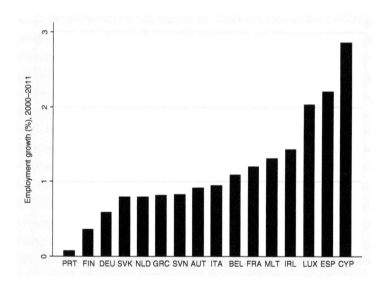

Figure 6.3 Employment growth across the EU in the decade before the programme

temporary and permanent employment. Employment *rates* at the start of the 2000s were in line with those of other EU countries, possibly as a result of relatively high activity rates. And yet, employment *growth* was the lowest, reflecting anaemic job creation (Figure 6.3), resulting in a comparatively high share of long-term unemployment. The segmentation of the Portuguese labour market made the overall rate of unemployment more sensitive to the cycle, so that the 2002 slowdown produced a substantial and protracted rise in unemployment. The 'sudden stop' in external financing in 2009 resulted in a major drop in domestic demand and surging unemployment.

While real wages grew broadly in line with productivity in the decade before the crisis, nominal unit labour costs grew faster than in partner countries, so that Portugal lost (cost) competitiveness which contributed to structural external imbalances. Moreover, wage differentials across sectors and firms did not sufficiently reflect productivity differences, being partly linked to rents, especially for workers of the public sector and for employees of firms shielded from foreign competition (Portugal 2015; Campos and Centeno 2012; European Commission 2014a).

In a nutshell, the labour market situation in Portugal at the time of the crisis was characterized by high and rising unemployment, persistently anaemic job creation, labour market segmentation, substantial cumulated competitiveness losses, a wage structure not adequately reflecting inter-sectoral and inter-firm productivity differences and an insufficient supply of skilled workers in a context of growing competitive pressures from low-wage emerging economies and by the need to expand high-skill sectors.

6.2.2 *Labour market institutions*

The weaknesses of the Portuguese labour market were partly rooted in labour market institutions, regulations and policies (e.g. OECD 2006). The Constitution provides strong guarantees to workers, reflecting ideals prevailing among constituent political groups at the time when Portugal returned to democracy. Constitutional principles are reflected in a Labour Code that regulates most aspects of labour relations, including wage setting.

(1) *Employment protection legislation* (EPL), namely the system of requirements to be fulfilled by employers in the case of redundancies and dismissals and to use fixed-term contracts, was at the time of the crisis one of the most stringent among OECD countries, especially for permanent contracts. In particular, the level of severance payments due by the Labour Code in case of individual and collective dismissals, both in the case of fair and unfair dismissal, was much above those found in other countries.[2] High EPL for permanent contracts go a long way towards explaining the dismal job creation and the segmentation of the Portuguese labour market (Figures 6.4 and 6.5).

(2) The Labour Code regulated working hours very strictly, with flexibility of adapting hours limited to derogations defined in collective contracts. Overtime pay in Portugal was among the highest in the OECD at the time of the crisis (OECD 2010).

(3) The *wage setting* system in Portugal was characterized by limited room for differentiating wages. On top of a statutory minimum wage, wage floors reflected collectively bargained minima, negotiated mostly at sector level. The limited relevance of firm-level bargaining reflects mostly the small size

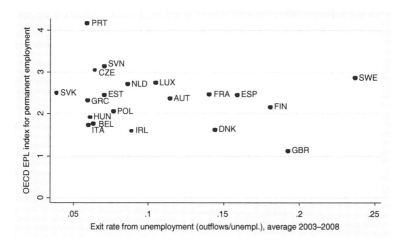

Figure 6.4 Employment Protection Index and exit rates from unemployment, a scatterplot across EU countries, pre-crisis period

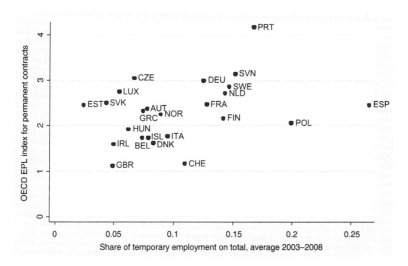

Figure 6.5 Employment Protection Index and share of temporary employment, a scatterplot across EU countries, pre-crisis period

of the average Portuguese firm in addition to labour market regulations. The practice of extending the wage conditions bargained in one sector to firms not belonging to the signatory employer association by means of administrative acts ('*portarias de extensao*') reduced the incentives for small firms to engage in collective bargaining and had a detrimental effect on employment, other things being equal (Guimaraes et al. 2014; Martins 2014).[3] Unions have the right to bargain collectively, but they can delegate such right to work councils.[4] The wage setting system prevailing in Portugal could have also contributed to the limited responsiveness of wages to changing macroeconomic conditions. The minimum wage, set by the government upon the proposal of social partners, increased rapidly as a share of the average wage in the first half of the 2000s, resulting in a growing and comparatively high share of workers whose remuneration was bound by the minimum wage (Figure 6.6). The renegotiation of collectively bargained wages was not incentivized due to the existence of a system of survival of expired collective wage contract (*'sobrevigência'*), whereby expired contracts could continue determining wage and non-wage conditions for several years.

(4) *Unemployment benefits* in Portugal were relatively generous in comparison with other countries at similar per capita income (Figure 6.7), but with relatively tight entitlement conditions in terms of past employment record. In

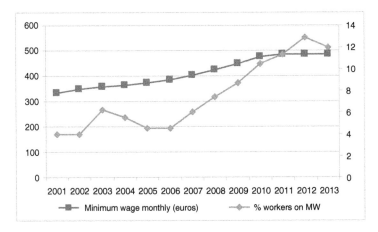

Figure 6.6 Evolution of nominal monthly minimum wage and share of workers paid the minimum wage

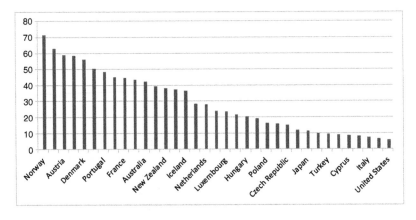

Figure 6.7 Average net replacement rates of unemployment insurance benefits during the first 5 years of unemployment, 2009

addition to unemployment insurance paid for relatively long periods and linked to seniority and age, the system foresees means-tested unemployment assistance for the long-term unemployed after the expiration of unemployment insurance, and social assistance for those not qualifying for unemployment assistance. Net replacement rates of unemployment insurance were linked to past wages, while unemployment and social assistance were linked to an index of cost of living ('social support index'). The long and unconditional duration of unemployment benefits, for some categories of workers, implied a risk of benefit dependence; the fact that benefits were linked to previous wages could generate unemployment traps for the unemployed with previously high wages.

(5) Concerning *Active Labour Market Policies*, i.e. the policies that favour the requalification and activation of jobless workers, Portugal had in place a well-developed system of training for the unemployed, with one of the highest expenditure as a share of GDP among EU countries. The system of counselling and activation of the unemployed, as well as the organization and functioning of Public Employment Services was however not up to the level of best practices (OECD 2017).

6.2.3 Reforms carried out before the financial assistance programme

The necessity of reforming certain aspects of the Portuguese labour market was debated among experts and policy makers already before the economic adjustment programme. In 2007, the Portuguese Labour Ministry presented a White Paper providing a comprehensive set of reform proposals. The Labour Code was reformed in 2009 following negotiations with social partners. The reforms concerned EPL (inter alia: reduction of the dismissal notice; elimination of reinstatement for dismissals with procedural irregularities; a cap to wage arrears in case of reinstatement); working time (possible introduction of bank of hours by means of collective bargaining); wage setting (possibility for unions to delegate bargaining to work councils in firms with more than 500 employees). A number of reforms concerned unemployment benefits, with the aim of strengthening the activation of the unemployed and reducing the risk of unemployment traps by capping net replacement rates.

In March 2011, the government agreed with social partners the so-called 'Initiative for Competitiveness and Employment', at a time when the possibility of an adjustment programme was already considered. The agreement envisaged an improved collective bargaining system, less restrictive employment protection legislation, increased flexibility of working hours and a more effective system of active labour market policies.

6.3 Labour market reforms in the adjustment programme: priorities and rationale

The overarching priority of the policy measures attached to the economic adjustment programmes was to ensure the repayment capacity of the economy. Even more than in other programme countries, the conditionalities required by the Portuguese programme were characterized by a substantial structural reform component: it was perceived that financial and fiscal measures alone would not have been sufficient to overcome the long-standing stagnation of productivity, to foster a sustainable export oriented recovery, and to reduce over time the high stock of foreign debt (see European Commission 2011). Improving competitiveness and re-orienting the economy towards exports is typically achieved by means of a devaluation of the currency. In the case of Portugal, the programme considered necessary to obtain the same effects by means of an 'internal devaluation'. A downward adjustment of labour costs was perceived not only as a key ingredient to foster external adjustment, but also for addressing surging unemployment.

The adjustment programme for Portugal was negotiated in May 2011 between the European Commission, the IMF and the European Central Bank, and the socialist government of Jose Socrates. The measures included in the Tripartite Agreement of March 2011 were reflected in the conditional policies of the adjustment programme regarding the labour market. These required measures were therefore specified at a high level of articulation and detail.

The programme however extended beyond the 2011 Tripartite Agreement, by including also additional measures aimed at fostering wage adjustment and reducing non-wage labour costs, and reforms of the education and training systems with the aim of enhancing the growth potential over the longer term.[5] This second set of measures was left to be determined in agreement with the institutions (EC, IMF, ECB), according to a pre-determined time frame for the delivery of analyses, action plans and legislation. The Memorandum of Understanding (MoU) envisaged a sufficiently long-time frame for enacting the measures, with a view to allow consultation with social partners and the preparation of the necessary technical work (see also the discussion in section 5).

The main elements of the agreed labour market measures were as follows (see also the Appendix).

6.3.1 Employment protection legislation

A number of measures concerned the level and design of *severance payments*. The measures were scheduled to take place in 3 steps.

(1) By July 2011 the government was asked to legislate a reform for newly hired workers in line with the March 2011 Tripartite Agreement. Severance payments for new permanent contracts had to be reduced from 30 to 20 days per year of tenure, and capped to 12 months. Severance payments for fixed-term contracts (initially set at 36 days per year of tenure for contracts shorter than 6 months and 24 days for longer contracts) had also to be reduced and made equal to those for permanent contracts. Half of the severance payments would be financed from a new employers' fund to be set up for this purpose.

(2) By the fourth quarter of 2011, the government was asked to legislate the alignment of severance payment entitlements for current employees with

those for new hires. The Memorandum of Understanding (MoU) made clear that, under the reform, the severance payments for current employees would grow in line with seniority, similarly to those of the newly hired employees, and be subject to a cap, without however being cut.

(3) By the first quarter of 2012, the government had to prepare a proposal aiming at: (a) reducing further the level of severance payments and aligning it to the EU's average; (b) make sure that severance entitlements paid out of the employers' fund were transferable across jobs. Legislation had to be prepared by the 3rd quarter of 2012.

Other measures concerned the *definition of fair dismissal*. By the first quarter of 2012, the Government was asked to present a legislation aimed at revising the definition of fair individual dismissal contained in the Labour Code. More specifically, the MoU required that: (a) individual dismissals justified by the unsuitability of the worker should be allowed even without the introduction of new technologies or other changes in the workplace; (b) individual dismissals due to the extinction of work positions should not necessarily follow a seniority rule; (c) individual dismissals should not be conditional on a previous attempt to transfer the worker to an alternative job.

The overall logic of the EPL reform was that of reducing barriers to the creation of permanent jobs, firms' restructuring and labour mobility, while preventing the risk of a large increase in lay-offs. The reduction of the level of severance payments for permanent contracts and their alignment to those of temporary contracts was a first step for reducing the segmentation of the labour market (Turrini 2011).

The large amount of financial resources required to liquidate severance payments (due in case of fair and unfair dismissals, and also in case of collective dismissals) implied increased risk of firms' bankruptcy, or non-compliant firms. For this reason, the March 2011 Tripartite Agreement contemplated the introduction of a fund financed by the employers to ensure the required financial resources. The reform further required this fund to be designed in such a way as to permit the transferability of payments across employers by means of notional individual accounts, building on the positive experience of the reforms of the severance payment system implemented by Austria, which allowed transferability of severance payment entitlements across employers (Hofer 2007). The aim was that of reducing the disincentives for labour mobility embedded in a system characterized by severance payments strongly linked to seniority.

6.3.2 Working time arrangements

The measures contained in the programme were aimed at enhancing the possibility for firms to use work hours in a flexible way and at reducing labour costs. To that purpose, the MoU asked the government to prepare by the end of 2011 a proposal to promote the use of flexible working time arrangements, including by means of a 'bank of hours' working arrangement by mutual agreement between employers and employees negotiated at plant level. Moreover, the government was asked to legislate by the first quarter of 2011 on the measures included in the March Tripartite Agreement concerning working time arrangements and short-time working schemes in cases of industrial crisis and to revise the minimum additional pay for overtime established in the Labour Code.

6.3.3 Wage setting

A series of measures aimed at making *wages more responsive to firm-level conditions.*

(1) The government was asked to define and enforce clear criteria to be followed for the extension of collective agreements by the second quarter of 2012. The representativeness of the negotiating organizations and the implications of the extension for the competitive position of non-affiliated firms were indicated to be among the criteria. The government was also asked not to extend collective contracts until criteria for granting the extension were established.
(2) The government was asked to implement the measures agreed in the Tripartite Agreement of March 2011 concerning the 'organised decentralisation'. These included the possibility for work councils to negotiate task, geographical mobility and working time arrangements, and the possibility for work councils to conclude firm-level agreements if delegated by unions with less restrictive conditions regarding firm size (the size threshold above which negotiations are allowed was reduced). The government was also required to present an action plan to promote the inclusion in sectoral collective agreements of conditions under which work councils can conclude firm-level agreements without the delegation of unions.

The *responsiveness of wages to changing macroeconomic conditions* was addressed by the following measures:

(1) Over the programme period, minimum wage increases had to be agreed in the framework of the programme and justified in light of economic and labour market developments.
(2) By the second quarter of 2012, the government was asked to prepare an independent review on: (a) how to enhance the effectiveness of the tripartite concertation on wages including with the establishment of norms for making wages more respondent to firms' conditions, as well as to general macroeconomic considerations together with procedures for monitoring compliance with such norms; (b) the desirability of shortening the survival (*sobrevigência*) of contracts that are expired but not renewed. On the basis of analysis and experts' views, the government legislated at the end of the programme a reduction in the time period allowed for the survival of expired contracts.

In order to decentralize wage bargaining, a key instrument considered was the introduction of criteria for granting the extension to firms not belonging to signatory employers' associations. Such criteria were in place in a number of EU countries such as Germany and the Netherlands, and generally included the requirement that the firms belonging to the negotiation employers' organization represent the majority of firms in the sector. A complementary objective was that of easing the conditions for firm-level collective bargaining, notably by enlarging the range of cases where collective contracts could be negotiated by work councils.

As in the case of EPL reforms, the programme envisaged different steps, with the implementation of the reforms already planned by the government and agreed with social partners. Wage setting reforms were among the most sensitive and hard to negotiate, and their prescriptiveness and degree of detail required a high degree of ownership by employers and unions. The text of the MoU was therefore explicit on the objectives but left room to the Portuguese authorities to find specific solutions in consultation with social partners.

6.3.4 Tax wedge

The tax wedge in Portugal at the time of the crisis was broadly in line with the EU average (amounting to about 40 percent of total labour cost for a single person with no children at the average wage, and with social contributions for employers about double those for employees).[6] The programme had two conflicting objectives regarding labour taxation. On the one hand, it wanted to ensure sufficient revenues in order to reduce the government deficit in line with the agreed time frame. On the other hand, it aimed at lowering labour costs with a view to recover competitiveness and reduce unemployment. The former was the most immediate priority, and consistently the tax wedge in the MoU was mentioned among the budgetary measures (not among the labour market measures). The programme targeted a budgetary-neutral 'recalibration of the tax system' to lower labour costs to be included in the 2012 budget law, without further specifying how this objective had to be achieved.

6.3.5 Unemployment benefits

In order to reduce the risk of benefit dependence and unemployment traps, the maximum duration of unemployment insurance benefits was capped to no more than 18 months, while the level of unemployment benefits was capped at 2.5 times the social support index (IAS) and was required to decline over the unemployment spell (a reduction of at least 10 percent in the benefit amount after 6 months). These measures were applied in such a way not to affect the currently unemployed and not to affect the existing rights of the employees. A number of measures eased the eligibility conditions for unemployment insurance, by reducing the required length of the contribution period from 15 to 12 months. The government was required to elaborate a proposal for extending eligibility to clearly-defined categories of self-employed workers providing services to a single firm on a regular basis ('bogus self-employed'). The government was asked to legislate by the first quarter of 2012.

6.3.6 Active labour market policies

At the time of the negotiation of the programme Portugal was already character-ized a by a comparatively high incidence of long-term unemployment. There was awareness that long-term unemployment would have further increased in light of the protracted recession. A strengthening of the Active Labour Market Policies (ALMPs) was therefore deemed a necessary step for tackling the risk of unemploy-ment hysteresis, complementing this way the measures aimed at preventing unem-ployment benefit dependence. The government was asked to review the current system of ALMPs and to present by end-2011 an action plan to strengthen the existing framework for active policies, including their mode of delivery, with a focus on the role of Public Employment Services.

6.4 Reform implementation over the programme

As in most adjustment programmes, conditions over structural reforms were among those meeting fiercer resistance in light of the opposition of interest groups. The Portuguese programme was particularly prone to encounter prob-lems on this front, with its relatively strong focus on structural reforms, and a long list of narrowly defined measures spanning a broad agenda (comprising, in addition to labour markets, the competition framework, public utilities and infrastructure, the management of state-owned enterprises, professions, the housing market, justice, education and vocational training and so on) to be adopted in line with a tight implementation schedule. Labour market reforms were among the most successful in terms of fulfilled targets, although some areas met strong resistance and implementation gaps remained substantial (European Commission 2014a).

The adjustment programme was implemented by a government different than the one that signed it. Following the elections of June 2011, the socialist govern-ment was replaced by a new coalition government led by Pedro Passos Coelho, where both the Social Democratic Party (which won the elections) and the People's Party (CDS-PP) of Paulo Portas were represented. Despite having won the elec-tions on the basis of an anti-programme platform, the new government broadly followed the adjustment programme, especially during the first 2 years. The execu-tion of the programme was helped by the technical profile of key ministries and state secretaries, and the effective coordinating role of a task force attached to the prime minister office. Reform conditionalities were updated throughout the pro-gramme in light of fulfilments and evolving agreed priorities.

A key reason underlying the smooth implementation of labour market measures during the first years of the programme was their design; notably the front-loading of the reforms already agreed with social partners. An additional factor that helped the timely implementation of reforms was the positive climate between the government and the social partners. A new Tripartite Agreement was agreed between the new coalition government and the social partners in January 2012. Although most of the measures aimed at revising the Labour Code were included in the January 2012 Tripartite Agreement, some measures aimed at decentralizing the wage setting system, notably the revision of the extension mechanism, were left out.

By the end of 2011, most of the measures requiring a revision of the Labour Code (namely, EPL, working time, some aspects relating to wage setting), as well as measures on unemployment insurance, had been legislated. Moreover, a downward adjustment of labour costs was favoured by fiscal savings obtained by the reduction of wages in the public sector.[7] However, by the second half of 2012 difficulties with the execution of the programme started becoming evident. The worsening of the economic situation implied lower than expected revenues and required larger budget cuts to meet the agreed targets. In July 2012, the Constitutional Court ruled wage cuts in the public sector and the suppression of a number of public sector benefits as unconstitutional. In September 2012, in light of worsening budgetary prospects, the government delayed the expected reduction in the tax wedge aimed at raising competitiveness. Reflecting concerns regarding social security funding, the government replaced cuts in social security contributions with a budgetary-neutral measure that reduced employers' contributions and raised employees' contributions by a roughly similar amount. The objective was to boost competitiveness and job creation without compromising fiscal consolidation. The proposal was met by protests by unions, who feared a loss of net wages, and the opposition of the employers' associations, who feared social tensions. The proposal was withdrawn soon after its announcement, and the tax wedge reform was subsequently dropped from the MoU conditionalities.

Reform fatigue became prevalent starting from the second half of 2012, in light of the protracted fiscal consolidation, the worsening recession and the surge in unemployment. Between 2011 and early 2013, exit rates from unemployment registered record-low numbers, which translated into a major increase in youth and long-term unemployment. The effectiveness of the programme was increasingly questioned in the public debate. By summer 2012, tensions in bond market started to decline and the financial sector creditworthiness improved. As the need of financial assistance became less urgent, the leverage of the international financing institutions for enforcing the programme weakened.

Criticisms of the programme were increasingly voiced not only by the political opposition but also from within the government majority, notably by members of the People's Party (CDS). In July 2013, there was a government re-shuffle, which resulted in Paulo Portas holding the position of deputy prime minister with a coordination role for the adjustment programme and the labour portfolio being held by a CDS minister. In July 2012, the Constitutional Court judged as unconstitutional most measures aimed at reducing wage and non-wage benefits in the public sector, and, in September 2013, rejected the Labour Code revisions concerning working time conditions and EPL, as well as the changes in the definition of unfair dismissal.

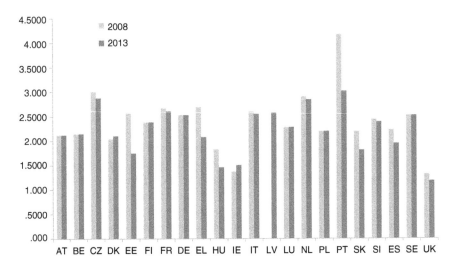

Figure 6.8 EPL indicator for permanent contracts

In a nutshell, a supporting political climate for labour market reforms was missing exactly when it was most necessary, since those reforms that still required an
agreement with social partners had yet to be implemented.

The execution of the programme in different areas is summarized in the
Appendix.

Reforms concerning EPL were overall far reaching. They led to the largest drop
in the OECD EPL index for permanent contracts among OECD countries (see
Figure 6.8). The reduction in unemployment since 2013 was among the strongest
recorded across the EU and not fully explained by the GDP recovery (Figure 6.1).

(1) The reduction of severance payments took place broadly as initially foreseen
     in the programme, both in terms of targets and timing, with the result of
     more than halving severance payments, and aligning payments due for
     permanent and temporary contracts.
(2) The definition of fair dismissals was reformed in line with the programme
     objectives. However, the Constitutional Court ruled the changes as uncon-
     stitutional. Following new MoU requirements, the government introduced
     lighter amendments to the labour code definition, in order to broaden the
     cases admissible for fair dismissal.
(3) Funds for the financing of severance payments were made available. But unlike
     what was originally envisaged, the entitlements were not made transferable.

Regarding the impact of the EPL reform, prima facie evidence shows that the
growth in employment since 2012 took place especially in terms of permanent jobs
(Figure 6.9). An analysis of the impact of the reforms using a matched

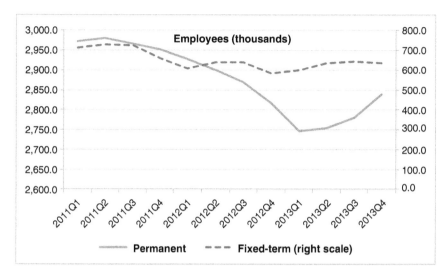

Figure 6.9 Number of employees by type of contract (thousands)

employer-employee administrative dataset for Portugal (*'Quadros de Pessoal'*) confirms that firms more concerned by the severance payment experienced a significantly larger increase of new hirings on permanent contracts, without also experiencing more firings, a result that was possibly due to the fact that the reform did not concern severance payment entitlements that were already accumulated (OECD 2017).

Working time arrangements were reformed according to the programme objectives. The new laws reforming EPL and working time arrangements also stated that the new Labour Code would have precedence over collective contracts. However, the Constitutional Court ruled out this possibility in September 2013. All in all, the labour code revision regarding overtime and working time arrangements implied that firms making use of overtime schemes reduced overtime labour costs by around 13 percent during the 2011–12 period (OECD 2017).

Reforms in the *wage setting* system were only partly successful, with some backtracking taking place before the termination of the programme. The reforms of the labour code aiming at wage decentralization took place according to the MoU's stipulations. New criteria for extending sectoral collective agreements to non-signatory parties were introduced by means of a government act only (with no legislation enacted), and after being met with strong opposition not only by unions but also by employers' organizations that were concerned about disparities in labour costs between members and non-members. As foreseen by the programme, a revision of the regime for the survival of expired collective contracts was also introduced.

The measures did not prove effective in fostering bargaining decentralization. Bargaining at firm level did not pick up and remained as infrequent as before

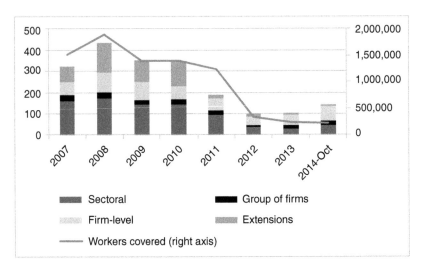

Figure 6.10 Number of collective contracts concluded and share of workers covered

the reforms. Sectoral collective bargaining instead froze after the start of the programme, as indicated by the fall in the number of new contracts concluded (see Figure 6.10).[8] The suspension of the reform of the extension mechanism, requiring the respect of a 50 percent representativeness threshold, implied that in some sectors collective contracts could not be extended.[9] The revision in the practice for extending collective contracts was identified among the reasons for the freeze in sectoral wage negotiations, as parties were not willing to negotiate under the new rules, possibly betting on a new reform restoring previous conditions. Accordingly, the government, with the aim of revitalizing sectoral collective bargaining, modified again the criterion for the coverage extension making it less binding.[10] Extensions granted dropped quite drastically between 2011 and 2014 (on average each year 15.5 contracts were extended) as compared with the pre-crisis period (151 contracts on average were extended each year between 2007 and 2010). The number of extensions rose in 2015 to 44 after the less-constraining extension criteria was introduced, remaining however well below the pre-crisis average. Preliminary evidence indicates that the drop in the extension of sectoral collective contracts may have helped maintaining employment.[11]

The freeze of sectoral wage negotiations resulted in a major increase in the number of individuals in the private sector whose wage did not change, while there was a non-negligible increase in the number of individuals whose wage fell as a result of reduced work time and lower entry wages for new hires (Bank of Portugal 2013). On aggregate, the growth of contractual wages in the private sector fell from 2.4 in 2010 to about 1.5 percent in 2011 and 2012, down to 1 percent in 2013 and 2014, implying real negative wage growth in 2011 and 2012 (OECD 2017).

The dynamics of overall nominal compensations per employee during the programme period were instead strongly affected by those in the government sector, where wage conditions were first reduced, and later re-established at previous levels following the ruling of the constitutional court that judged such cuts unconstitutional.

Reforms concerning *unemployment benefits* reflected the objectives of the adjustment programme and were broadly in line with the conditions included in the MoU. The reforms aimed at tackling different risks of the system: that of unemployment traps linked to high replacement rates for some categories of jobseekers; the risk of benefit dependency for permanent workers with long employment history that benefited from long-lasting benefits; and the risk of insufficient coverage, especially for precarious workers and young workers with short employment history. Preliminary evidence on social security records suggests that the reform may have played in the direction of reducing unemployment traps and benefit dependence (OECD 2017). Comparing unemployed individuals whose benefits were subject to the cap introduced by the reform and those that were not, it was found that the exit rate from unemployment was higher for jobseekers subject to the cap, although the difference is not statistically significant. Moreover, jobseekers that were subject to a 10-percent reduction of benefits after 6 months from becoming unemployed exhibited higher exit rates as compared with jobseekers whose benefits were not reduced (no statistically significant difference though).[12] Concerning the degree of protection provided by unemployment benefits, it turns out that the ratio of jobseekers entitled to unemployment insurance or unemployment assistance to the total number of jobseekers rose slightly between 2011 and 2013 from 45 to 47 percent, partly reflecting the easing of access to unemployment insurance associated with the reforms of the programme,.

The measures taken in the fields of ALMPs were quite far-reaching. Training programmes were refocused on the basis of their effectiveness, which implied the replacement of programmes of long duration with programmes of shorter duration. Public employment services were reformed and their offer revised. New hiring subsidies targeted to the young and the long-term unemployed were introduced and new scheme for apprenticeship was launched. Overall, the participation in the training and subsidized hiring schemes increased substantially after their introduction, and analysis based on administrative data from the Public Employment Service suggests that hiring subsidies and, to a lesser extent, training schemes, were followed by a higher probability of being employed for participants, as compared with a control group (OECD 2017).

6.5 Lessons for policy design

In contrast to other EU countries that implemented adjustment programmes, Greece in particular, the Portuguese authorities already shared the view that reforms were needed before the signing in programme, and proposals were already under discussion with social partners. The time frame of the programme was conceived so as to allow the discussion and elaboration of new measures with social partners and stakeholders. While this element strengthened ownership, it also implied back-loading of a number of reforms. This turned out to be detrimental for implementation, since the commitment to reforms weakened during the programme period.

Overall, the experience of Portugal provides a number of lessons for policy design.

(1) *Bold reforms are easier to implement in time of crises.* Despite the fact that there was a large consensus that Portugal needed bold reforms well before the 2011 crisis, it was only after the start of the debt crisis that the authorities tackled labour market reforms in a resolute way. The crisis therefore appears to have raised the cost of the status quo and contributed to remove resistance to reforms (Drazen and Grilli 1993). This happened despite the fact that initial conditions were not supportive of bold reforms; namely tight fiscal constraints and proximity to elections. The lack of fiscal space left no alternative to taking bold steps to consolidate public finances and reform the economy at the same time (Tanzi 2015).

(2) *Reforms that are the result of a domestic debate are more likely to ensure ownership of a consistent reform programme.* The existence of a pre-crisis debate on labour market reforms and awareness of reform needs among policy makers were key factors for the achievements of the programme, as this allowed broad convergence of views on the main objectives of the labour market measures at the start of the programme among experts (Rodrik 1996). Such a consensus also facilitated the maintenance of reform objectives even after the change in government following the 2011 political elections. A similar path of deep and broadly consistent labour market reforms carried out by subsequent governments was also observed in other countries where a debate on desirable reform avenues predated an acceleration of reform activity in a context of financial assistance programmes (e.g. Spain) or financial market pressures (e.g. Italy).

(3) *Ownership helps the feasibility and sustainability of reforms.* In the case of the post-crisis Portugal, endorsement by the social partners was key for the revising the labour code. By contrast, the absence of consensus was a major obstacle for reforming the wage setting system. In this respect, lack of support to the reform of the extension mechanism by the social partners also contributed to its limited effectiveness and actually led to the partial backtracking towards the end of the programme.

(4) *Phasing in the impact of reforms helps to overcome resistance.* Designing the measures in such a way as to prevent loss of existing rights minimized resistance and limited the social impact of the programme, confirming evidence from a number of existing analyses (e.g. Boeri 2005). In the case of Portugal, this was notably the case of the reforms carried out in the severance payments system and unemployment insurance fields.

(5) *A gradual approach has advantages but also disadvantages.* Adopting the measures backed by social partners first and back-loading other measures was aimed at building consensus and permitting the necessary elaboration by policy authorities. However, back-loading proved problematic in key areas at the stage of execution, as reform fatigue kicked in and incentives by the authorities to comply with programme conditionality weakened as financial market pressure started easing. This raises a general issue on the optimal timing of reforms in the context of adjustment programmes (e.g. gradual vs. 'cold-turkey' approach) which has probably received insufficient attention.

(6) *Concreteness helps, the best can be the enemy of the good.* The definition of easily identifiable targets (such as in the case of the reform of the Labour Code) appears to have helped achieving reform objectives. Conversely, sophisticated reform conditions turned out to be out of reach (such as a fund for financing severance payments with portable entitlements). This suggests that attempts to micro-manage structural reforms by mean of programme conditions have limitations if not backed by strong ownership and administrative capacity.

Notes

1 The views expressed in this paper do not reflect necessarily those of the European Commission. Useful comments were received by Antonio de Lecea, Antonio Dias da Silva, Martin Hallet and Stefan Kuhnert.

2 For the case of permanent jobs, severance payments for fair dismissal in Portugal were 30 days of wage per each year of tenure, almost three times what was paid on average in other OECD countries. The cases justifying fair dismissals were narrowly defined in the Labour Code. Unfair dismissals implied a severance payment higher than that in case of fair dismissals or, if this is what the employee preferred, reinstatement in the previous job and back pay up to one year.

3 A different type of administrative extension prevailing in Portugal is the one used to address sectors where collective contracts are not present. The Ministry of Labour can extend to these sectors the same conditions found in collective contracts of other sectors.

4 Note that work councils are firms-level organizations representing the work force that may or may not refer to existing unions. Note also that in Portugal, contracts bargained at a lower level prevail over those negotiated at a higher level. Hence, the prevailing practice of extending contracts might not necessarily come at the detriment of wage decentralization in the presence of a well-developed system of collective bargaining at firm level. However, the very limited prevalence of firm level bargaining in Portugal did not result in wage decentralization on this front.

5 The Memorandum of Understanding mentioned that 'reforms in labour and social security legislation will be implemented after consultation of social partners, taking into account possible constitutional implications, and in respect of EU Directives and Core Labour Standards' (European Commission 2011, p. 77)

6 Source: data from the OECD-European Commission tax and benefit project.

7 The 2011 budget included a 5 percent cut in public sector wages; the MoU required their nominal freeze relative to the 2012–13 period. Additional cuts in public sector wages were legislated in Autumn 2011 with the suspension of the payment of the 13th and the 14th allowance for wages above a certain threshold.

8 Sectoral bargaining started recovering in 2014 and 2015, but the number of new contracts negotiated did not reach the typical level before the crisis.
9 More specifically, the representativeness criterion required that the firms affiliated with the signatory employers' organization to employ at least 50 percent of total employees in the sector. The extension criterion also took into account considerations linked to the competitiveness of the sector and the share of SMEs in the sector.
10 The criterion was modified in the last period of the programme in such a way as to include the possibility of extending collective contracts to all sectors where the share of SMEs on the firms affiliated with the signatory employers' organization is above a threshold of 30 percent, irrespective of the representativeness of the agreement.
11 Hijzen and Martins (2016) analyze a matched employer-employee database and find that not extending collective contracts that were normally extended before the reform implied stronger employment growth in the firms not affiliated to the employers' organization that concluded the agreements.
12 The effects of the cut in benefit duration carried out during the programme has not been assessed, as useful evidence is not yet available, since the reform does not concern individuals unemployed at the time of the reform and does not reduce rights already accumulated by employees via their contribution history. However, analyses on a reform carried out in Portugal in 1999, which lengthened unemployment insurance, found that the jobseekers that could not benefit from the reform had exit rates from unemployment 60 to 80 percent higher (Addison and Portugal 2008).

Bibliography

Addison, J. T., and Portugal, P. (2008) How Do Different Entitlements to Unemployment Benefits Affect the Transitions From Unemployment to Employment? *Economics Letters*, 101(3), 206–209.

Arpaia, A., Kiss, A., and Turrini, A. (2014) *Is Unemployment Structural or Cyclical? Main Features of Job Matching in the EU After the Crisis*. European Commission Directorate General for Economic and Monetary Affairs. Economic Paper No. 527.

Bank of Portugal (2013) *Recent Wage Developments in Portugal*. Bank of Portugal, Economic Bulletin, Autumn. Available from: https://www.bportugal.pt/en/publications/banco-de-portugal?page=18&mlid=778

Blanchard, O. (2006) *Adjustment Within the Euro. The Difficult Case of Portugal*. MIT Department of Economics. Working Paper No. 06–04.

Boeri, T. (2005) *Reforming Labour and Product Markets: Some Lessons From Two Decades of Experiment in Europe*. IMF. Working Paper No. 05/97.

Campos, M., and Centeno, M. (2012) *Public-Private Wage Gaps in the Period Prior to the Adoption of the Euro: An Application Based on Longitudinal Data*. Bank of Portugal. Working Paper No. 1/2012.

Centeno, M., Duarte, C., and Novo, A. (2011) *The Impact of the Minimum Wage on Low Wage Workers*. Bank of Portugal. Economic Bulletin, Autumn 2011. Available from: https://www.bportugal.pt/en/comunicado/economic-bulletin-autumn-2011-projections-portuguese-economy-2011-2012

Drazen, A., and Grilli, V. (1993) The Benefit of Crises for Economic Reforms. *American Economic Review*, 83(3), 598–607.

European Commission (2011) *The Economic Adjustment Programme for Portugal, European Economy*. European Commission. Occasional Paper No. 79.

European Commission (2013) *Labour Market Developments in Europe*. European Commission Directorate General for Employment, Social Affairs and Inclusion. Economic Paper No. 6.

European Commission (2014a) *The Economic Adjustment Programme for Portugal*. European Commission Directorate General for Economic and Financial Affairs. Occasional Paper No. 202.

European Commission (2014b) *Government Wages and Labour Market Outcomes*. European Commission Directorate General for Economic and Financial Affairs. Occasional Paper No. 190.

Guimaraes, P., Martins, F., and Portugal, P. (2014) *Upward Nominal Wage Rigidity*. IZA. Discussion Paper No. 10510.

Hijzen, A., and Martins, P. (2016) *No Extension Without Representation? Evidence From a Natural Experiment in Collective Bargaining*. IZA. Discussion Paper No. 10204.

Hofer, H. (2007) *The Severance Pay Reform in Austria ('Abfertigung Neu')*. CESifo. DICE Report 4/2007.

IMF (2010) *Portugal: Staff Report*. IMF. Country Report No. 10/18.

IMF (2015) *Portugal: Selected Issues*. IMF. Country Report No. 15/127.

Martins, M., and Portugal, P. (2010) *Price and Wage Formation in Portugal*. ECB. Working Paper No. 1259.

Martins, P. (2014) *30,000 Minimum Wages: The Economic Effects of Collective Bargaining Extensions*. IZA. Discussion Paper No. 8540.

OECD (2006) *Economic Survey: Portugal 2006*. OECD. Available from: http://www.oecd.org/fr/portugal/economicsurveyofportugal2006puttingpublicfinancesonasustainablepath.htm.

OECD (2010). *Employment Outlook*. OECD. Available from: http://www.oecd.org/els/employmentoutlook-previouseditions.htm.

OECD (2017) *Labour Market Reforms in Portugal 2011–2015. A Preliminary Assessment*. OECD. Available from: http://www.oecd.org/employment/labour-market-reforms-in-portugal-2011-15-9789264269576-en.htm.

Portugal, P. (2006) *Wage Setting in the Portuguese Labour Market: A Microeconomic Approach*. Bank of Portugal. Economic Bulletin, Autumn 2006. Available from: https://www.bportugal.pt/en/publications/banco-de-portugal/all/381?page=4.

Portugal, P. (2015) *The Portuguese Economic Crisis: Policies and Outcomes*. Policy Brief, Bertelsmann Stiftung.

Rodrik, D. (1996) Understanding Economic Policy Reforms. *Journal of Economic Literature*, 34(1), 9–41.

Tanzi, V. (2015) Crises, Initial Conditions and Economic Policies. In: *Structural Reforms and Fiscal Consolidation: Trade-offs or Complements?* German Federal Ministry of Finance and IMF (March 25), Berlin, Germany Federal Ministry of Finance.

Traxler, F., and Behrens, M. (2002) *Collective Bargaining Coverage and Extension Procedures*. EurWORK [Online]. Available from: https://www.eurofound.europa.eu/observatories/eurwork/comparative-information/collective-bargaining-coverage-and-extension-procedures.

Turrini, A. (2011) *EPL Reforms in Europe: A Portuguese Way to Single Contract Outcomes?* VoxEU. [Online]. Available from: http://voxeu.org/article/labour-market-reforms-lessons-portugal.

Appendix

Labour market measures in the 2011 financial assistance programme for Portugal

Measures in 17 May 2011 Memorandum of Understanding	*Measures taken by the government*
Employment protection legislation	
Severance payments.	
• The Government will submit **by end-July 2011** legislation to Parliament to implement a reform in the severance payments for new hires in line with the March 2001 Tripartite Agreement. Severance payments of open-ended contracts will be aligned with those of fixed-term contracts. The reform will re-design the system for severance payment entitlements as follows:	Observed by deadline.Comment. The MoU in 2014 after the 11th review included the request for government to consider, together with social partners, ways to align severance payments for unfair dismissals to those for fair dismissal. No measure was taken.
• Total severance payments for new open-ended contracts will be reduced from 30 to 10 days per year of tenure (with 10 additional days to be paid by an employers' financed fund) with a cap of 12 months and elimination of the 3 months of pay irrespective of tenure;	
• Total severance payments for fixed-term contracts will be reduced from 36 to 10 days per year of tenure for contracts shorter than 6 months and from 24 to 10 days for longer contracts (with 10 additional days to be paid by an employers' financed fund);	
• Implementation of the fund agreed in the March Tripartite Agreement to partly finance the cost of dismissals for new hires.	The measure was delayed until October 2013, see below.
• By **Q4–2011**, the Government will present a proposal to align severance payment entitlements for current employees in line with the reform for new hires, (taking into account the revised link between entitlement and seniority and the cap to total entitlements) without reducing accrued-to-date entitlements. This plan will lead to draft legislation to be submitted to Parliament by **[Q1–2012]**.	Legislation adopted by deadline, taking effect starting from November 2012.

Measures in 17 May 2011 Memorandum of Understanding	Measures taken by the government
• By **Q1–2012**, the Government will prepare a proposal aiming at:	
• aligning the level of severance payments to that prevailing on average in the EU;	Legislation was adopted in December 2012. The alignment would bring severance payments from 20 to 12 days of pay per year worked and would take place in two stages.
• allowing the severance pay entitlements financed from the fund agreed in the Tripartite agreement to be transferable to different employers by means of the creation of notional individual accounts.	In October 2013 two compensation funds were put in place: a firm defined at the level of the firm, and a fund working on a mutual basis and non-transferable benefits receiving a minority of contributions.

On the basis of this proposal, draft legislation will be submitted to Parliament no later than **Q3–2012**.

Definition of Dismissals

The Government will prepare by **Q4–2011** a reform proposal aimed at introducing adjustments to the cases for fair individual dismissals contemplated in the Labour Code with a view to fighting labour market segmentation and raise the use of open-ended contracts. This proposal will lead to draft legislation to be submitted to Parliament by **Q1–2012**.

• Individual dismissals linked to unsuitability of the worker should become possible even without the introduction of new technologies or other changes to the workplace (art. 373–380, 385 Labour Code). Inter alia, a new reason can be added regarding situations where the worker has agreed with the employer specific delivery objectives and does not fulfil them, for reasons deriving exclusively from the workers' responsibility;	Legislation was adopted by the deadline. The reform also implied that the new Labour Code could prevail on the conditions established in collective contracts. Comment. Some measures relating to the definition of fair dismissals were ruled as unconstitutional by the Constitutional Court in 2013 and replaced with alternative
• Individual dismissals linked to the extinction of work positions should not necessarily follow a predefined seniority order if more than one worker is assigned to identical functions (art. 368 Labour Code). The predefined seniority order is not necessary provided that the employer establishes a relevant and non-discriminatory alternative criteria (in line with what already happens in the case of collective dismissals);	Labour Court formulations with in the programme framework. It was also ruled out the possibility for the new Labour Code to prevail on the conditions established in collective contracts.

(Continued)

Measures in 17 May 2011 Memorandum of Understanding	Measures taken by the government

- Individual dismissals for the above reasons should not be subject to the obligation to attempt a transfer for a possible suitable position (art. 368, 375 Labour Code). As a rule, whenever there are work positions available that match the qualifications of the worker, dismissals should be avoided.

Working time arrangements

The Government will prepare an assessment regarding the use made of increased flexibility elements by the social partners associated with the 2009 Labour Code revision and prepare an action plan to promote the use of flexible working time arrangements, including on modalities for permitting the adoption of "bank of hours" working arrangement by mutual agreement of employers and employees negotiated at plant level. **[Q4–2011]**

Observed by deadline. The reform also implied that the new Labour Code could prevail on the conditions established in collective contracts.

Draft legislation will be submitted to Parliament **by Q1–2012** on the following aspects:
- implementation of the commitments agreed in the March Tripartite Agreement regarding working time arrangements and short-time working schemes in cases of industrial crisis, by easing the requirements employers have to fulfil to introduce and renew these measures;
- revision of the minimum additional pay for overtime established in the Labour Code: (i) reduction to maximum 50% (from current 50% for the first overtime hour worked, 75% for additional hours, 100% for overtime during holydays); (ii) elimination of the compensatory time off equal to 25% of overtime hours worked. These norms can be revised, upwards or downwards, by collective agreement.

Legislation was adopted by deadline.

Comment. The Constitutional Court in 2013 ruled out the possibility for the new Labour Code to prevail on the conditions established in collective contracts.

Wage setting and competitiveness

Minimum wage

The Government will commit that, over the programme period, any increase in the minimum wage will take place only if justified by economic and labour market developments and agreed in the framework of the programme review.

Observed throughout the programme.

Comment: the minimum wage was raised in October 204 and subsequently in January 2015.

Extension of collective wage contracts.

The government will define clear criteria to be followed for the extension of collective agreements and commit to them. The representativeness of the negotiating organizations and the implications of the extension for the competitive position of non-affiliated firms will have to be among these criteria. The representativeness of negotiating organizations will be assessed on the basis of both quantitative and qualitative indicators. To that purpose, the Government will charge the national statistical authority to do a survey to collect data on the representativeness of social partners on both sides of industry. Draft legislation defining criteria for extension and modalities for their implementation will be prepared by Q2–2012;

Observed by November 2012. The government adopted a Council of Ministers Resolution requiring that for granting an extension to a sectoral collective contract the employers' association that concluded the agreement must employ at least 50 % of employees in the sector.

Comments.
- A new conditionality was added requiring the government to use the available discretion not to extend collective contracts until the criteria for extension are defined. Such conditionality was not always observed throughout the programme.
- Action by government on the extension mechanism was delayed. The MoU conditionalities evolved by indicating a minimum 50% representatives threshold as a condition for granting the extension.
- An additional criterion was introduced by the government in June 2014, i.e. the extension would also be feasible if at least 30% of firms of the firms affiliated with the signatory employers' organization in a sector are SMEs, irrespective of representativeness.

Wage Norm

The government will prepare an independent review by Q2–2012 on how the tripartite concertation on wages can be reinvigorated with the view to define norms for overall wage developments that take into account the evolution of the competitive position of the economy and a system for monitoring compliance with such norms.

Observed by deadline. Not followed by measures.

(*Continued*)

(Continued)

Measures in 17 May 2011 Memorandum of Understanding	Measures taken by the government

Duration of collective contracts

By **Q2–2012** the government will prepare and independent review on the desirability of shortening the survival (sobrevigência) of contracts that are expired but not renewed (art 501 of the Labour Code).

Observed in Q1 2014.Comment: The survival of expired collective agreements was reduced from 18 to 12 months and the time needed for collective agreements that make their expiry dependent on the existence of a new agreement to enter into a period of survival was reduced from 5 to 3 years.

Firm-level bargaining

- By **Q4–2011** the government will implement the commitments in the Tripartite Agreement of March 2011 concerning the 'organised decentralisation', notably concerning: (i) the possibility for works councils to negotiate functional and geographical mobility conditions and working time arrangements; (ii) the creation of a Labour Relations Centre supporting social dialogue with improved information and providing technical assistance to parties involved in negotiations; (iii) the lowering of the firm size threshold above which works councils can conclude firm-level agreements to 250 employees. Action for the implementation of these measures will have to be taken by **Q4–2011**.
- The government will promote the inclusion in sectoral collective agreements of conditions under which works councils can conclude firm-level agreements without the delegation of unions. An action plan will have to be produced by **Q4–2011**.
- By **Q1–2012** the Government will present a proposal to reduce the firm size threshold for works councils to conclude agreements below 250 employees, with a view to adoption by **Q2–2012**.
- By **Q1–2012** the Government will present a proposal to reduce the firm size threshold for works councils to conclude agreements below 250 employees, with a view to adoption by **Q2–2012**. Draft legislation will be submitted to Parliament by **Q1–2012**.

Legislation was adopted by deadline.Comments.
- The firm size above which works councils can conclude collective contracts was lowered more than requested in the MoU, namely to 150 workers.
- The MoU, in light of limited use of firm-level bargaining, introduced in Q2 2014 the request to study ways to foster collective agreement in dialogue with social partners. The possibility to temporarily suspend sectoral agreements at firm level with the consent of the original signatories was introduced.

Tax wedge

The 2012 budget will include a budget neutral recalibration of the tax system with a view to lower labour costs and boost competitiveness.

The measure was not implemented. The MoU was revised after the third review, and the implementation by the Portuguese of alternative measures to reduce firms' costs was acknowledged.

Measures in 17 May 2011 Memorandum of Understanding	*Measures taken by the government*

Unemployment benefits

The Government will prepare by **Q4–2011** an action plan and adopts draft legislation by Q1 2012 to reform along the following lines the unemployment insurance system:
- reducing the maximum duration of unemployment insurance benefits to no more than 18 months. The reform will not concern those currently unemployed and will not reduce accrued-to-date rights of employees;
- capping unemployment benefits at 2.5 times the social support index (IAS) and introducing a declining profile of benefits over the unemployment spell after six months of unemployment (a reduction of at least 10 percent in the benefit amount). The reform will concern those becoming unemployed after the reform;
- reducing the necessary contributory period to access unemployment insurance from 15 to 12 months;
- presenting a proposal for extending eligibility to unemployment insurance to clearly-defined categories of self-employed workers providing their services to a single firm on a regular basis.This plan will lead to draft legislation to be adopted by the government by **Q1 2012**.

Measures were taken within the deadline.

Comment. The reduction in the maximum duration of unemployment benefits was not to 18 but to 26 months, and unemployment benefit duration maintained a substantial link to age.

Active labour market policies

The Government will present by **[Q4–2011]**:
- a report on the effectiveness of current activation policies and other ALMPs in tackling long-term unemployment, improving the employability of the young and disadvantaged categories, and easing labour market mismatch;
- an action plan for possible improvements and further action on activation policies and other ALMPs, including the role of Public Employment Services.

Observed by deadline. Further evaluation reports and action plans produced by Q2 2012.

Comment. The action plans were followed by revised ALMP programmes and a new organization of the Public Employment Service.

The table is compiled using information on the MoU conditionalities and measures taken by the Portuguese government available in European Commission, The Economic Adjustment Programme for Portugal, European Economy, Occasional paper, various issues.

7 Some unpleasant labour arithmetics

A tale of the Spanish 2012 labour market reform

Carlos Cuerpo, Federico Geli and Carlos Herrero[1]

7.1 Introduction

From 1995 to 2007, the Spanish economy enjoyed a long period of strong economic growth that gave rise to a large expansion in the labour market. The unemployment rate fell to historically low levels (8 percent in 2007). This fall in unemployment was, however, not entirely of a structural nature, as there were some signs of persistent dysfunctionalities in the labour market, such as its dual structure, with a share of temporary workers above 30 percent, excessive rigidities in wage setting, especially collective bargaining arrangements, and extreme volatility particularly in employment (the extensive margin of the labour market). With the onset of the economic and financial crisis in 2008, these structural weaknesses were fully revealed, contributing to the sharp increase in the unemployment rate that reached 18 percent already by the end of 2009 and peaked at 26 percent in 2013.

This evolution can be partially explained by the growth pattern of the Spanish economy during this period: it mainly relied on the expansion of credit and the dynamism of the construction sector. Nevertheless, in countries experiencing a similar growth pattern, the rise of unemployment was not so intense (Estrada et al. 2009). This suggests that the adjustment to negative shocks in the Spanish labour market was particularly acute via changes in employment instead of hours (the intensive margin) and/or wages. This, together with the counter-cyclical behaviour exhibited by productivity in Spain, is explained up to a certain extent by the existing labour market institutions (Bentolila et al. 2011): strong protection for insiders would be preventing adjustment to shocks through changes in hour and wages and encouraging pro-cyclical variations mainly in temporary employment that, which in turn, gave rise to counter-cyclical productivity.

The rise and the persistence of unemployment prompted the Spanish government to implement two labour market reforms in 2010 and 2011, whose scope was quite limited. In 2012, however, a newly elected absolute majority government passed a new reform that introduced more far-reaching changes in labour market institutions.

This chapter aims at analyzing the macroeconomic impact of the 2012 labour market reform. It is organized as follows. The first section reviews the labour market reforms enacted during the economic crisis, explaining some political economy issues and describing some of its effects by looking at simple indicators. The second section focuses on the 2012 reform and goes a step further: it implements a comprehensive econometric analysis, presenting new evidence on its macroeconomic impact. We find evidence suggesting that the reform has encouraged wage moderation, reduced labour market frictions and increased the resilience of the labour market to negative shocks. Paradoxically, however, the results also hint to an exacerbation of the duality problem in the labour market.

7.2 The labour market reforms during the economic crisis

Since the return to democracy in 1978, there have been several reforms intended to improve the performance of the Spanish labour market. Over the last few years in particular, due to the challenges posed by the economic crisis, there have been different attempts to reduce existing inefficiencies. In particular, there were two reforms of limited scope and impact in 2010 and 2011, followed by a more encompassing one in 2012. This section reviews their main characteristics.

7.2.1 The 2010 and 2011 reforms

In September 2010 and July 2011, the Government implemented a set of measures intended to: (a) reduce duality in the labour market; (b) improve efficiency in the matching of jobs and workers; and (c) enhance firms' internal flexibility and collective bargaining (Wölfl and Mora-Sanguinetti 2011).

Regarding the first objective, the 2010 reform tried to reduce the gap between dismissal costs for permanent and for temporary contracts. The reform broadened the conditions under which a dismissal could be defined as 'fair' (with a severance payment of 20 days' wages per year of seniority, against 45 days' in the case of unfair dismissals) and extended the pool of workers that could be hired under a permanent contract with a reduced unfair severance payment of 33 days' wages per year of seniority. The 2010 reform also implemented some limitations to the use of temporary contracts and raised the compensation paid by the firm at termination of temporary contracts from 8 to 12 days. Such increase was gradual: the compensation would increase one additional day of compensation per year, reaching 12 days in 2015.

Moreover, in order to improve the efficiency in the matching process, the 2010 reform allowed private agencies to provide placement services (previously only non-profit agencies were allowed to do so).

As far as internal flexibility and collective bargaining are concerned, the 2010 labour market reform eased the requirements to opt out from collective agreements. It allowed firms to modify working conditions (such as working hours, shifts and duties) if they reached an agreement with their employees. It also eased the conditions to opt out from wage clauses established at higher level collective agreements (sectorial or regional): an agreement between the company and its employees would be sufficient. In this vein, the 2011 reform gave firm-level collective agreements priority over agreements at higher levels on subjects such as wages and working conditions. However, such priority was *de facto* prevented, since higher level agreements were still allowed to exclude bargaining at company level.

The impact of these reforms was quite limited. The number of fair dismissals rose slightly after the 2010 reform but this was mainly due to the fact that the economic crisis made it easier to define dismissals as fair. Likewise, there was no evidence of an increase in permanent hirings (see Conde-Ruiz et al. 2011).

Bentolila et al. (2011) argue that these two reforms were put into place due to the external pressures coming from international financial markets, in the context of the Eurozone sovereign debt crisis. Since neither the Government, nor social partners (trade unions and employers' associations) were fully committed to these reforms, they did not significantly reduce the divide between insiders (workers on a permanent contract) and outsiders (unemployed and workers on a temporary contract). In the same vein, Dolado et al. (2010) argue that duality in the Spanish labour market and the conflict of interests between insiders and outsiders discourage the implementation of reforms that improve labour market flexibility.[2]

In sum, the 2010 and 2011 reforms aimed at improving the labour market response to shocks, shifting the adjustment mechanism from changes in employment to variations of hours and wages. Both reforms were implemented in a context of a timid recovery after the deep 2008–09 recession. In fact, the Spanish government expected that these reforms would lay the foundations for a solid recovery of employment. However, as the economy entered a double-dip recession and macroeconomic conditions deteriorated, after the financial turmoil of the summer of 2011, unemployment began to hike again. In fact, in the summer of 2011, with the Spanish economy under strong financial pressures, the government passed a new package of labour market reforms. Among other measures, it implemented a new training contract for young unemployed and, quite unexpectedly, suspended some of the limitations to the use of temporary contracts that were included in the 2010 reform.

7.2.2 The 2012 reform

After the December 2011 elections, the new majority Government passed a more comprehensive labour market reform already in February 2012. This new reform, although more far-reaching, shared the same main goals than the previous ones; that is, to reduce labour market duality and to improve companies' internal flexibility and enhance collective bargaining.

Regarding labour market duality, the 2012 reform introduced substantial changes in employment protection legislation. First, severance payment for unjustified dismissals was reduced from 45 days per year of seniority (up to 42 months) to 33 days per year of seniority (up to 24 months). Second, the causes of justified dismissal (with a severance payment of 20 days per year of seniority) were further clarified and, to some extent, quantified (for instance, dismissals based on economic reasons are defined as fair if the firm experiences a decline in profits or revenues for three consecutive quarters). Third, the so-called *despido exprés*, a legal procedure that allowed a firm to declare a dismissal as unfair and to pay the severance payment upfront (45 days per year of seniority), was eliminated. Finally, the reform removed the payment of the interim wages between the date of dismissal and the final court ruling if the dismissal was defined as unfair in court.

As regards collective bargaining, the 2012 labour market reform removed the possibility for higher level agreements to exclude company-level agreements. Therefore, it gave collective agreements at firm level total priority over higher level ones, either sectorial or regional, as far as wages and working time were concerned. In addition, the indefinite extension of collective agreements in absence of a new agreement (the so-called *ultractitividad*) was limited to 2 years. It is worth noting that all workers in Spain are covered by the relevant collective bargain agreement, even if they do not belong to a union. For instance, a collective agreement bargained at a sector or firm-level covers all the workers that belong to a particular sector or firm. This so-called *eficacia general* principle makes collective bargaining a very powerful instrument. Therefore, any improvement in the structure of collective bargaining should have strong effects on the performance of the labour market.

Furthermore, the 2012 reform implemented new mechanisms of internal flexibility that made easier for firms to opt out from collective agreements: companies can claim economic (such as a decline in sales for two consecutive quarters), technical (such as new working methods or skills required) or production reasons (such as a substantive change in the demand) to opt out from wages' and other working conditions' clauses agreed in higher level collective agreements. Finally, the mandatory requirement for an administrative authorization in cases of working time reductions and for suspending contracts was removed, and the scope of causes that justify them was relaxed to include some generic reasons such as changes in firms' competitiveness, productivity and working methods.

The 2012 reform also included other measures targeted at addressing other shortcomings in the Spanish labour market. For instance, regarding hirings, it extended the length of the training contract (*contrato para la formación*) from 2 to 3 years and raised from 25 to 30 years the maximum age at which a worker can be hired under this contract. It also introduced a new permanent contract for start-ups, aimed at Small and Medium–Sized Enterprises (SMEs), with no severance payment for the first year trial period. Finally, in order to improve the matching process, the reform allowed private agencies to run professional training courses (previously this could be done only by firms' and workers' organizations) and allowed private agencies to provide placement services for temporary jobs.

In July 2012, the Government implemented a fiscal adjustment package which also included some measures intended to improve the activation of the unemployed. In particular, the replacement rate of unemployment benefits was reduced from 60 percent to 50 percent after an unemployment spell of six months.

Several factors contributed towards making this reform more far-reaching than the previous ones. On the political economy side, it is worth noting that: (a) the reform was passed by a new Government which enjoyed an absolute majority in both chambers; and (b) there was a very high external pressure for structural reforms following the economic recession, the accumulation of macroeconomic imbalances (e.g. large current account deficits, loss of productivity vis-à-vis trade partners, highly indebted household sector etc.) and the perceived weakness of the financial sector, which altogether led to a sharp increase of the sovereign debt risk premium. Moreover, the continuous deterioration of labour market conditions since 2008 eroded the resistance of social partners to further reform efforts, as the share of permanent workers over total labour force declined.

7.3 First look at the data: what have we seen so far

In the previous section, we have summarized the key elements of the 2012 labour market reform. As previously mentioned, the reform had two main objectives: to reduce labour market duality and to enhance collective bargaining and internal flexibility. If the reform was successful in reducing labour market duality, we should observe a decline in the share of temporary workers. On the other hand, a better functioning of collective bargaining should give rise to a shift from collective agreements at regional and sectoral level towards agreements at the firm level. In addition, a higher degree of flexibility in labour market institutions, due to lower employment protection, and an improved functioning of collective agreements should shift the adjustment process from quantities (i.e. unemployment) to prices (i.e. wage moderation) and reduce structural unemployment. We should also observe an alignment of wages and productivity growth.

Several papers have already tried to evaluate the size of these effects.[3] Some of the earlier attempts to evaluate the reform were made by the Spanish Ministry of Employment and Social Security (2013) itself and by Izquierdo et al. (2013). The Ministry of Employment and Social Security (2013) estimated a dynamic labour demand equation and found that the evolution of private employment from the second quarter of 2012 to the first quarter of 2013 was better than forecasted. This study attributed the better than expected evolution of employment to the effects of the reform. Izquierdo et al. (2013) showed that wage moderation increased from the second quarter of 2012 to the second quarter of 2013. In order to explain this higher wage moderation, they estimated a wage equation and found that the most recent evolution of wages was not explained by the explanatory variables in the wage equation (past inflation, unemployment rate and productivity) and could be attributed to the effects of the labour market reform.

During the summer of 2013, the Spanish government commissioned the OECD to perform an evaluation of the impact the 2012 labour market reform. The report (OECD 2013) used regression-discontinuity models to evaluate the effects of the reform on labour costs, on labour market flows and on labour market duality. The findings were mainly positive: the reform seemed to have improved internal flexibility, contributed to wage moderation and increased permanent hiring. In particular, regarding wage moderation, the report found that the reform had led to a deceleration of unit labour costs in the business sector of between 1.2 and 1.9 percent. Moreover, it was estimated that the reform increased hiring rates by 8 percent and reduced separation rates by 24 percent. Finally, the results showed that the exit rate from unemployment into a permanent contract increased by 24 percentage points. The IMF (2015) also found that the 2012 reform has contributed to wage moderation and, as a consequence, it has made the labour market more resilient, reducing job losses following negative shocks to labour demand.

A first look at the evolution of the main indicators of the Spanish labour market since 2012 offers some additional insights on the impact of the reform, as two more years have passed since the report was conducted and more observations are now available. Figure 7.1 looks at the structure of collective bargaining. The

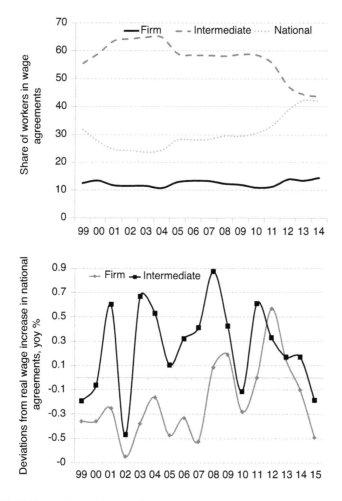

Figure 7.1 Collective bargaining structure

upper panel shows the distribution of workers between different bargaining levels (company, region and national) and the lower panel reflects the agreed wage increases at each level. The share of workers covered by collective agreements at regional level has steadily declined since 2011. However, they have mainly been replaced by agreements at national level, while the prevalence of collectively bargained agreements at company level has slightly increased. These developments are at odds with the expected effects of the reform, but should be welcome interpreting the pre-reform intermediate structure as the less beneficial state. This is because agreements at national and firm level are more likely to be associated to wage moderation due to either internalization of the employment consequences of wage increases or to more competition (see Calmfors and Driffill 1988). One possible explanation of this paradox is that social partners were negotiating agreements at national level that, although unable to incorporate firm-specific factors, were superior at internalizing their macroeconomic effect (e.g. impact on inflation, productivity growth, exports etc.). In this sense, the Agreement on Employment and Collective Bargaining 2012–14 (AECB), which was signed by social partners just before the 2012 reform was passed, defined some guidelines for collective bargaining on key issues such as internal flexibility and established limits of bargained wages growth for this period (0.5 percent in 2012 and 0.6 percent in 2013). The AECB 2015–17, signed by social partners in 2015, stablished new limits of bargained wages growth for this period (1 percent in 2015 and 1.5 percent in 2016). On the other hand, small- and medium-size enterprises may prefer to opt out from some of the working conditions established by higher level agreements, in key issues such as wages and hours, instead of conducting their own negotiating, since it is less burdensome. In 2014 and 2015, almost 65 percent of the opt-outs from higher level collective agreements referred to wage clauses and 95 percent of the firms that opted-out had less than 250 workers (Ministry of Employment and Social Security 2016). Regarding the differences of agreed wage increases at each level of negotiation, the wage moderation impact achieved at national level by the AECB 2012–14 seemed to have faded already: For firm-level agreements, as of 2014, wage increases became again smaller than at national level.

Figure 7.2 shows further insights in the evolution of agreed wages. While nominal agreed wages have remained almost flat since 2013, real agreed wages have become more responsive to both GDP growth and changes in employment (see upper panel): they fell in 2012 as the economy entered in a double-dip recession, and started to grow again as the economy recovered. The double-dip recession starting in 2009 seems to mask different dynamics in agreed wages and its impact in real variables. The mild decrease in the growth rate of agreed wages in 2009 and 2010 was not enough to prevent a sharp rise in the pace of real wages in 2009 while the economy was entering into a full scale recession, since the fall in price inflation turned out to be larger and faster than expected by market participants. However, as of 2012 changes in agreed wages and price developments translated into an evolution of real wages in line with GDP growth, first decreasing during the economic bust and then increasing its pace of growth during the recovery phase. This pro-cyclical response of real wages could be interpreted as consistent with the sequence of the 2012 reform: the increase of labour market flexibility and the improvement of collective bargaining would have made real wages more responsive to cyclical conditions. In fact, the dysfunctionalities of the Spanish labour market became evident at the beginning of the crisis, between 2008 and 2010, when real agreed wages rose despite the fact that GDP growth and employment plummeted. However, it should be mentioned that price developments as of 2009 also contributed to ease some pressure wage dynamics, requiring a lower nominal adjustment as inflation remained subdued. Furthermore, the lower panel in Figure 7.2 suggests that neither agreed wages nor compensation per employee have become more responsive to productivity changes.

As far as permanent/temporary workers duality is concerned, the upper panels of Figure 7.3 shows that both the number of temporary workers and the share of

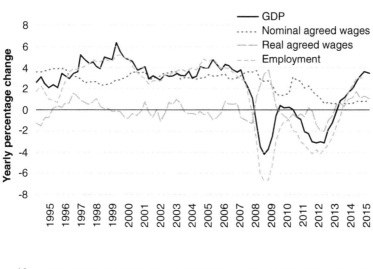

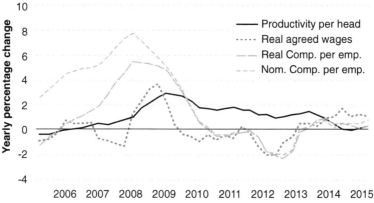

Figure 7.2 Wage, employment and productivity developments

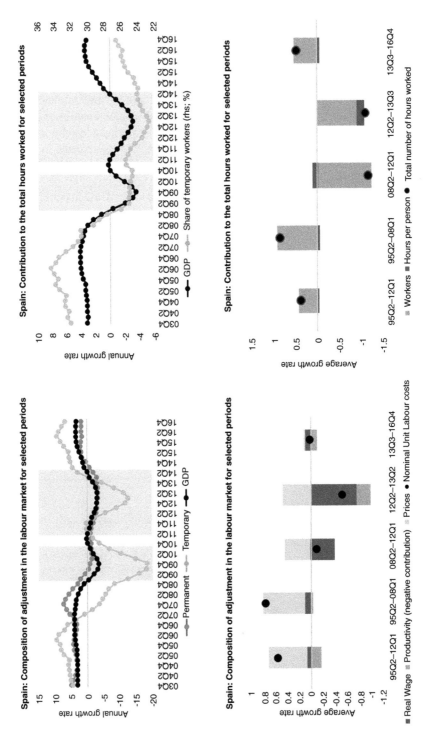

Figure 7.3 Duality and shock absorption capacity

temporary workers fell strongly in 2012. However, this seems to be explained by cyclical developments: as the economy entered a double-dip recession, the burden of the adjustment fell on temporary workers, who were the first to be dismissed. The share of temporary workers actually started to grow again in 2013, as the economy began to recover. While the share of temporary workers has not reached the pre-crisis level, it seems that a large share of employment is being created via temporary contracts. If this is the case, it would imply that the 2012 reform has not sensibly contributed to remedy the dual structure of the Spanish labour market as temporary workers still bear most of the brunt of the adjustment.

Post-reform data also signals a more balanced adjustment path from the extensive (employment) to the intensive (hours) margin, in particular during the years of negative growth following the reform. The lower left panel of Figure 7.3 shows the decomposition of the evolution of unit labour costs. There it can be seen that since 1995 and until the 2012 reform, the labour market adjustments to positive shocks were mainly channelled via changes in the price component of wages (i.e. changes in nominal wages not related to changes in productivity or real wages but rather to consumer inflation) and to negative shocks via productivity losses. However, in the post-reform period one third of the adjustment has been made via changes in real wages. Moreover, the lower right panel of Figure 7.3, which shows the average contribution to changes in total compensation of employees for selected periods, also highlights that after the reform firms started to use the possibility of reducing the number of hours worked rather than the number of workers. In fact, during the recessionary period between 2012Q2 (start of the reform) and 2013Q3 (end of recession) approximately 20 percent of the decrease in total compensation of employees is due to a reduction in the average hours worked per person. Nevertheless, it is possible that the impact of the reform was somehow limited due to the duality problem, since temporary contracts cannot easily benefit from measures that tend to improve the intensive margin but rather face adjustment via termination or non-renewal.

This descriptive analysis of the recent evolution of the Spanish labour market shows mixed results: there have been some changes in the structure of collective bargaining which may have encouraged wage moderation, but duality still seems to be a problem which limits the capacity to absorb shocks in a more balanced way. Any assessment of the impact of the reform requires netting out the effects of other factors such as cyclical developments. In order to do so, the next section presents an econometric analysis of the macroeconomic impact of the reform.

7.4 Estimating the macroeconomic impact of the reform

Despite recent improvements in the Spanish labour market, the still very high unemployment rate remains the key macroeconomic imbalance and an important challenge for the years to come.[4] Looking ahead, an accurate diagnosis of the interplay between the business cycle and the labour market should thus be aimed at understanding whether these improvements are likely to stay in the future (i.e. they can be qualified as structural gains) or are simply due to cyclical developments. In this context, the 2012 labour market reform could, in theory, play a major role in tilting the balance towards making the improvements long-lasting.

In order to gauge the impact of the reform, this section reviews three stylized facts, providing an overarching view of the connection between the labour market dynamics and the business cycle. First, we look at the Phillips Curve, which depicts a negative relation between the change in nominal wages and the rate of unemployment (see Phillips 1958). Second, we consider the Beveridge Curve, which assesses the efficiency of the matching process between jobs and workers, and describes a negative relationship between unemployment and vacancy rates. Third, we estimate an equation for the Okun's Law (1962), which vindicates a negative relationship between the change in the unemployment rate and GDP growth.

7.4.1 Wage developments

As it can be seen in Figure 7.4, the large reduction in unemployment rates witnessed from 1995 to 2008 was accompanied by a substantial increase in the private sector wage level. Since the beginning of the crisis, there has been a deceleration in wage increases (more moderate slope), as unemployment soared (slope turning positive). However, despite the recovery in terms of unemployment which started in mid-2013, wage dynamics have remained subdued. Two other factors were at play since 2012, on top of cyclical developments. First, social partners reached a 2-year agreement on wage moderation and in favour of job creation. Second, the 2012 reform, which contained elements oriented towards promoting a better alignment between wages and productivity, such as higher internal flexibility and decentralization in collective bargaining processes.

The estimation of a wage curve for the Spanish economy helps in depicting potential structural gains due to the reform and singling them out of cyclical

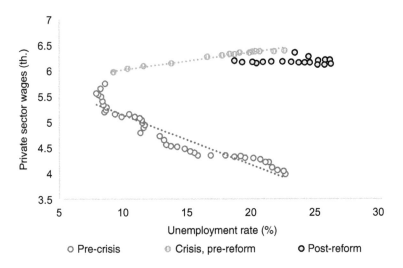

Figure 7.4 Wage curve, 1995Q1–2016Q4

dynamics. The wage curve is often considered an alternative to the traditional Phillips Curve when representing the negative correlation between unemployment and wages.[5] Wages are considered in levels, however, contrary to the Phillips Curve, where wages are set up in growth rates. The estimated equation relates the private sector nominal wages to its main determinants: (a) prices; (b) productivity; and (c) unemployment, as in equation (1).[6] The elasticity of wages to unemployment (a measure of wage flexibility or responsiveness to labour market conditions) amounts to –0.11, in line with previous results for Spain (see Sanromá and Ramos 2005 for an application to Spanish micro data).

$$W_t = -2.612 + 0.97^{***} CPI_{t-1} - 0.11^{*} U_{t-1} + 0.007^{***} \Delta Prod_t + \varepsilon_t, \qquad (1)$$
$$(0.103)\ (0.024)\ (0.059)\ (0.003)$$

The evolution of the residuals since the implementation of the reform (see Figure 7.5) gives an indication of potential structural changes in the wage-unemployment relation. Indeed, persistent negative residuals since 2012 could be a sign of missing elements contributing to wage moderation, such as the labour market reform.[7] In order to check whether the impact of this additional factor is significant, the regression is augmented with a dummy variable for the post-reform period, which turns out to be significant and negative. Figure 7.5 shows the residuals obtained from the previous wage equation. In the post-reform period the residuals show a negative bias. This indicates that from 2012 to 2015 nominal wages in Spain were lower than the level implied by their main determinants (prices, productivity and employment). As can be seen in Figure 7.5, this negative bias in the residuals disappears once correcting for the dummy. We also use the above wage equation to forecast nominal wages from 2012, just prior to the reform, onwards. Similarly, in-sample forecasts also reflect the omission bias when the dummy is

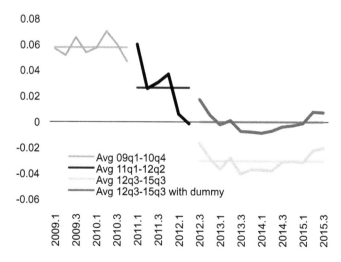

Figure 7.5 Wage equation residuals

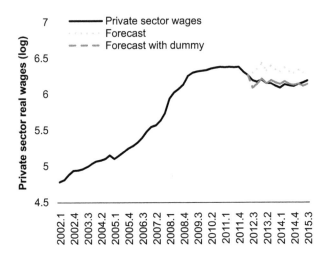

Figure 7.6 Private sector wages, forecast comparison

not taken into account, as the nominal wage forecast would be consistently higher than observed values (see Figure 7.6).

7.4.2 Matching efficiency

The Beveridge Curve (BC) provides a complementary tool to evaluate the extent to which movements in the labour market are of cyclical or of a permanent/structural nature. The theory and the empirical evidence postulate a negative relationship between the unemployment and the vacancy rates, as can be seen in the case of Spain in Figure 7.7 for the pre-crisis period.

Movements along this curve represent the impact of cyclical conditions. In this vein, the evolution between 1995 and 2007 could be considered of cyclical nature, with higher aggregate demand leading to a larger vacancy rate (v, defined as the number of posted vacancies over total job post) and ultimately to a lower unemployment rate (u) as it became easier to find a job.

Moreover, the position of the BC in the (u, v) space is typically related to the degree of 'frictions' existing in labour market and, more generally, to its institutional setting: the closer the curve to the axes, the lower the percentage of vacant jobs per unemployed worker and – *ceteris paribus* – the lower market 'frictions'. With the beginning of the crisis, the curve shifted outwards, potentially signalling an increase in structural unemployment as the matching between new jobs and workers became less efficient. Figure 7.7 also shows how, since the implementation of the reform, there has been a turnaround in the unemployment-vacancies locus and the curve is shifting inwards, partially undoing the impact of the crisis and possibly indicating efficiency gains attached to the 2012 labour market reform.[8] Several aspects of the 2012 reform could have had an impact on the efficiency of

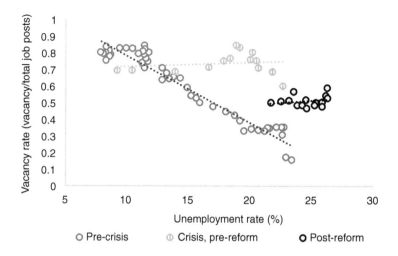

Figure 7.7 Beveridge curve, 1995Q1–2015Q3

the matching process between jobs and workers either directly (such as changes in the employment protection legislation and in the placement services regulation) or indirectly, via their effect on wage bargaining process.[9]

Beyond a graphical inspection of the Beveridge Curve, we test the statistical significance of the identified structural shifts by estimating the curve for the Spanish economy using quarterly data available since 1980. The specification follows Bonthius and Jarvis (2013). The unemployment rate is regressed on its lagged value, in order to capture its persistence, on the vacancy rate, on its squared value, in order to capture the convexity of the curve and potential non-linearities, and on a dummy variable for the crisis, in order to capture efficiency losses due to, for example, an increase in long-term unemployment or to the heavy sectoral reallocation that took place since 2008. The estimation results (see equation[10](2)) are in line with Bonthius and Jarvis (2013). The coefficient associated to the lagged dependent variable is large and highly significant, showing the persistent nature of unemployment. The coefficient of the vacancy rate and its squared value show a negative and convex significant relationship with the unemployment rate.

$$U_t = 2.13 - 4.33^{***} Vac_t + 2.87^{***} Vac_t^2 + 0.94^{***} U_{t-1} + 1.09^{***} dummycrisis + \varepsilon_t \qquad (2)$$
$$ (0.25)\ (0.92)\quad (1.06)\qquad (0.01)\qquad (0.13)$$

$$U_t = 1.85 - 3.54^{***} Vac_t + 1.99^{***} Vac_t^2 + 0.95^{***} U_{t-1} + 1.43^{***} dummycrisis - 0.94^{***} dummyref + \varepsilon_t \quad (2')$$
$$ (0.24)\ (0.85)\quad (0.96)\qquad (0.01)\qquad (0.13)\qquad\qquad (0.17)$$

When the equation is augmented with a dummy variable reflecting the impact of the reform (see equation 2'), as with the estimation of the wage curve, the coefficient associated with the reform dummy is highly significant and negative, possibly reflecting lower market frictions and higher efficiency attributable to the implementation of the reform. In addition, the estimated impact of the crisis becomes stronger.[11]

7.4.3 *The cost of reducing unemployment*

Overall, a better labour market performance in terms of higher flexibility and more efficient matching between workers and jobs, as evidenced in the previous sections, could potentially be reflected into the employment performance along the cycle. That is, the impact of the 2012 reform should be reflected in changes in the Okun's curve.

Okun's original contribution posited a negative relationship between unemployment and output, suggesting that a 2–3 percent drop in GDP growth was associated with a 1 percent increase in the unemployment rate (Okun 1962). The version in differences of Okun's curve Law relates contemporaneous changes in both variables, as in equation (3), where each change, expressed in percentage points, in real GDP, is associated with a proportional change in unemployment, estimated by the coefficient β.[12] Moreover, the ratio $\left(\frac{-1-\alpha}{\beta}\right)$ reflects the GDP growth rate that is consistent with a 1 pp. drop in the unemployment rate.[13]

$$\Delta U_t = \alpha + \beta \Delta GDP_t + \varepsilon_t,$$ (3)

The dynamics depicted by the Okun relationship are represented in Figure 7.8, in which three different patterns can be identified: (a) pre-crisis (1980–2007);

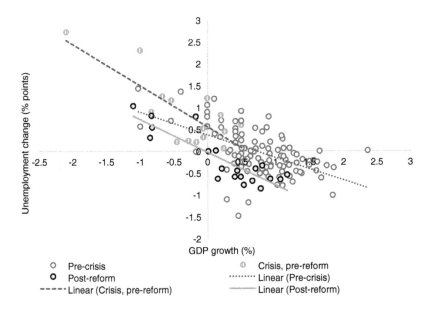

Figure 7.8 Okun's Law, 1980Q1–2016Q4

(b) post-2008 (2008–12); and (c) post-reform. With the advent of the crisis, the Okun curve shifts up and becomes steeper, possibly reflecting a higher average unemployment rate and a larger sensibility of unemployment to changes in output than in the pre-crisis period respectively. The observations following the 2012 reform seem to show, however, a distinct pattern. On the one hand, the constant (α) drops and it is lower than in the pre-crisis and (pre-reform) crisis periods. On the other hand, the slope after the reform appears to become flatter, although not enough to reach pre-crisis values.

This descriptive examination is complemented with an empirical exercise. In order to obtain an econometric estimation of the impact of the 2012 reform, a time-varying version of equation (3) is estimated, allowing for the parameters of the relationship to vary over time.[14, 15]

Results are shown in Figures 7.9 and 7.10 for the constant (α) and the slope (β) respectively. The econometric exercise confirms the existence of a parameter insta-bility at the end of sample.[16]

In particular, the case for the constant is clear-cut as there is a sudden increase following the crisis, which is more than compensated in the post-2012 period in the case of the specification which includes a dummy variable for the post-reform years. The constant term is traditionally interpreted as depending on structural factors of the economy or institutional features of labour market (see Anderton et al. 2014). Therefore, a sudden drop associated with the reform could be inter-preted as a structural improvement associated with it. The slope presents a mirror image, with a break occurring after the crisis as the coefficient almost doubled on average and came back later on (albeit not fully recovering pre-crisis values),

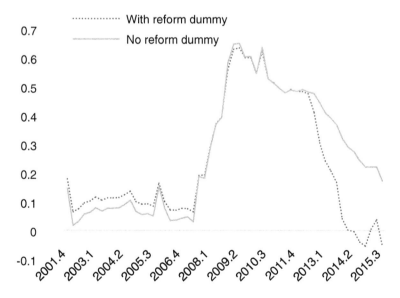

Figure 7.9 Constant, α

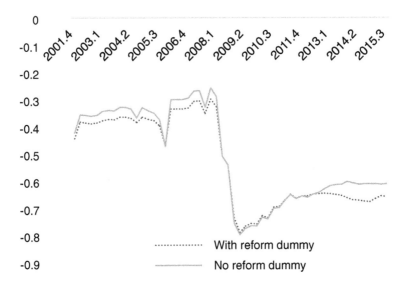

Figure 7.10 Slope, β

although in this case, the estimation with and without the reform dummy are mostly in line (they do not present significant differences).

The combined effect of the estimated increase (in absolute terms) in the slope and decrease in the constant implies a reduction of the unemployment-decreasing threshold $\left(\frac{-\alpha}{\beta}\right)$ in terms of GDP growth. In other words, the post-reform Spanish labour market would need lower GDP growth to start reducing unemployment or to prevent unemployment from increasing. In particular, the average estimate for the whole sample, the post-2008 and the post-reform period yield striking differences; 2.9 percent, 2.2 percent and 1.7 percent growth of real GDP respectively.

Finally, Okun estimates can be used to focus on the potential impact of the reform on the duality of the labour market. For this purpose, following Ball et al. (2013), an employment (L_T) version of equation (3) is estimated for both temporary and permanent workers, as in (4) with changes in employment depending on the growth rate of GDP:

$$\Delta L_t = \alpha_t + \beta_t \Delta GDP_t + \varepsilon_t \qquad (4)$$

As can be seen in Figures 7.11 and 7.12, the constant has increased for both types of contracts in the specification including the reform dummy (as a mirror image of the drop in the original Okun's curve). However, the response is significantly larger in the case of temporary workers, whose long-run growth rate experiences a sharp increase.

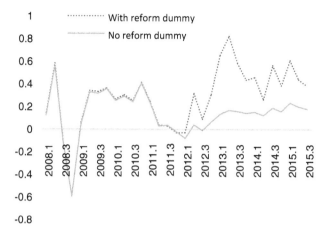

Figure 7.11 Temporary contracts, α

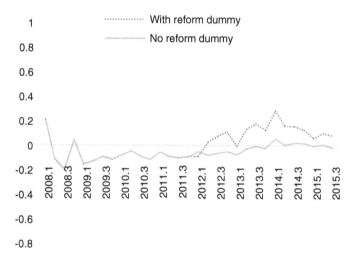

Figure 7.12 Permanent contracts, α

7.5 Conclusion

The 2008 economic and financial crisis and its posterior EU banking and sovereign debt dimensions highlighted some unresolved structural issues in the Spanish labour market, exacerbating unemployment, particularly in its young and long-term components. Duality between permanent and temporary workers, excessive rigidities in wage setting and collective bargaining arrangements and extreme volatility, particularly in employment, stand amongst the most commonly cited structural dysfunctionalities (Bentolila et al. 2011; Estrada et al. 2009).

After two reforms of limited scope and impact implemented in 2010 and 2011, the 2012 labour market reform aimed at mitigating these institutional flaws and achieving a more efficient and resilient labour market, focusing particularly on reducing labour market duality and enhancing collective bargaining as well as internal flexibility (Wölfl and Mora-Sanguinetti 2011; OECD 2013).

A bird's eye view of the raw data presents mixed evidence on the impact of the reform. There have been some changes in the structure of collective bargaining that have encouraged wage moderation, but duality still seems to be a problem which limits the capacity to absorb shocks in a more balance way. First, collective agreements have been on the rise at the national level, at the expense of the intermediate sectoral ones. This behaviour was probably influenced by the Agreement on Employment and Collective Bargaining 2012–14 (AECB) and the easing of opting-out mechanisms, which allowed more flexibility for firms. Nominal wage developments were subdued, particularly at the national level, also favoured by the AECB. Real wages, in turn, have become more responsive to cyclical conditions, despite low inflation. Moreover, it seems that the labour market has shifted towards a more balanced response to negative shocks, via less pressure on the number of employed people and leaving the lion's share of the adjustment to wages and hours. However, it is possible that the impact of the reform in this area has been somehow limited due to the exacerbation of duality. After a strong cyclical correction in 2012, the share of temporary workers started to grow again in 2013, as the economy began to recover, hampering one of the original objectives of the reform.

A robust assessment of the potential macroeconomic impact of the 2012 reform and of the likelihood that these effects will remain (i.e. their structural nature) was also performed via an econometric analysis of three overarching stylized facts: (a) the Wage Curve; (b) the Beveridge Curve; and (c) Okun's Law. Overall, the main findings of the econometric approach provide evidence of significant structural gains that are in line with the descriptive analysis. The reform has encouraged wage moderation, reduced labour market frictions and increased the resilience of the labour market to negative shocks. Paradoxically, however, the results also hint to an exacerbation of the duality problem in the labour market. As long as the past lacklustre growth of labour productivity reflects this duality, the increase in the creation of temporary contracts relative to permanent ones may have adverse effects on the Spanish rate of productivity growth in the future.

Having said that, the Spanish case can still provide some policy lessons. First, side (unwanted) effects can potentially limit the effects of a reform. The evidence of the Spanish case shows that the reform might have contributed to the exacerbation of duality. Overall, it is possible that the combined effect of the reform effectively increased the gap between the cost of hiring temporary and permanent workers, and hence limited its impact. Complementary measures geared towards a decrease of duality, such as those intended to equalize hiring and firing costs of temporary and permanent jobs, especially in relatively low productive jobs, or towards the investment in higher productivity sectors, could potentially address the problem. A second lesson points towards the timing of reforms. Even in a recession, the best policy option might still be to go ahead and implement the institutional changes. Although the reform was introduced in a recessionary period, evidence shows that the implementation of the reform quickly improved the nature of the adjustment process from the extensive to the intensive margin, and hence contributed to reduce dismissals. In addition, the gap between the growth of the economy and employment creation was reduced by the reform. The latter can be inferred from the evidence that shows that job creation kicked off before the recovery started. In the same vein, the timing of complementary measures also seems to matter, as it shown by the simultaneous implementation of the AECB 2012–14, which helped to ease wage pressures, giving more time to economic agents to fully internalize the impact of the reform.

With regard to political economy issues, it is important to point out that social partners and civil society in general might be more lenient towards accepting reforms in bad times, while unemployment figures are high and structural deficiencies are more evident. In this vein, national ownership can also help. In Spain, the signature of the AECB 2012–14 by almost all social partners contributed to its social acceptance, something which was missing in previous reforms, as they were often perceived by a large part of society as an external imposition.

Notes

1 The views expressed in this document are those of the author(s) and do not necessarily represent the views of the Spanish Independent Authority for Fiscal Responsibility or the Spanish Ministry of Finance. The authors would like to thank Paolo Manasse and Dimitris Katsikas for their very helpful comments to an earlier draft and also the participants of the Athens Workshop on Crisis and Structural Reforms in Southern Europe organized by the Eliamep.
2 They construct an index to measure the extent to which labour markets reforms that increase labour flexibility would be acceptable. This index, defined as the share of workers on a permanent contract over the total labour force, fell strongly in the earlier 1990s, when several labour market reforms that introduced a higher degree of flexibility were accepted by the social partners.
3 García Pérez and Jansen (2015) provide a comprehensive summary of the main evaluations of the 2012 labour market reform. They also raise further questions about its effects.
4 See European Commission (2016) for a recent and detailed diagnosis of the remaining macroeconomic imbalances in the Spanish economy.
5 See Blanchflower and Oswald (1990) for the original contribution and Blanchflower and Oswald (2005) for a revamp.
6 The estimated relation between wages and unemployment is kept in levels, as Johansen cointegration tests point to the existence of a cointegrating vector between the explanatory variables and the level of nominal wages. Productivity is transformed in year on year changes, meant as a smoothed version of its level, while keeping the same order of integration I (1). *, ** and *** indicate significance at the 10,5 and 1% level respectively.
7 Similar results are found in Izquierdo et al. (2013).
8 The number of vacancies is taken from the Macroeconomic Database of the Spanish Economy (REMSDB) and its construction follows the methodology described in Díaz (2007).
9 See Nickell et al. (2002) for a recollection of the variables expected to influence equilibrium unemployment-vacancy locus.

10 Note that *, ** and *** indicate significance at the 10, 5 and 1 percent level respectively.
11 The dummy for the crisis is defined as 1 for every period after 2007Q4 while the dummy reform only starts at 2012Q3.
12 The constant α represents the long-run 'trend' growth in the unemployment rate, $\alpha = -\beta\Delta GDP^*$, where GDP^* is stands for potential output. Therefore, in the long run, if the GDP grows at its potential rate, unemployment will be constant and equal to its structural rate (provided that the structural rate of unemployment is constant (Ball et al. 2013)).
13 Similarly, $\left(\frac{-\alpha}{\beta}\right)$ represents the growth rate that is consistent with a stable unemployment rate (i.e. $\Delta U_t = 0$).
14 The estimation is carried out following Ciapanna and Taboga (2011), who perform Bayesian time-varying estimation, obtaining at the same time the degree of parameter instability and the paths for the parameters (the median path is taken for the purpose of this analysis). Aksoy and Manasse in Chapter 4 of the book estimate a similar relationship, which specifically relates the change in parameters to the implementation of structural reforms.
15 As the coefficients estimated from equation (3) might be biased due to endogeneity issues, two alternative specifications were estimated for robustness. In the first case, the lagged values of the changes in unemployment and GDP were included in the equation, yielding similar results. In the second case, a model was estimated based on GDP and unemployment gaps: $\Delta(U_t - U_{t_t}^*) = \Delta(U_t - U_{t_t}^*) + \varepsilon_t$, where unemployment and GDP trends were obtained by means of a HP filter. Under this specification, the parameter β also gets larger (in absolute terms) after the reform (except for the last quarter, most probably due to the end point problem usually present in the HP filter).
16 In particular, according the stability measures based on the posterior probabilities as defined by Ciapanna and Taboga (2011).

Bibliography

Anderton, R., Aranki, T., Bonthius, B., and Jarvis, V. (2014) *Disaggregating Okun's Law Decomposing the Impact of Expenditure Components of GDP on Euro Area Unemployment*. ECB. Working Paper No. 1747.
Ball, L., Leigh, D., and Loungani, P. (2013) *Okun's Law: Fit at 50?* IMF. Working Paper No. 13/10.
Bentolila, S., Dolado, J. J., and Jimeno, J. F. (2008) *Two Tier Employment Protection Reforms: The Spanish Experience*. CESifo. DICE Report No. 4/2008.
Bentolila, S., Dolado, J. J., and Jimeno, J. F. (2011) *Reforming an Insider-Outsider Labor Market: The Spanish Experience*. IZA. Discussion Paper No. 6186.
Blanchflower, D., and Oswald, A. (1990) The Wage Curve. *Scandinavian Journal of Economics*, 92(2), 215–235.
Blanchflower, D., and Oswald, A. (2005) *The Wage Curve Reloaded*. IZA. Discussion Paper No. 1665.
Bonthius, B., and Jarvis, V. (2013) *What's Going on Behind the Euro Area Beveridge Curve(s)?* ECB. Working Paper No. 1856.
Boscá, J. E., Bustos, A., Díaz, A., Doménech, R., Ferri, C. J., Pérez, E., and Puch, L. (2007) *The REMSDB Macroeconomic Database of The Spanish Economy*. Documentos de trabajo Secretaría de Estado de Presupuestos y Gastos. Available from: http://www.sepg.pap.minhafp.gob.es/sitios/sepg/en-GB/Presupuestos/Documentacion/Paginas/BasedatosmodeloREMS.aspx.
Calmfors, L., and Driffill, J. (1988) Bargaining Structure, Corporatism, and Macroeconomic Performance. *Economic Policy*, 6, 14–61.

Ciapanna, E., and Taboga, M. (2011) *Bayesian Analysis of Coefficient Instability in Dynamic Regressions*. Banca d'Italia. Working Paper No. 836.

Conde-Ruiz, J. I., Felgueroso, F., and García Pérez, J. I. (2011) *Reforma Laboral 2010: Una primera evaluación y propuestas de mejora*. FEDEA. Colección de Estudios Económicos 01–2011.

Díaz, A. (2007) *Obtención de las variables del mercado de trabajo en la ecuación de matching del modelo REMS*. Ministerio de Economía y Hacienda. Mimeo.

Dolado, J. J., Felgueroso, F., and Jansen, M. (2010) *El conflicto entre la demanda de flexiblidad laboral y la Resistencia a la reforma del Mercado de trabajo en España*. FEDEA. Colección de Estudios Económicos 06–2010.

Estrada, A., Izquierdo, M., and Lacuesta, A. (2009) *El funcionamiento del mercado de trabajo y el aumento del paro en España.* Banco de España. Boletín Económico Julio-Agosto 2009.

European Commission (2016) *Country Report, Including an In-Depth Review on the Prevention and Correction of Macroeconomic Imbalances*. European Commission. Staff Working Document 02–2016.

García Pérez, J. I., and Jansen, M. (2015). *Reforma laboral de 2012: ¿Qué sabemos sobre sus efectos y qué queda por hacer?* FEDEA. Policy Paper 2015/04.

IMF (2015) *IMF Country Report No. 15/233*. Available from: ttps://www.imf.org/external/pubs/ft/scr/2015/cr15233.pdf.

Izquierdo, M., Lacuesta, A., and Puente, S. (2013) *La reforma laboral de 2012: un primer análisis de sus efectos sobre el mercado de trabajo*. Bank of Spain. Economic Bulletin September 2013.

Ministry of Employment and Social Security (2013) *Report Evaluating the Impact of the Labour Reform*. [Online]. Available from: www.empleo.gob.es/es/destacados/HOME/impacto_reforma_laboral/.

Ministry of Employment and Social Security (2016) *Anuario de Estadísticas 2015*. [Online]. Available from: http://www.empleo.gob.es/es/estadisticas/anuarios/2015/CCT/CCT.pdf.

Nickell, S. J., Nunziata, L., Ochel, W., and Quintini, G. (2002) The Beveridge Curve, Unemployment and Wages in the OECD from the 1960s to the 1990s. In: Aghion, P., Frydman, R., Stiglitz, J. and Woodford, M. (eds.) *Knowledge, Information, and Expectations in Modern Macroeconomics: Essays in Honor of E. S. Phelps*, Princeton, NJ, Princeton University Press.

OECD (2013) *The 2012 Labour Market Reform in Spain: A Preliminary Assessment*. [Online]. Available from: www.oecd.org/employment/spain-labourmarketreform.htm.

Okun, A. (1962) Potential GNP: Its Measurement and Significance. *Proceedings of the Business and Economics Statistics Section*, American Statistical Association, pp. 98–103.

Phillips, A. W. (1958) The Relation Between Unemployment and the Rate of Change of Money Wage Rates in the United Kingdom, 1861–1957. *Economica*, 25(100), 283–299.

Sanromá, E., and Ramos, R. (2005) Further Evidence on Disaggregated Wage Curves: The Case of Spain. *Australian Journal of Labour Economics*, 8(3), 227–243.

Spanish Ministry of Employment and Social Security (2016). *Avance Anuario de Estadísticas 2015*. Available from: http://www.empleo.gob.es/es/estadisticas/anuarios/2015/CCT/CCT.pdf.

Wölfl, A., and Mora-Sanguinetti, J. S. (2011) *Reforming the Labour Market in Spain*. OECD Economics Department. Working Paper No. 845.

8 Balancing adjustment policies and structural reforms in Greece

The case of product markets

Athanassios Petralias[1], Marianthi Anastasatou[2] and Dimitris Katsikas

8.1 Introduction

The Greek crisis has proven the most difficult episode of the wider Eurozone crisis. More than 7 years after its outbreak, the country is going through its third bailout programme, but a sustainable recovery is not yet in sight. During the crisis, the country received an extraordinary amount of money in the context of consecutive rescue packages, and yet the economy fell into the deepest recession an advanced country has experienced during the post-war period. One of the most important aspects of the crisis, and one which could go a long way towards explaining the difficulty of recovery, is the inherent weakness of Greece's growth model before the crisis, which was largely consumption-driven and financed through private and public debt (Katsikas and Filinis 2015; Manasse 2015). The economy was subject to numerous structural impediments and rigidities such as low productivity, a small export sector and a heavy burden of regulation and red tape, all of which led to low levels of competition, dynamism and extroversion in domestic product markets (for a recent review of these issues see Masourakis and Gortsos 2014). Accordingly, achieving recovery in the short-term and sustainable growth in the long-term would require addressing these problems. In this context, structural reforms in product markets and the wider business environment were bound to be a priority of the bailout programmes.

Indeed, the country has been called upon to implement a programme of structural reforms which has gradually increased in scope and comprehensiveness to include substantial product market and business regulation reforms. However, at the beginning of the adjustment process, the preferred policy for addressing low competitiveness and for restarting the economy (through the expected increase in exports) was that of internal devaluation, that is, the improvement of cost competitiveness through a depression of wages and labour costs, which was pursued through reforms in the labour market.[3] At the same time, the country has had to implement one of the most ambitious fiscal consolidation programmes, compared both to the other Eurozone countries undergoing a crisis (Daude 2016), but also to any other developed country that undertook substantial fiscal consolidation in recent decades (Anastasatou 2017). The aim of this chapter is to examine the policy mix between fiscal policies and structural reforms, with an emphasis in business regulation and product markets.

The hypothesis we want to test is whether policy makers got the balance right. Judging from the results, the mix and timing of policies described above, may have been counterproductive, as fiscal consolidation measures and internal devaluation policies led the Greek economy to a deep and long depression, which undermined the effectiveness of reforms, while the timing and sequencing of product market and business reforms themselves was likely not optimal.[4] To test the overall adjustment strategy, this chapter will examine how fiscal measures on the one hand, and reforms to remove rigidities and obstacles to competition on the other hand, affected the performance of the Greek economy as reflected on selected macroeconomic variables associated with the capacity of the Greek economy to compete internationally and stage a recovery, namely employment and inflation. We control for the impact of labour market reforms (some of which were part of the internal devaluation 'agenda'), as well as other factors which affected the macroeconomic environment, including political and economic (i.e. over Grexit) uncertainty, which has been a key feature of the crisis from its beginning until today. Given the differences in the timing of implementation of different reforms and fiscal measures, the findings could also provide us with insights about the appropriateness the programme's timing and sequencing.

For this analysis, we rely on linear regression models and apply a model selection method to identify which of the reforms and fiscal measures and at which time lags, affected our macroeconomic variables, controlling for other factors as described above.

The remainder of the chapter proceeds as follows: in the next section, arguments and evidence on the structural origins of the crisis in Greece and its handling to-date will be presented. Next, the difficulties of combining adjustment policies and structural reforms will be discussed. The following sections will present the model that will be employed to examine the relative impact of adjustment policies and structural reforms on the dependent variables, as well as the data used and the results of the exercise. A final section summarizes the findings and offers policy recommendations.

8.2 The origins and handling of the Greek crisis: international competitiveness, business environment and product markets

Weak competitiveness is at the core of Greece's economic woes. The World Economic Forum's (WEF) global competitiveness index shows that Greece's international competitiveness has deteriorated over time starting from the mid-2000s (Figure 8.1).

This picture is consistent with the course of Greece's external balance, which also gradually deteriorated during the 2000s, with the current account deficit peaking in 2008 at 14.9 percent of GDP. This development, also observed in other countries in the EMU periphery, was initially interpreted as something to be expected, a 'catch-up' process related to European integration (e.g. Blanchard and Giavazzi 2002). However, a closer look would reveal that, at least in Greece's case, the deterioration

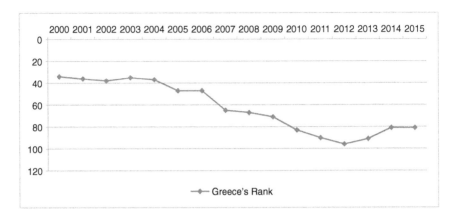

Figure 8.1 WEF global competitiveness index (2000–08)

Source: World Economic Forum

Note: The number of countries examined varies from year to year (the average for the years 2000–15 is 120). Although this makes the scores not directly comparable, the trend is clear. Besides, the inclusion of more countries in the index improves the accuracy of the overall picture; if this trend moves Greece lower in the rankings, this would only mean that Greece is even less competitive than previously thought.

Note: The WEF index until 2004 refers to the Growth Competitiveness Index and thereafter to the Global Competitiveness Index.

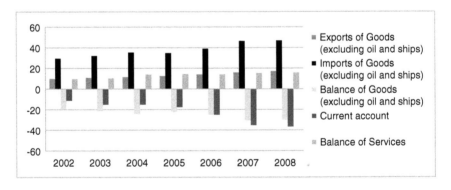

Figure 8.2 Greek external sector imbalances, 2002–08 (billion euros)

Source: Bank of Greece

of Greece's external balance was for the most part due to deterioration of its trade balance, which in turn reflected the fact that while imports increased steadily during the period 2002–08, its exports were stagnating at a low level (Figure 8.2).

On the one hand, these trends reflected the poor export performance of Greek companies; on the other hand, they reflected the fact that Greece's export base remained very small; for the period 1995–2012, Greek exports as a percentage of

GDP were only 22.3 percent, making Greece the most closed economy in the EU (Böwer et al. 2014). The closed nature of the Greek economy is also evident by the lack of Foreign Direct Investment (FDI) into the country; for the period 2004–12, Greece ranked last in attracting FDI flows in the EU-27 (Papazoglou 2014).

The inability to increase the economy's extroversion and competitiveness is due to a number of factors, most of them structural in nature (Papazoglou 2014; Vettas and Kouranti 2014; Böwer et al. 2014). Some of these factors are related to Greek labour costs; according to the Bank of Greece (2012), increased labour costs were responsible for half of Greece's loss of competitiveness before the crisis. The loss of competitiveness however, was also due to other factors, such as the low technological content of Greek exports, the small size of Greek businesses, the low levels of inward Foreign Direct Investment (FDI) and the low levels of competition in domestic product (goods and services) markets (Mitsopoulos 2014; Papazoglou 2014; Zografakis and Kastelli 2017; Vettas and Kouranti 2014).

Many of these problems are due to the adverse regulatory environment in Greek product markets, which suffer from excessive and low-quality regulation (Katsoulacos et al. 2015). This has been registered by a number of international indicators. Before the crisis, OECD's Product Market Regulation (PMR) Index, consistently ranked Greece as a country with excessive product market regulation and high barriers to entrepreneurship (Figure 8.3). In World Bank's 'Doing Business' rankings, Greece received low scores, even when compared to developing countries, for most aspects of its business environment (Table 8.1).

Excessive regulation has increased the administrative costs for businesses, and legal uncertainty has deterred investment (Mitsopoulos 2014). Restrictive regulation and barriers to entry (Vettas and Kouranti 2014), as well as weak competition authorities and policies (Katsoulacos et al. 2015), have limited the ability of Greek firms to compete domestically and globally.

In view of these problems, one would think that product markets' reforms would be among the top priorities of the bailout programmes. However, this was not the

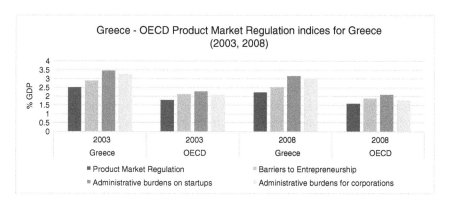

Figure 8.3 OECD Product Market Regulation indices for Greece (2003, 2008)
Source: OECD

Table 8.1 Greece, doing business 2008 (rank: 1–178)

Activity	Rank
Starting a business	100
Dealing with licenses	42
Employing workers	142
Registering property	93
Getting credit	84
Protecting investors	158
Paying taxes	86
Trading across borders	65
Enforcing contracts	87
Closing a business	38
Ease of doing business (overall score)	100

Source: World Bank

case, at least not from the beginning. Terzi (2015) and Terzi and Wolff (2014) show that product markets reforms were largely absent from the first Greek programme and only became a significant component of policy conditionality in the second one. As Katsikas et al. (2017) show using IMF's MONA database, private sector reforms (excluding financial sector and labour market reforms) in the first programme represented only 4.4 percent of the total actions (which effectively meant only two actions), while in the second, the share of private sector reforms rose to 10.3 percent of the total number of actions.

The overwhelming priority of the first adjustment programme was fiscal consolidation. Although the first Memorandum of Understanding (MoU) signed between the Greek government and its debtors acknowledged that the resolution of both the fiscal and competitiveness problems of Greece should be the programme's two main objectives,[5] it nonetheless went on to pronounce fiscal adjustment as the 'cornerstone of the programme'.[6] Moreover, fiscal adjustment continued being the top priority in the adjustment programmes that followed.[7] It is telling that the fiscal consolidation that was achieved was the biggest in a developed country in recent decades (Figure 8.4a), and it was achieved in a very short period of time (Figure 8.4b), compared to other similar adjustments (Anastasatou 2017).

Fiscal considerations were predominant also for the choice of structural reforms; approximately 30 percent of the reforms in the first two programmes referred to fiscal sustainability issues, such as the restructuring of the tax administration, the budget process, the fiscal control and transparency of public entities etc. (Katsikas et al. 2017).

The overall economic situation made the implementation of structural reforms politically difficult since, typically, reforms hurt the interests of specific groups, whose members lobby the government in order to prevent the welfare loss linked with the reform. As a result, some reforms in product markets did not proceed at

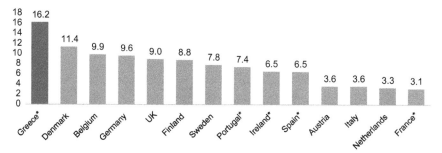

Figure 8.4a Biggest fiscal consolidation

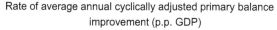

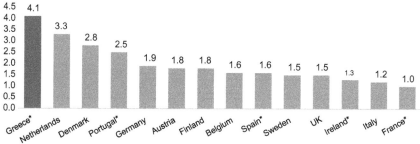

Figure 8.4b Fastest fiscal consolidation

Source: Anastasatou (2017)

Note: The cases of fiscal adjustment have been defined along the criteria set by the OECD (OECD Economic Outlook 81, May 2007)

* Excluding financial sector support

all and others were partially implemented, while others were legislated but not implemented in practice (for examples see Katsoulacos et al. 2015; Vettas and Kouranti 2014; Petralias 2017). Despite these problems, the new drive towards structural reforms in the product markets seemed to pay some dividends, as indicators of market regulation showed some improvement (Figure 8.5 and Table 8.2).

While product markets' reforms progressed gradually, a substantial labour market reform was implemented early on; among other things, this reform relaxed the norms for firing and hiring workers and reduced minimum wages in the private sector. The idea was to address Greece's low competitiveness by reducing labour costs. Indeed, the second MoU signed in early 2012, acknowledged some progress in bringing down unit labour costs, but noted a competitiveness gap of about 15–20 percent; accordingly, it stated that 'more emphasis (is needed) on securing reductions in unit labour costs and improvements in competitiveness, through a combination

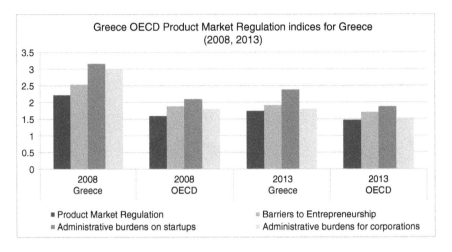

Figure 8.5 OECD Product Market Regulation indices for Greece (2008, 2013)

Source: OECD

Table 8.2 Greece, doing business (2008, 2016; rank: 1–189)

Activity	2008	2016
Starting a business	100	54
Dealing with construction permits	–	60
Getting electricity	–	47
Registering property	93	144
Getting credit	84	79
Protecting minor investors	–	47
Paying taxes	86	66
Trading across borders	65	27
Enforcing contracts	87	132
Resolving insolvency	–	54
Ease of doing business (overall score)	100	60

Source: World Bank

of upfront nominal wage cuts and structural labour market reforms'.[8] Labour costs, declined substantially, helped by the reforms, but also (and perhaps primarily) by the deep and prolonged recession of the economy (Figure 8.6).

However, this was not always translated into lower prices; in services' markets where wage costs are often the largest part of total production costs, prices followed the decline in wages; however, this was not the case in other sectors. Other factors, such as increased cost of capital, higher energy costs and increased taxation seem to have outweighed the drop in labour costs. Until 2012 the export prices of goods continued to increase despite the significant decline in unit labour costs

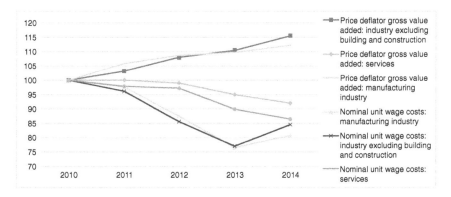

Figure 8.6 Wages and prices during the crisis

Source: Ameco, European Commission; authors' calculations

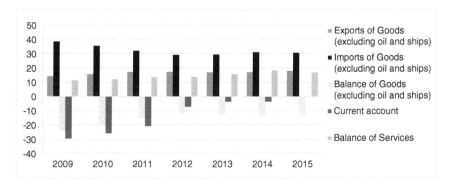

Figure 8.7 Greek external sector imbalances, 2009–15 (billion euros)

Source: Bank of Greece

(Zografakis and Kastelli 2017).[9] At the same time, the penetration of Greek exports to foreign markets did not increase with the exception of some low-technological intensity products mainly in non-EU markets (Zografakis and Kastelli 2017). In this context, it is not surprising that the elimination of the current account deficit was not so much due to an improved export performance, but rather to the fall of imports which followed the collapse of domestic demand (Figure 8.7).

The export performance of the Greek economy indicates that despite the improvement in the product market regulation indicators, the country's inward-looking, low value-added growth model hasn't yet changed substantially. Indeed, until 2013, 90 percent of the new businesses that were established were activated in low value-added, non-tradable sectors of the economy, such as restaurants, bars and retail shops (Endeavor Greece 2013).[10] This trend is also corroborated by data from the Ministry of Labour, Social Insurance and Social Solidarity, which shows that the sectors and professions in which employment increased during the crisis were related to services catering to the domestic market, typically in low specialization and value-added activities (Katsikas and Filinis 2015).

8.3 Adjustment policies and structural reforms: an uneasy relationship

As outlined in the previous section, the adjustment programme sought to address the twin imbalances in the public budget and the external sector through a heavy front-loaded fiscal consolidation programme and an internal devaluation policy respectively (the latter largely based on labour market reforms). This policy mix, combined with the impact of political and economic uncertainty, reduced incomes and led to a collapse of domestic demand, which drove the economy into a prolonged and deep depression and unprecedented levels of unemployment (Figure 8.8).

In this recessionary environment, the reforms were expected to unleash the potential of the real economy, which was previously constrained by over-regulation and rigidities. However, the theory cautions against many aspects of this strategy. In terms of timing, although the contractionary impact of fiscal adjustment materializes instantaneously, structural reforms are typically expected to produce their beneficial results in the medium-to-long term (Anderson et al. 2014).[11] Moreover, tight fiscal (Helbling et al. 2004) and constrained monetary policies (Eggertsson et al. 2013) are likely to undermine the effectiveness of structural reforms, while adverse economic conditions are likely to minimize any positive

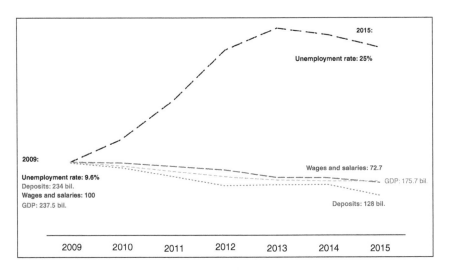

Figure 8.8 Key macroeconomic indicators of the Greek Economy (2009–15)

Sources: Unemployment rate, wages and salaries and GDP: ELSTAT; private deposits: Bank of Greece; authors' calculations

effects or even lead to negative short-term effects (Bordon et al. 2016; OECD 2016). Moreover, there is evidence to suggest that some labour market reforms (primarily EPL relaxation) may reduce or even reverse the effectiveness of product market reforms, if they are implemented before them (Bouis et al. 2012; Bouis et al. 2016; Fiori et al. 2012).

Therefore, given that the potential positive effects of structural reforms take some time to materialize and that they are affected by their mix and sequencing, while adjustment policies can have an immediate and negative effect, the hypothesis under examination, is that adjustment policies plunged the economy into a recession, which in combination with the counterproductive timing and sequencing of reforms, limited the latter's impact.

8.4 Testing the balance between adjustment policies and structural reforms

In this section, we examine the timing and the relative impact of fiscal measures and reforms in product markets on two key macroeconomic variables, namely employment and inflation. We control for other factors, such as labour market reforms and economic climate indicators, which may impact the dependent variables

8.4.1 The dependent variables

The dependent variables in our analysis are employment and inflation. We focus on these variables for a number of reasons. First, there are theoretical arguments that link these variables to reforms in the product markets. Increased competition reduces mark-ups and applies downward pressure on prices.[12] Moreover, reforms that lower entry barriers and remove impediments to competition are expected to lead to an increase in the number of businesses and in the scope/volume of their activity respectively, which would in turn increase employment (for a review of the evidence see Boeri et al. 2015).[13]

Another crucial aspect is timing. Prices and employment should be more rapidly affected by reforms in product markets compared to other variables (e.g. consumption which is affected only indirectly through the effects on prices or employment). This is important because the focus here is on short-term effects. It should be noted that there is a growing empirical literature on the short-term effects of structural reforms, which indicates that both prices and employment variables can indeed be affected in the short-term by structural reforms in product markets (e.g. Bouis et al. 2012; Bordon et al. 2016; Bouis et al. 2016; OECD 2016).

Also, improving competition both by facilitating new entrants in domestic markets and by removing obstacles to business activity (e.g. price, geographical and technical restrictions) was repeatedly mentioned as a key objective of the reforms, as it was expected to lead to increasing price flexibility and employment.[14] Finally, low prices are important both for improving international competitiveness and for boosting real incomes domestically.

8.4.2 Description of the product market reforms and fiscal adjustment measures

We examine the most important and wide-ranging reforms in product markets and the business environment that took place during the implementation of the first two bailout agreements (2010–14). These were the 'one-stop-shop' reform, whose aim was to reduce the regulatory burden and time needed for starting a new business and the reform which reduced the capital required for starting certain types of companies. Before the reform, the process of starting a new business was both lengthy and expensive. According to the Doing Business report of the World Bank, Greece's ranking in that particular category was a depressing 152 (out of 178 countries), as there were 15 different procedures required, which took on average 38 days to complete; the process cost approximately 23 percent of per capita income, while the minimum capital required amounted to 104 percent of per capita income (World Bank 2007).[15] More specifically, the minimum capital requirements for the two main types of companies in Greece, a limited liability company (EPE) and the typical Société Anonyme, were 4,500 and 60,000 euros respectively.

The 'one stop-shop' reform was intended to simplify the start-up process and was combined with the launch of a new General Electronic Commercial Registry (GEMI) for all companies, which acts both as an information repository, and the operator of the main online platform necessary for the delivery of many of the services associated with the 'one-stop-shop' reform. The 'one-stop shop' reform and GEMI became operational in April 2011. On the other hand, the minimum capital required for EPE and Société Anonymes was substantially reduced gradually from the 1st to the 3rd quarter of 2013, to zero and 24,000 euros respectively.[16] The reforms improved the situation substantially; by 2016 Greece's ranking in the 'starting a business category' had improved to 54. The number of procedures required was reduced to five, the number of days needed to complete them dropped to 13, while the cost of the entire process amounted to only 2.2 percent of per capita income (World Bank 2016). As we saw, the minimum capital was greatly reduced and in some cases, it even fell to zero.

The other major reform that is examined here is the first 'OECD toolkit'. The 'OECD toolkits' are packages of measures that aim to reduce the regulatory burden in product and services markets. They address the findings of comprehensive studies of several key sectors. In the Greek programmes, there have been three waves of such studies, the first taking place from January to November 2013, the second from September to December 2014 and the third from February to November 2016. In total, the toolkits identified 1,276 regulations which inhibited competition and proposed 773 measures relating to 14 major sectors of the Greek economy (SEV 2016). Here, we focus on the first toolkit, which comprised 332 proposals and was voted (for the most part) in March 2014. According to a study by the industrial employers' association, 87 percent of the first toolkit's proposals have been implemented, with 91 percent of these taking place already by the end of 2014 (SEV 2016).

Regarding the fiscal adjustment measures, we are particularly interested in the pro-cyclical effect of the policies adopted at the same time. As noted in Figure 8.4, the size of the adjustment was unprecedented; the General Government primary deficit (programme definition) decreased by more than 11 percentage points of GDP in the period of interest. The measures are estimated around 30 p.p. of GDP equally split between the revenue and expenditure side.[17]

8.4.3 Methodology

We consider a separate linear regression model for the log-differences of each dependent variable, (denoted by Y_t), in our case, price inflation and employment.

$$Y_t = c + \sum_{k=1}^{K} a_k S_{k,t} + \sum_{i=1}^{I} \sum_{l_i=0}^{3} \theta_{i,l_i} Z_{i,t-l_i}, \quad e_t \sim N\left(0, \sigma^2\right)$$

where $S_{k,t}$ refer to K factors affecting Y_t contemporaneously, and $Z_{i,t-l_i}$ to I factors affecting Y_t, each with lags (l_i) up to three quarters. For a given set of variables and lags ($S_{k,t}$ and $Z_{i,t-l_i}$), the parameters to be estimated are $\left\{c, a_k, \theta_{i,l_i}, \sigma^2\right\}$. An analogous specification in a Bayesian context, has been employed by Petralias and Prodromidis (2015) and Petralias and Katsikas (2017). We perform forward stepwise model selection to choose the variables to be included in the model out of a list of potential candidates $S_{k,t}$ and $Z_{i,t-l_i}$ and their lags.

Stepwise selection is an automatic procedure used in order to choose the independent variables which will enter the model (see for example, Draper and Smith 1981). Forward stepwise starts with only the constant in the model and then variables are added and subtracted at sequential steps based on a statistical criterion (the p-value in our case). Taking into account the large number of potential candidate factors, under this approach, only the statistically significant variables with their associated distinct lags remain in the final model, increasing the robustness of the results and reducing multicollinearity. Statistically significance for model selection was set at 5 percent.

The pool of potential regressors aims to capture the typical determinants for employment and inflation suggested by theory, as well as variables related to the adjustment programme that Greece implemented in the period under examination. The independent variables are classified into five categories: (a) business environment and product market reforms, (b) labour market reforms, (c) fiscal adjustment measures, (d) macroeconomic environment and (e) seasonality and political uncertainty dummies, as well as a measure of economic sentiment (see Appendix). The $Z_{i,t-l_i}$ vector includes the variables that measure the business environment and product market reforms. The $S_{k,t}$ vector includes the control variables related to the fiscal adjustment, labour market reforms as well as variables controlling for the macroeconomic environment including uncertainty.

This is because in our specification, lags apply only to the reforms, i.e. the Dummies, associated with the OECD toolkit and the 'one-stop-shop', which we are mainly interested in. The rest of the variables are taken to affect the dependent variables contemporaneously, since there is no strong theoretical reason to expect lagged effects of other variables, but also to facilitate the estimation process and avoid increasing the model dimension; note that in such a case, other more complex methods (i.e. Bayesian estimation) would be required, which is beyond the scope of this paper. Nonetheless, alternative specifications were tested, by including lags in other variables, which did not alter the results with respect to the effect of the reforms; moreover, lags of variables associated to labour market reforms did not turn out to be statistically significant.

8.4.4 The data

The data are on quarterly basis and cover the period from the first quarter of 2005 to the last quarter of the 2015. Thus, approximately half of our sample observations come before the crisis and half of them during the crisis. In what follows we give a brief description of the variables used. Detailed information about the variables used is given in the Appendix. The dependent variables are the (log-differences of the) consumer price index (CPI) and employment (number of employees). Regarding the determinants of inflation and employment, the choice of explanatory variables is partially dictated by the availability of data. Data limitations are significant when it comes to quarterly frequency, especially when one is interested in qualitative indicators of institutional arrangements. Another criterion used is the degree to which a candidate regressor allows us to identify the impact of certain policy changes.

The first dependent variable is price inflation. In order to choose the specific channels through which price developments occurred in Greece during the period of interest, we start from the international empirical literature,[18] or studies focusing on Greece.[19] A key determining factor is the labour cost, which is measured by three variables: wages costs, which includes wages and salaries, the labour costs other than wages and salaries, and the minimum wage.[20] Next, in order to control the extent to which indirect tax hikes have been passed-through to consumers, we test as potential regressors the VAT rates and the special fuel taxes on heating oil and unleaded gasoline. The impact of price developments abroad is captured in our model by the import price deflator, the oil prices, the exchange rate of Euro to the US dollar and the international food commodity prices.[21] The lagged inflation rate controls for possible persistent effects.

The determinants of employment are chosen among the factors suggested by the literature.[22] We use a set of variables capturing the role of policies and labour market institutions i.e. the replacement rate, the employment protection legislation and the wage costs (measured as before). Also, we use lagged employment to allow for possible hysteresis effects. We also control for the credit available to the private sector.

In order to proxy the product market reforms, we use two dummy variables, one for the quarter that the OECD toolkit was legislated, and one for the General Electronic Commercial Registry (GEMI) and 'one-stop-shop' for new business start-ups. Moreover, we use the amounts required to establish an anonymous company or a limited company.

In order to control for the fiscal stance, we use the primary expenditure and total revenue of the General Government. Finally, in both regressions we control for the impact of the level of economic activity using the GDP growth rate and the capacity utilization index – proxy for the output gap.

In both regressions, seasonal dummies are included, as well as a dummy for elections (taking value 1 for the quarters when elections took place) and a crisis dummy (taking value 1 from April 2010 onwards, when Greece requested a bailout). It is noted that the inclusion of seasonal dummies is imposed on the stepwise regression (i.e. we do not allow their removal during the model selection procedure) given the well-documented seasonality exhibited in prices (e.g. Riley 1961) and employment (e.g. Marshall 1999). Finally, we include an Economic Sentiment indicator in order to capture the assessment/expectations of economic agents. All variables (dependent and independent) except dummies were converted to indices with year base 2010 = 100, and log-differences were taken. This simplifies the explanation of results (using indices with same base year), decreases multicollinearity (as opposed to taking levels), whereas residuals were normal in all regressions with no significant autocorrelation or heteroscedasticity.

8.4.5 Empirical results

In this section, we present the empirical results of the Stepwise regression estimations. The results for employment are reported in Table 8.3. The impact of economic

Table 8.3 Stepwise regression for employment

Variable		
C	−0.009	(−4.07)***
DUMMY_Q1	0.018	(5.74)***
DUMMY_Q2	0.011	(2.11)**
DUMMY_Q3	−0.002	(−0.46)
EMPLOYMENT(-1)	0.553	(6.09)***
GDP_VOLUME	0.144	(3.48)***
DUMMY_OECD_TOOLKIT(-3)	0.021	(3.44)***
DUMMY_OECD_TOOLKIT	0.014	(2.36)**
PRIVATE_LOANS	0.076	(1.92)*
R^2 adjusted 0.85		

Notes:
1 The values in the parenthesis are *t*-statistics.
2 The set of candidate predictors are presented in the Appendix.
3 Selection method: Stepwise forwards, Stopping criterion: *p*-value forwards/backwards = 0.05/0.05
4 *Statistically significant at the 10 percent level. ** Statistically significant at the 5 percent level. *** Statistically significant at the 1 percent level.
5 **EMPLOYMENT** corresponds to the number of employed persons, **DUMMY_Q1-Q3** to seasonal dummies for first, second and third quarter, **GDP_VOLUME** to Gross domestic product at market prices, **DUMMY_OECD_TOOLKIT** to dummy for the legislation of the OECD toolkit (taking value 1 in 2014 Q3) and **PRIVATE_LOANS** to total amount of private loans provided by private banks. All variables (except dummies) were converted to indices with year base 2010 = 100, and log-differences were taken.

growth is significant with 1 percent increase of slowdown leading to 1.4 percent decrease of employment. The significance of the lagged value suggests hysteresis effects. The dummy controlling for the OECD's toolkit seems to impact employment contemporaneously, but also with three quarters lag suggesting that product market reforms have a positive impact on employment. However, the size of the coefficients suggests that the (negative) effect of the recession on the employment has been much bigger compared to that (positive) effect of the product market reforms. Finally, credit to the private sector also impacts employment positively. It is worth noting that no labour market reform or labour cost variables appear to affect employment growth. This finding is unusual and might indicate that some other factor which is not being controlled for (e.g. increased corporate income tax for the crisis period, or inability to roll over the heightened tax burden to the consumers) may be offsetting the impact of the reduced labour cost. The variables describing institutions of the labour market typically exhibit a very low variability in the data, and this may explain the lack of statistical significance. Moreover, the fiscal variables, total revenues and primary expenditure are not statistically significant, possibly because their impact on employment is already captured by the GDP growth rate.

Concerning the timing of reforms, we find that the OECD toolkit's measures have a significant and positive effect with a lag of three quarters. Moreover, given that the OEDC toolkit was introduced in 2014 and that employment is predominantly affected by its lagged performance and the GDP growth rate, the evidence is consistent with a scenario where the impact of product market reforms is too little and comes too late, as the recession has already taken its toll on the economy. However, given the positive relation between product market reforms and employment, the implemented reforms may have alleviated to some degree the negative consequences of the recession, while it is reasonable to expect that, *ceteris paribus*, they will facilitate a faster a recovery of the economy.

The results for consumer prices are reported in Table 8.4. The lagged value of the dependent variable has a significant impact suggesting high inflation persistence. Product market reforms adopted during the crisis are negatively related to prices with one period lag. Also, lower levels of the minimum capital needed for the establishment of an anonymous company correlate with lower consumer prices. The special fuel tax on unleaded oil and international oil prices have a positive relation to the CPI as expected. Finally, prices are positively linked with elections on the quarter the latter take place. Although the effect is relatively small and of borderline significance, it could be related to expectations for increased spending following the election of a new government or to loosening of the administrative control mechanisms during the election period. As in the case of employment, the fiscal stance is not selected by the stepwise procedure. The same holds for the GDP growth rate. We interpret these two results as an indication that lagged inflation captures the impact of the real economy developments. Also, a rather surprising finding is the fact that the VAT rate, which showed a significant increase during this period, is not statistically significant and is dropped from the regression. A possible interpretation is that the impact of VAT rates on prices is diluted in the case of quarterly data. If prices change immediately when the new rates are legislated, then the bulk of the impact on CPI occurs immediately. Given that during

Table 8.4 Stepwise regression for CPI

Variable		
C	0.019	(12.12)***
DUMMY_Q1	−0.031	(−10.55)***
DUMMY_Q2	−0.000	(−0.16)
DUMMY_Q3	−0.039	(−11.80)***
CPI(-1)	0.424	(4.30)***
DUMMY_OECD_TOOLKIT(-1)	−0.018	(−3.93)***
MINIMUM_CAPITAL	0.018	(3.52)***
SPECIAL_FUEL_TAX	0.045	(3.50)***
EUROPE_BREND_SPOT	0.011	(2.59)**
DUMMY_ELECTIONS	0.003	(1.99)*
R^2 adjusted 0.91		

Notes:
1 The values in the parenthesis are *t*-statistics.
2 The set of candidate predictors are presented in the Appendix.
3 Selection method: Stepwise forwards, Stopping criterion: *p*-value forwards/backwards = 0.05/0.05
4 *Statistically significant at the 10 percent level. ** Statistically significant at the 5 percent level.
   *** Statistically significant at the 1 percent level.
5 *CPI* corresponds to domestic consumer price index, *DUMMY_Q1-Q3* to seasonal dummies for first,
   second and third quarter, *DUMMY_OECD_TOOLKIT* to dummy for the legislation of the OECD
   toolkit Crisis (taking value 1 in 2014 Q3) *MINIMUM_CAPITAL_ANONYMOUS* to the minimum
   capital required for an anonymous company (in euros), *SPECIAL_FUEL_TAX_UNLEADED* the
   value of the special fuel tax for gasoline (euros per ton), *EUROPE_BREND_*SPOT to the oil
   price ($ per barrel) and *DUMMY_ELECTIONS* to a dummy taking value 1 for the quarters when
   elections took place. All variables (except dummies) were converted to indices with year base 2010 =
   100, and log-differences were taken.

the crisis period prices were falling, the quarter average may not reflect the policy change as a price increase in one month is cancelled out by negative inflation rates during the following two months. This interpretation seems reasonable in light of other papers finding significant impact of VAT on prices when using monthly data (see Petralias and Prodromidis 2015).

In order to ensure the completeness of the analysis, we have tested a number of alternative specifications, which include GDP, investment and private consumption as dependent variables. Reforms did not seem to have a statistically significant direct impact on any of these variables during the period examined. This is to a great extent an expected outcome. First, it is reasonable to assume that reforms impact private consumption and GDP only indirectly through prices and employment. Second, many factors were at play during the same time, so that the direct effects of product market reforms on consumption, GDP and investment may be difficult to isolate and estimate precisely.

8.5 Conclusions

Before the crisis, the Greek economy was characterized by burdensome and costly regulation, which reduced competition, kept prices high and stifled innovation, extroversion and ultimately growth. The reforms in the regulatory framework of product markets, pursued in the context of the bailout programmes, were for the most part much needed and long overdue. However, their implementation does not seem to have changed the situation on the ground; the competitiveness and extroversion of the Greek economy remain low, while growth has not picked up.

To explain this outcome, the aim of this chapter has been to test the following hypothesis: the policy mix pursued in the context of the Greek bailout programmes was counterproductive. A harsh fiscal consolidation programme, especially when accompanied by internal devaluation policies, is likely to lead to a recession in the short run, while structural reforms typically produce results in the medium to long term. To test the hypothesis, we used a stepwise regression model to examine the impact of product market reforms, fiscal consolidation measures and internal devaluation policies on employment and prices.

Summarizing the main results of our analysis, we conclude that the product markets reforms adopted during the crisis have played a positive role in supporting employment and reducing prices, although the effect has been quite small compared to the impact of the adverse economic environment. Regarding employment, the recession had a significant effect in the opposite direction of product market reforms. Moreover, the significant reduction of the provision of credit to the private economy, itself the result of the troubles of the banking sector, has also adversely affected employment. On the other hand, prices were affected adversely primarily by the cost of energy (including indirect taxation on fuel), while the big slowdown in economic activity imparted a downward bias to inflation. In a nutshell, the recession exerted downward pressure to prices similarly to product market reforms, but the indirect tax hikes pushed them to the opposite direction preventing thus a quicker fall of prices which would have alleviated the loss of real disposable income.

One could argue that given the extraordinary fiscal imbalances, some degree of austerity policies was inevitable and that product markets reform could help alleviate part of the negative effects. However, this would have required a different timing of reforms. As we saw, the reform that had the largest positive impact on employment is the OECD toolkit, but this was only implemented in 2014, 4 years after the country entered a bailout programme and 6 years after the economy had entered a recession. In addition, this reform impacts the economy with a lag, which means most of its effects were effectively felt from early 2015 onwards. Given the preceding deterioration of domestic demand, on which so much of the economy depends, the increase in energy costs and the loss of access to credit, reforms reducing red tape and competition impediments at this late stage, can only be evaluated as too little, too late.[23]

The first policy lesson that we can draw is that macroeconomic conditions are indeed important for the effectiveness of reforms, as suggested by the literature. The adverse macroeconomic conditions present at the time when the reforms were finally introduced undermined their effectiveness. On the one hand, fiscal consolidation swamped the positive employment effects of the reforms, while the credit crunch severely imposed liquidity constraints of both households and companies, in turn affecting adversely demand for both consumption and investment.

The second lesson is that the timing of structural reforms is very important. Reforms should be an early priority. Because they work with a lag, they should be introduced first, in order to help alleviate the contractionary effects of fiscal consolidation.[24] Regarding the issue of sequencing with other reforms, our results do not hold much insight, as labour market reforms did not appear to have a distinct, direct effect on our dependent variables.

On a political economy note, stressing growth-enhancing reforms early on in an adjustment programme would also likely increase the political feasibility of reforms, as they would be implemented in a more accommodating economic environment. Indeed, some of the product market reforms were amongst the most difficult to implement politically, as they run against vested interests, in contrast to the early labour market reforms, where the burden of the adjustment process fell on the private sector employees, whose representation is fragmented and weak. In other words, instead of starting from the most politically convenient reforms, it may better to start from the reforms most likely to yield the best economic results (probably a mix of labour market and product market reforms); such a process could reduce uncertainty and increase acceptance of later reforms (Rodrik 1989, 2016).

Notes

1 The author contributed to the chapter before his joining the Bank of Greece. The views in this chapter are those of the author and do not necessarily reflect those of the Bank of Greece.
2 The author contributed to the chapter before her joining the Bank of Greece. The views in this chapter are those of the author and do not necessarily reflect those of the Bank of Greece.
3 Obviously, the unprecedented depression of the Greek economy was also responsible for a large (perhaps the largest) part of the wages' adjustment.
4 For arguments on the suboptimal timing and sequencing of reforms in the Greek case, see Manasse (2015) and Terzi (2015).
5 *Greece – Memorandum of Economic and Financial Policies*, May 3, 2010, p. 2.
6 Ibid., p. 2.
7 A practice which demonstrates the primacy of fiscal adjustment objectives is the fact that failure to meet reforms' targets typically meant that they were moved to the next assessment (often as prior actions) – while failure to meet fiscal targets meant that the assessment could not be completed and funding was withheld.
8 *Memorandum of Understanding between the European Commission Acting on Behalf of the Euro-Area Member States, and the Hellenic Republic*, 2012, par.2, p. 2.
9 Beyond the factors mentioned above, this is also due to the high import component of Greek exports.
10 Beyond the rigidities and obstacles of the business environment, this development is also due to a number of other factors including the credit crunch in the Greek banking system, which has arguably influenced investment decisions towards sectors and activities with low capital requirements (see for example Katsikas and Filinis 2015, p. 22).
11 While the long-term impacts of structural reforms are widely held to be positive (Nicoletti and Scarpetta 2003; Bouis and Duval 2011; Fiori et al. 2012), their impact in the short-term is more ambiguous.
12 These effects may be due to increased efficiency effects (see for example Nickell 1996), or simply because deregulation removes costly obstacles and restrictions.

13 The overall employment effect depends to some degree on the structure of the market. In markets characterized by big players and low levels of competition before the reform, such as network and utility industries, increased competition from new companies (following privatization or abolition of barriers to entry) may lead incumbents to shed personnel to increase cost competitiveness with potentially negative unemployment effects; in markets where deregulation is expected to facilitate the entry of more efficient players (e.g. retail trade), the employment effects are not expected to be negative (OECD 2016). In Greece, given that the market reforms examined affect a very wide range of businesses including competitive sectors such as retail trade and professional services (but not privatizations), we would expect employment gains in the short run, *ceteris paribus*.

14 See for example, *Memorandum of Understanding Between the European Commission Acting on Behalf of the Euro-Area Member States, and the Hellenic Republic*, 2012, paragraphs 28 and 30.

15 Indicatively, for the other European countries that also went through a crisis, the scores for number of procedures, days required, cost and minimum capital were as follows: Ireland: 4, 13, 0.3, 0.0; Italy: 9, 13, 18.7, 9.8; Spain: 10, 47, 15.1, 13.7; Portugal: 7, 7, 3.4, 34.7 (World Bank 2007).

16 At the same time, a new type of company, a private capital company (IKE) was formed, with a minimum capital requirement of 1 euro and a number of innovative features that reduced red tape and increased flexibility for its owners.

17 Source: Ministry of Finance.

18 See, among others, Andersson et al. (2009), Dwyer and Leong (2001).

19 See, among others, Sideris and Zonzilos (2005) and Albani et al. (2007).

20 The three variables are selected on the grounds that they allow to disentangle the impact of different labour market reforms, i.e. the deregulation of the labour market in general, the size of the social security contributions and net taxes of the employers, and the decrease of the minimum wage.

21 The food prices, which might seem as a more specific regressor compared to the rest of the variables, is included as it has been shown to be particularly significant for inflation developments in Greece (Albani et al. 2007).

22 Actually, the regressors are typical determinants of unemployment (see, among others, Bassanini and Duval 2006; Bertola 2016). Additional determinants of employment's development are the driving factors of labour participation. These typically vary across population groups. Some examples are child benefits of public expenditure on childcare for prime-age females, or the loss (gain) of net pension wealth from continuing to work for old workers. However, such data are not available on quarterly frequency and such a group specific approach is beyond the scope of this paper.

23 According to Anderson et al. (2014), structural reforms in the euro periphery would anyway take several years before structural reforms could reasonably be expected to offset the near-term negative impact on activity arising from the required fiscal consolidation.

24 It has to be said however, that given the European and international political and economic circumstances when the crisis broke out, the feasibility of the latter option for Greece at the time is highly debatable.

Bibliography

Albani, M., Zonzilos, N., and Bragoudakis, Z. (2007) *An Operational Framework for the Short-term Forecasting of Inflation*. Bank of Greece. Economic Bulletin No. 29.

Anastasatou, M. (2017) Is It Possible to Attain High Primary Fiscal Surpluses for Many Years? In: Katsikas, D., Filinis, K. and Anastasatou, M. (eds.) *Understanding the Greek Crisis: Answers to Key Questions About the State, the Economy and Europe*, Athens, Papazisis Publications (in Greek).

Anderson, D., Hunt, B., and Snudden, S. (2014) Fiscal Consolidation in the Euro Area: How Much Pain Can Structural Reforms Ease? *Journal of Policy Modelling*, 36, 785–799.

Andersson, M., Masuch, K., and Schiffbauer, M. (2009) *Determinants of Inflation and Price Level Differentials Across the Euro Area Countries*. ECB. Working Paper No. 1129.

Bank of Greece (2012) *Governor's Annual Report*. Athens, Bank of Greece.

Bassanini, A., and Duval, R. (2006) *Employment Patterns in OECD Countries: Reassessing the Role of Policies and Institutions*. OECD Social, Employment and Migration. Working Paper No. 35.

Bertola, G. (2016) *European Unemployment Revisited: Shocks, Institutions, Integration*. CESifo. Working Paper No. 6170.

Blanchard, O., and Giavazzi, F. (2002) Current Account Deficits in the Euro Area: The End of the Feldstein-Horioka Puzzle? *Brookings Papers on Economic Activity*, 2, 147–209.

Boeri, T., Cahuc, P., and Zylberberg, A. (2015) *The Costs of Flexibility-Enhancing Structural Reforms: A Literature Review*. OECD Economics Department. Working Paper No. 1264.

Bordon, A. R., Ebeke, C., and Shirono, K. (2016) *When Do Structural Reforms Work? On the Role of the Business Cycle and Macroeconomic Policies*. IMF. Working Paper No. 16/62.

Bouis, R., Causa, O., Demmou, L., Duval, R., and Zdzienicka, A. (2012) *The Short-Term Effects of Structural Reforms: An Empirical Analysis*. OECD Economics Department. Working Paper No. 949.

Bouis, R., and Duval, R. (2011) *Raising Potential Growth After the Crisis: A Quantitative Assessment of the Potential Gains From Various Structural Reforms in the OECD Area and Beyond*. OECD Economics Department. Working Paper No. 835.

Bouis, R., Duval, R., and Eugster, J. (2016) *Product Market Deregulation and Growth: New Country-Industry-Level Evidence*. IMF. Working Paper No. 16/114.

Böwer, U., Michou, V., and Ungerer, C. (2014) *The Puzzle of the Missing Greek Exports*. European Commission. Economic Paper No. 518.

Daude, C. (2016) *Structural Reforms to Boost Inclusive Growth in Greece*. OECD Economics Department. Working Paper No. 1298.

Draper, N., and Smith, H. (1981) *Applied Regression Analysis*, 2nd Edition, New York, John Wiley and Sons, Inc.

Dwyer, J., and Leong, K. (2001) Changes in the Determinants of Inflation in Australia. In: Bank for International Settlements. *Empirical Studies of Structural Changes and Inflation*, 3, 1–28. Basel, Bank of International Settlements.

Eggertsson, G., Ferrero, A., and Raffo, A. (2013) Can Structural Reforms Help Europe? *Journal of Monetary Economics*, 61, 2–22.

Endeavor Greece (2013) *Entrepreneurship and Investment Opportunities in Greece Today*, Athens, Endeavor Greece.

Filinis, K., and Georgakopoulos, A. (2017) The Reform of the Greek Labour Market. In: Katsikas, D., Anastasatou, M., Nitsi, E., Petralias, A. and Filinis, K. (eds.) *Structural Reforms in Greece During the Crisis (2010–2014)*, Athens, Bank of Greece (forthcoming in Greek).

Fiori, G., Nicoletti, G., Scarpetta, S., and Schiantarelli, F. (2012) Employment Effects of Product and Labour Market Reforms: Are There Synergies? *The Economic Journal*, 122(558), F79–F104.

Helbling, T., Hakura, D., and Debrun, X. (2004) Fostering Structural Reforms in Industrial Countries. In: IMF (ed.) *World Economic Outlook*, Washington, DC, International Monetary Fund, pp. 103–146.

Katsikas, D., Anastasatou, M., Nitsi, E., Petralias, A., and Filinis, K. (2017) *Structural Reforms in Greece During the Crisis (2010–2014)*, Athens, Bank of Greece (forthcoming in Greek).

Katsikas, D., and Filinis, K. (2015) *Crisis and Sustainable Growth: On the Inability to Reform the Production Model of the Greek Economy*. Centre of Planning and Economic Research (KEPE). Greek Economy No. 21 (in Greek).

Katsikas, D., Filinis, K., and Anastasatou, M. (eds.) (2017) *Understanding the Greek Crisis: Answers to Key Questions About the State, the Economy and Europe*, Athens, Papazisis Publications (in Greek).

Katsoulacos, Y., Genakos, C., and Houpis, G. (2015) Product Market Regulation and Competitiveness: Towards a National Competition and Competitiveness Policy in Greece. In: Meghir, C., Pissarides, C., Vayanos, D. and Vettas, N. (eds.) *Reforming the Greek Economy*, Cambridge, MA, MIT Press (forthcoming).

Manasse, P. (2015) *What Went Wrong in Greece and How to Fix It*. VoxEU. [Online]. Available from: http://voxeu.org/article/what-went-wrong-greece-and-how-fix-it.

Marshall, K. (1999) Seasonality in employment. *Perspectives on Labour and Income*, 11(1), 16–22.

Masourakis, M., and Gortsos, C. V. (eds.) (2014) *Competitiveness and Growth: Policy Proposals*, Athens, Hellenic Bank Association (in Greek).

Mitsopoulos, M. (2014) Manufacturing, Competition and Business Environment. In: Masourakis, M. and Gortsos, C. V. (eds.) *Competitiveness and Growth: Policy Proposals*, Athens, Hellenic Bank Association (in Greek).

Nickell, S. (1996) Competition and Corporate Performance. *Journal of Political Economy*, 104, 724–746.

OECD (2016) Short-term Labour Market Effects of Structural Reforms: Pain Before the Gain? In: *OECD Employment Outlook 2016*, Paris, OECD Publishing

Papazoglou, C. (2014) Greek Export Performance: Competitiveness and FDI. In: Masourakis, M. and Gortsos, C. V. (eds.) *Competitiveness and Growth: Policy Proposals*, Athens, Hellenic Bank Association (in Greek).

Petralias, A. (2017) Is It True that Reforms Are Pursued Only for Fiscal Reasons or to Serve Particular Interests? The Case of the Product Markets. In: Katsikas, D., Filinis, K. and Anastasatou, M. (eds.) *Understanding the Greek Crisis: Answers to Key Questions About the State, the Economy and Europe*, Athens, Papazisis Publications (in Greek).

Petralias, A., and Katsikas, D. (2017) Reforms in the Business Environment and the Product Markets. In: Katsikas, D., Anastasatou, M., Nitsi, E., Petralias, A. and Filinis, K. (eds.) *Structural Reforms in Greece During the Crisis (2010–2014)*, Athens, Bank of Greece (in Greek).

Petralias, A., and Prodromidis, P. (2015) Price Discovery Under Crisis: Uncovering the Determinant Factors of Prices Using Efficient Bayesian Model Selection Methods. *Empirical Economics*, 49(3), 859–879.

Riley, H. E. (1961) Some aspects of seasonality in the consumer price index. *Journal of the American Statistical Association*, 56(293), 27–35.

Rodrik, D. (1989) Credibility of Trade Reform: A Policy Maker's Guide. *The World Economy*, 12(1), 1–16.

Rodrik, D. (2016) The Elusive Promise of Structural Reform. *Milken Institute Review*, 18(2), 26–35.

SEV (2016) *The implementation of the OECD toolkit for the assessment of competition in Greece . . . in numbers. Progress of implementation and new recommendations. Key facts & figures*. Athens, Business Environment Observatory, SEV-Hellenic Federation of Enterprises (in Greek).

Sideris, D., and Zonzilos, N. (2005) *The Greek Model of the European System of Central Banks Multi-Country Model*. Bank of Greece. Working Paper No. 20.

Terzi, A. (2015) *Reform Momentum and Its Impact on Greek Growth*. Bruegel. Policy Contribution 2015/12.

Terzi, A., and Wolff, G. (2014) *A Needle in a Haystack: Key Terms in Official Troika Documents*. Bruegel Blog. [Online]. Available from: http://bruegel.org/2014/03/a-needle-in-a-haystack-key-terms-in-official-troika-documents/.

Vettas, N., and Kouranti, F. (2014) Competition, Competitiveness and Extroversion. In: Masourakis, M. and Gortsos, C. V. (eds.) *Competitiveness and Growth: Policy Proposals*, Athens, Hellenic Bank Association (in Greek).

World Bank (2007) *Doing Business 2008*. Washington, DC, The International Bank for Reconstruction and Development/The World Bank.

World Bank (2016) *Doing Business 2016: Measuring Regulatory Quality and Efficiency*. Washington, DC, World Bank.

Zografakis, S., and Kastelli, I. (2017) Is It True that Reducing Labour Costs Is Sufficient to Improve the Competitiveness of the Greek Economy? In: Katsikas, D., Filinis, K. and Anastasatou, M. (eds.) *Understanding the Greek Crisis: Answers to Key Questions About the State, the Economy and Europe*, Athens, Papazisis Publications (in Greek).

Appendix

Dependent variables

- Employment: Number of employed persons, in thousands (Source: ELSTAT).
- Consumer prices: Domestic consumer price index (Source: ELSTAT).

Independent variables

Product market reforms

- Dummy for the legislation of the OECD toolkit Crisis (taking value 1 in 2014 Q3).
- Dummy for the establishment of the General Electronic Commercial Registry (GEMI) and 'one-stop-shop' for new business start-ups (taking value 1 in 2011Q2).
- Minimum capital required for a limited company, in euros.
- Minimum capital required for an anonymous company, in euros.

Labour market reforms

- Labour costs index: includes wages and salaries, business economy (Source: Eurostat).
- Wages cost index: includes labour costs other than wages and salaries, business economy (Source: Eurostat).
- Minimum wage.
- Replacement rate: it is estimated as the ratio of the unemployment benefit over the mean ordinary income of a full-time employee. For further details, see Filinis and Georgakopoulos (2017).
- Employment protection legislation: based on the annual data of OECD – Employment Protection Legislation Version 2. The quarterly data are estimated according to the date that any amendment to the status quo was legislated. For years 2014–15 for which no data are available the index is assumed to remain constant at the level of 2013. For further details, see Filinis and Georgakopoulos (2017).

Fiscal measures

- Primary expenditure, General Government, million euros (Source: ELSTAT).
- Total revenue, General Government, million euros (Source: ELSTAT).
- VAT: the series was constructed as a weighted average of the VAT rates corresponding to each subcategory (4-digit) of the CPI at each month. Subgroup weights are those used by ELSTAT to construct the CPI (source: legislation and ELSTAT).
- Special fuel tax for gasoline.
- Special fuel tax for heating oil.

Macroeconomic variables

- GDP growth rate: gross domestic product at market prices, volume (Source: Eurostat).
- Capacity Utilization: capacity utilization in industry (Source: Eurostat).

- Import prices: price index of imports of goods and services (implicit deflator), percentage change compared to same period in previous year, euro, unadjusted (Source: Eurostat).
- Oil prices: Europe Brend oil spot prices ($ per barrel) (Source: US Energy Information Administration).
- International prices of food commodities: food price index (Source: FAO).
- Total amount of private loans provided by private banks (source: Bank of Greece).
- Loans to the private sector (source: Bank of Greece).

Political and Economic uncertainty
- Dummy Crisis (taking value 1 from April 2010 onwards, when Greece officially requested a bailout).
- Dummy Elections (taking value 1 for the quarters when elections took place).
- Economic sentiment indicator (Source: IOBE).

Notes: All variables except dummies are converted to indices with base period the average of 2010 = 100. For these variables log-differences are taken.

Part III

The political economy of structural reforms in southern Europe

9 The political economy of Cyprus's financial sector reform

Sofronis Clerides

9.1 Introduction

The collapse of the Cypriot banking system captivated the world in March 2013. The economic circumstances leading to this event have been analyzed extensively and are by now well understood.[1] In short, large capital inflows in the period 2004–08 created an environment with abundant liquidity that led to excessive lending and risk taking. Cypriot banks financed consumer loans and a construction boom in Cyprus, and real estate prices skyrocketed. The two major banks also expanded rapidly abroad, especially in Greece, where they created extensive branch networks and invested in government bonds. The onset of the global crisis burst the bubble, led to large public deficits and laid bare the problems in the banks' loan books.

This narrative is certainly not unique to Cyprus. Similar boom-and-bust episodes have occurred many times in history, as documented by Reinhart and Rogoff (2009). What makes Cyprus stand out is the culmination of the crisis in a bail-in of bank depositors in March 2013. The haircut of deposits in the two largest Cypriot banks was unprecedented in both conception and scale. The total amount of the bail-in was 9.4 billion euros (52.0 percent of 2013 Cyprus GDP), while the total recapitalization bill came to 12.9 billion euros (71.3 percent of GDP).[2] By comparison, the largest fiscal costs (direct fiscal outlays due to financial sector rescue packages) reported in Laeven and Valencia's (2013) database of systemic banking crises during 1970–2011 are 55.1 percent and 56.8 percent for Argentina (1980) and Indonesia (1997) respectively. Cyprus's crisis had a significantly larger total cost, but only 19.2 percent came from state coffers; the rest was shouldered by depositors and bondholders.

The objective of this paper is to analyze the political economy factors that led to this catastrophic outcome. A political economy approach recognizes that state actors do not necessarily take decisions with the objective of maximizing a universally agreed social welfare function. Politicians may put different weight on the welfare of different groups based on their personal interest or preferences. Accordingly, Katsikas (this volume) defines political economy considerations as those regarding 'the distribution of costs and benefits of structural reforms'. Times of crisis provide fertile ground for testing political economy theories because multiple reforms with potentially significant distributional impacts are implemented within relatively short periods.

The paper shows that political economy considerations operated at multiple levels in the Cyprus crisis. Domestic politics played an important role in the build-up to the crisis by delaying corrective action, allowing bank troubles to go past the point of no return, and putting the haircut option on the table. At that point, political economy constraints at the European level came into play and ensured that the bail-in option would eventually win out. Political economy factors at various levels were important in shaping the precise nature of the remedy and had huge consequences in how the economic burden of the adjustment was distributed. It will also be argued that additional considerations such as ideology, personal relations, egos and inadequate understanding of complex issues played an important role.

Section 2 of the paper gives an overview of the build-up of Cyprus' economic boom to its 2008 peak and the descent into crisis that culminated in 2013. Section 3 gives an account of the events of March 2013 and discusses their implications. Section 4 discusses the main political economy factors that shaped the crisis and its outcome, and section 5 concludes.

9.2   The makings of a boom-and-bust

9.2.1   The run-up to 2008

Up until 2008, Cyprus was a great success story. In 1974, it had lost 37 percent of its territory and more than half its productive capacity (primarily agriculture and tourism at the time) that had come under Turkey's control. The small island economy rebounded quickly, initially by riding its tourism industry and then by successfully positioning itself as a financial and business centre. The main attraction was a low corporate tax rate for international businesses, which was complemented by an attractive location and high quality services provided by Cyprus's legions of UK-educated accountants and lawyers. The sector took off in the 1990s and became an important engine of growth, alongside tourism. Entry into the EU in 2004 gave a significant boost to the attractiveness of Cyprus as an international business centre. The provision of accounting, legal and financial services boomed and there was growth of important niche activities such as shipping.

The growth of the international business sector was accompanied by a large expansion of the banking sector. In 1990, the banking sector (measured as total assets) was just slightly higher than the country's GDP; in 2004 it was about five times GDP and by 2009 it had reached nine times GDP.

The banks used their plentiful liquidity to finance consumer loans and a construction boom in Cyprus. Excessive lending to the construction sector and to households led to a sharp rise in property prices; the Central Bank's residential property price index doubled between 2002 and the 2008 peak. It also resulted in extraordinarily high levels of private debt held by households and businesses (300 percent of GDP). In addition, the banks expanded aggressively overseas. Greece was a natural target due to the historic and cultural links between the two countries and the presence of a large Cypriot community there. The two large banks – Bank of Cyprus (BoC) and Laiki – created extensive branch networks and invested in Greek government bonds. They also set up a presence in several other countries, mostly in the Balkans and Eastern Europe.

Public finances were on a positive trajectory in the years up to 2008. In 2003, the government had run a 6.6 percent deficit and public debt stood at 69.6 percent of GDP. The government of Tassos Papadopoulos (leader of the centrist DIKO party) made adoption of the euro a key policy target and took measures to bring the fiscal targets in line with the Maastricht criteria. Its efforts were successful, culminating in 2 years of budget surpluses (2007 and 2008) and a reduction of public debt to 48.9 percent of GDP by end-2008 (Figures 9.1 and 9.2). But the surpluses were largely a mirage created by windfall revenues from a tax amnesty, the real estate

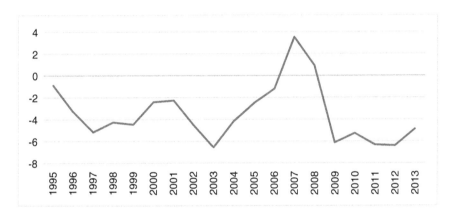

Figure 9.1 Fiscal balance

Source: IMF World Economic Outlook, October 2014

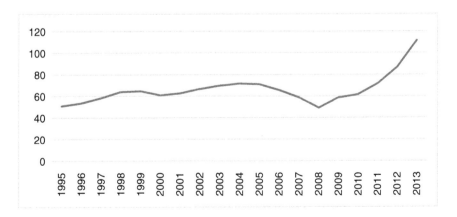

Figure 9.2 Public debt

Source: IMF World Economic Outlook, October 2014

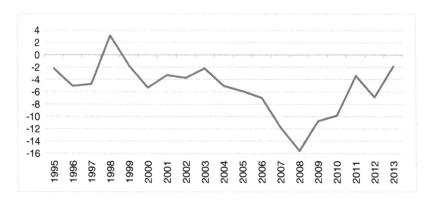

Figure 9.3 Current account balance

Source: IMF World Economic Outlook, October 2014

bubble and unsustainable consumption levels (Clerides 2014). The current account deficit exploded during this period, reaching the phenomenal level of 15.6 percent in 2008 (Figure 9.3).

Presidential elections were held in 2008, with three candidates tied up in a very close race. The fiscally conservative incumbent Tassos Papadopoulos lost and Demetris Christofias was elected president. Christofias was the leader of AKEL, a workers' party that evolved from the former Cyprus Communist Party. In order to assuage concerns about his economic policy, Christofias appointed the non-partisan former banker Charilaos Stavrakis as finance minister.

Two significant developments in the financial sector in this period are worth noting. One was the 2006 takeover of Laiki by the Greek bank Marfin, part of the Marfin Investment Group (MIG). This led to a change in Laiki's management, with Greek financier Andreas Vgenopoulos becoming the key figure in the new group. The second development was the appointment by President Papadopoulos of Athanasios Orphanides as the new governor of the Central Bank of Cyprus (CBC). Orphanides, whose term started in May 2007, was a highly-regarded monetary policy expert and senior adviser at the Board of Governors of the Federal Reserve System.

On the surface, Cyprus presented a rosy picture in 2008; it had been growing fast and had low public debt and budget surpluses. But under the hood, trouble was brewing. The huge capital inflows in the period 2004–08 had caused a bubble in real estate and construction, reckless expansion of banks overseas and overconsumption by households, businesses and the sovereign. A correction was on the cards, but no-one could have predicted what was to happen.

9.2.2 The unravelling: 2008–13

The world went into crisis mode in September 2008. Cyprus did not suffer any immediate consequences as its banks did not hold toxic assets and were not dependent on inter-bank lending, which had frozen. This led some to believe that the country would escape the crisis altogether. Such was likely the expectation of President Christofias, who took office in March 2008. His government was eager to deliver on its promises of increased social spending and in 2009 government expenditure increased by 7.8 percent. Government revenues in the same year registered an 8.5 percent decline, turning 2008's budgetary surplus into a 6.1 percent deficit. Contrary to expectations, the economy contracted by 1.85 percent in 2009.

The deteriorating fiscal situation prompted calls for corrective measures from CBC governor Athanasios Orphanides, local economists and even the biggest opposition parties, DISY and DIKO.[3] In standard political economy analysis elected governments try to implement reforms and the opposition tries to stop them (see Terzi, this volume). Cyprus at this juncture was unique in that the opposition was essentially offering to share the political cost of reform, but the government would not take up the offer. As a result, budget deficits in 2010 and 2011 remained at high levels, at 5.3 percent and 6.3 percent respectively.[4] Public debt rose from 48.9 percent of GDP in 2008 to 71.1 percent in 2011 and 85.8 percent in 2012. This was pure fiscal deterioration; no public funds had been used up to this point to support banks.

The first signs of impending trouble in the banking sector appeared in 2010, when the size of Cypriot banks' holdings of Greek government bonds (GGBs) became known. BoC and Laiki were downgraded by Moody's in July and the Cypriot sovereign was downgraded by Standard and Poor's (S&P) in November. S&P cited the risk associated with the banks' exposure to GGBs and the high private debt as the main reasons for the downgrade. In February 2011 Moody's also downgraded Cyprus' rating, citing exposure to Greece and domestic fiscal problems as the reasons.

The banking sector's troubles presented the government with an alibi for not reducing public expenditure. It was argued that ordinary citizens should not be made to pay for the banks' mistakes. The government's antagonistic stance towards banks further strained relations with CBC governor Orphanides, who defended the banking system and kept urging the government to tackle the deficit. Relations were so bad that Orphanides was essentially not on speaking terms with either Christofias or Stavrakis. In December 2010, Orphanides and ECB president Mario Draghi jointly sent a letter to the president sounding warning bells and urging immediate corrective action.

Parliamentary elections were held on May 22, 2011. A few days later (May 31), Fitch downgraded its rating of the Cyprus sovereign, essentially locking the country out of international markets. The government shifted to a strategy of (more expensive) short-term financing from the domestic market. On July 11 a huge explosion destroyed the country's biggest power station, leading to severe power cuts and knocking the economy back into recession. There were mass protests against the Christofias government, whose handling of large amounts of confiscated explosives was deemed responsible for the explosion. A few days later, on July 21, the European Union Council proposed a 'voluntary' haircut of up to 21 percent on GGBs in order to reduce Greece's unsustainable debt burden. This implied a substantial loss for the two major Cypriot banks (a combined total of the order of 1 billion euros, or 5.5 percent of GDP). Although this was a major hit, the CBC maintained that the banks had sufficient buffers to absorb the blow.

In August Stavrakis resigned and was replaced by Kikis Kazamias, a respected AKEL veteran. Kazamias understood the gravity of the situation and developed a good working relationship with Orphanides. He was able to leverage his AKEL credentials to convince the government to approve a package of fiscal measures in December 2011. But it was too little, too late. The government's financing problems due to its inability to borrow from international markets had become pressing. On October 4, the government came to an agreement with the Russian Federation to take out a 2.5 billion euros loan. The loan was to be repaid in its entirety in 5 years and the amount was calculated to cover financing needs through the end of Christofias' term in February 2013.

On October 26, 2011, the EU Council increased the nominal haircut of GGBs to 50 percent. Eventually this was finalized at 53.5 percent, which for some creditors corresponded to more than 70 percent in present value terms. The loss for the two major Cypriot banks from this decision was a massive 4.5 billion euros (25 percent of GDP). On December 8, the European Banking Authority (EBA) announced the results of its capital adequacy exercise. It revealed a capital shortfall of 1.97 billion euros for Laiki and 1.56 billion euros for BoC (a total of 20 percent of GDP).[5] Banks were given until June 2012 to raise the required capital. This appeared feasible for BoC because it had issued convertible securities, but not for Laiki. Laiki had been losing deposits throughout 2011 (this was not widely known at the time). Following this development, the CBC ousted Laiki strongman Vgenopoulos and CEO Efthimios Bouloutas.[6] Well-regarded former finance minister Michael Sarris was put at the helm of Laiki with the unenviable task of trying to find investors for the beleaguered bank.[7]

In March 2012 Kazamias suddenly resigned after just six months in his post, citing health reasons. He was replaced by Vassos Shiarly, who – like Stavrakis – was a former top executive at the Bank of Cyprus. In April 2012 president Christofias appointed Panicos Demetriades, a professor of economics at Leicester University, to replace Orphanides at the helm of the CBC. Demetriades had been openly critical of Cypriot banks and the CBC in articles published in the press prior to his appointment.[8] Upon his taking office, the CBC's approach towards banks became much tougher. Demetriades echoed the government position that the banks had caused the crisis and he was sympathetic to the co-operative banking sector. Unlike Orphanides, he supported the Christofias government's opposition to a long-standing IMF recommendation that supervision of the co-operative sector should come under the CBC. In June 2012, in one of his first speeches as Central Bank governor, he praised the co-operative sector for suffering fewer problems during the crisis because of better practices.[9] In another speech in December 2012, he referred to Cypriot banks' practices as 'casino banking'.[10]

The situation started unravelling in May 2012. The June 2012 deadline for banks to meet their capital targets was approaching and Laiki had been unable to attract investors. In May the government announced that it intended to recapitalize Laiki with 1.8 billion euros of public money. On June 19 BoC unexpectedly disclosed at its annual general meeting that it was still 200–300 million euros short of meeting the recapitalization target set by the EBA. A week later, on June 27, it submitted a formal request for 500 million euros in state assistance. In the meantime, on June 25 Fitch became the last of the three major rating agencies to downgrade Cyprus to junk status, which meant that the ECB could no longer accept Cypriot bonds as collateral. Unable to raise funds to capitalize the banks, the government had no choice but to formally request assistance from European institutions.

The Fitch downgrade came with an estimate that the total amount required to recapitalize the Cypriot banking sector would be 5.8 billion euros. Rumours circulating in Cyprus were putting the amount at 8–10 billion euros. The CBC hired PIMCO to conduct a due diligence exercise to determine the banking system's needs. The final report was published in March 2013 but the key results became known in the fall of 2012. They showed total capital needs of 6.0 billion euros in the base scenario and 8.9 billion euros in the adverse scenario, a huge 33 percent and 50 percent of GDP respectively.

In the meantime, negotiations with the Troika dragged on for months as the government was trying to avoid compromise on some of its core policies such as spending, wage indexation, opposition to privatizations and separate supervision of the co-op sector. On November 25, 2012, the government finally agreed to a draft MoU. But by now it was too close to the presidential elections coming up in February, so it was left to the new government to finalize the details.

9.2.3 The external environment

By the end of 2012 the basic figures had crystallized. Cyprus would need about 10 billion euros to recapitalize its banks and another 7 billion euros to finance deficits and honour upcoming debt obligations. The IMF's debt sustainability analysis (DSA) indicated that if Cyprus were to borrow the entire required amounts its debt burden would reach 145 percent, much higher than the Fund's unofficial maximum of 120 percent. The IMF had been heavily criticized for agreeing to the Greek programme in 2010 even though its own analysis questioned the sustainability of the country's debt. It was highly unlikely that it would show the same flexibility again in the case of Cyprus. This placed a fairly hard constraint of 10 billion euros on the amount Cyprus could borrow from the institutions. The remaining 7 billion euros would have to come from fiscal measures or other sources. At almost 40 percent of GDP, this was a herculean task.

At the same time, the external climate was turning sour. After Greece, Ireland and Portugal, bailout fatigue was beginning to set in in many European capitals. There was increasing frustration in EU and international policy circles for Cyprus's apparent lack of urgency in tackling its problems and for taking a loan from Russia rather than seeking help from its European partners. The negative climate started spilling into the public domain in late 2012. In November, a story broke out in the German press about a 'secret German intelligence report' claiming that anti-money laundering rules were not being properly applied in Cyprus and that Russian oligarchs who laundered their money through the island would be the primary beneficiaries of a Cyprus bailout (Dettmer and Reiermann 2012). This was quickly picked up by German opposition politicians looking for issues on which Chancellor Merkel might be vulnerable ahead of the September 2013 elections.

Although neither the report nor any evidence were ever made public, the issue remained in the limelight for weeks and severely damaged Cyprus's image. German finance minister Wolfgang Schäuble made several references to Cyprus as a haven for Russian oligarchs (Parkin 2013). He stated that Cyprus's 'business model' had failed and it had to chart a new course,while French finance minister Pierre Moscovici called Cyprus 'a casino economy'.[11] They were both referring to Cyprus's status as a low-tax jurisdiction serving as a financial and business centre. This strategy has been followed by several other EU countries (such as Ireland, Malta and Netherlands) but is disliked by some of the more influential European countries. Germany in particular has long been in favour of tax harmonization across Europe. This was an opportunity to make a forceful point about low-tax jurisdictions.

The conditions leading to the bail-in were now in place. A full bailout of Cypriot banks was impossible because it would make its debt unsustainable and because several European countries were against using public money for what they perceived to be a bailout of Russian oligarchs. These considerations capped the amount to be lent to Cyprus at 10 billion euros, when the country's needs were 17 billion. Thus, the possibility of a depositor bail-in began to be entertained as an option in the fall of 2012. The idea became a subject of open discussion for at least three months prior to its actual execution. This further destabilized the Cypriot banking system; 6 billion euros in deposits left Cyprus during the three months leading up to March 15, including 3.4 billion euros (largely held by foreigners) in the first two weeks of March alone.

9.2.4 Summary

A number of conclusions emerge from the analysis presented thus far. First, the Cyprus economy had built up large imbalances during the prosperous 2000s. The banks had overextended themselves and the sovereign happily played along, oblivious of the risks. A correction was inevitable, and it would have been painful no matter what. Second, the delay in addressing the mounting economic challenges had enormous consequences. It made the overall price tag much greater but also had a distributional impact: it gave better informed individuals time to take their money out of the banks, thereby increasing the burden on everyone else.

It seems clear ex post that the crucial milestone was October 2011, when the large haircut of GGBs was decided. At that time, Cyprus could have credibly argued that its two major banks should be recapitalized by the Hellenic Financial Stability Fund (like Greek banks) on account of the facts that (a) about half their loan portfolios were in Greece and (b) Laiki was managed by a Greek group since the merger with MIG and Egnatia. Even if that appeal was unsuccessful, Cyprus should have immediately asked for support.

The opportunity was missed because the government was desperate to avoid a programme. It knew that seeking assistance would require giving up on some of its key policies on public spending, wage indexation, privatizations and labour market reform. It was not willing to do that. Sour relations between the executive and the Central Bank hindered the development of a proper policy response to the crisis. Although Kazamias had developed a good working relationship with Orphanides, he was unable to convince the president to heed the governor's concerns. Orphanides's confrontational style and public criticism of the government did not make it easy for an understanding to be reached.

9.3 The reckoning: March 2013

The February 2013 elections produced a new president, Nicos Anastasiades of the centre-right DISY party. Anastasiades, who had campaigned on a promise not to allow a deposit haircut, took office on March 1, 2013. One of his first decisions was to appoint the experienced Michael Sarris as finance minister. A Eurogroup meeting was scheduled to discuss the Cyprus situation on March 15. Sarris prepared a plan for fiscal measures and privatizations that would cover a large part of the 7 billion euros financing gap and hoped that the Eurogroup would show some flexibility in order to bridge the remaining difference.

It became obvious early on in the Eurogroup meeting of March 15 that there was no such appetite and that some kind of depositor contribution would be necessary. After long and tense negotiations, the controversial decision was reached shortly before dawn on March 16. The key aspect of the decision was the imposition of a 'solidarity levy' on all deposits in Cypriot banks. The levy was set at 6.75 percent for deposits up to 100,000 euros and 9.9 percent for amounts exceeding that threshold. It was intended to raise 5.8 billion euros.

The decision was met with heavy criticism from analysts across the world, mostly for taxing insured deposits (amounts up to 100,000 euros). By March 18 the EU backtracked; after an emergency Eurogroup teleconference it essentially gave Cyprus a free hand to raise the required 5.8 billion euros from deposits using any formula it wished but strongly encouraged excluding the first 100,000 euros.[12]

The only alternative on the Eurogroup's table was the IMF's proposal to merge BoC and Laiki and capitalize the merged entity with a haircut on deposits that was estimated to reach as much as 40 percent.[13] This option was supported by Germany and a small number of other countries. The solidarity levy on deposits at *all* banks, not just BoC and Laiki, was proposed by the European Commission as a way to spread the burden and to lower the level of the haircut. Cyprus supported this proposal and, after much wrangling, Germany and the IMF eventually acquiesced.

What remained to be decided was the precise formula that would raise 5.8 billion euros. No-one claims responsibility for the inclusion of insured deposits in the levy, but there is broad consensus among news reports that the European Commission and Cyprus (represented by Commissioner Ollie Rehn and President

Anastasiades) were keen on keeping the top rate below 10 percent.[14] This made a levy on insured deposits inevitable, as the numbers would not otherwise add up.

All opposition parties in Cyprus railed against the government for agreeing to the haircut of deposits and the March 18 Eurogroup statement went largely unnoticed. Pleas extended to parliament by CBC governor Demetriades and local economists to devise a new formula fell on deaf ears. The government did not have a majority in parliament and it was lukewarm in its support of its own decision. Parliament rejected the levy on March 19, even though there was no backup plan. On March 20, an agreement was reached to sell Cypriot banks' operations in Greece to the Bank of Piraeus. A new Eurogroup on March 24 decided the basic terms of the rescue package and a final political agreement was reached on April 5.

The key elements of the MoU for the financial sector were: (a) resolution of Laiki bank into a good bank and a bad bank; the good bank would be folded into BoC and the bad bank would be run down over time;[15] (b) recapitalization of BoC via a bail-in of depositors and junior bondholders; (c) consolidation of the co-operative sector and recapitalization with 1.5 billion euros of programme money; (d) improvement of the legal framework to facilitate the proper functioning of banking operations (foreclosure, insolvency etc.); and (e) imposition of capital controls in order to prevent a run on the banks until confidence in the system was restored.

The precise level of depositor contribution was determined several weeks later. Beyond the 100,000 euros that were protected, Laiki's depositors lost almost all of their money while BoC's depositors lost 47.5 percent. Total depositor losses amounted to 7.8 billion euros. Another 0.2 billion euros of senior debt and 1.3 billion euros in subordinated debt were bailed in, giving a total of 9.4 billion euros or 52.0 percent of 2013 GDP (18.07 billion euros).[16]

9.3.1 Bailout versus bail-in

The bail-in was sharply criticized in Cyprus and most Cypriots still feel very bitter about it. Yet, it had one very significant advantage compared to the alternative of a bailout. A full bailout using taxpayer money would have meant that the entire cost of supporting the banks would be borne by Cypriot taxpayers. The bail-in was borne by depositors, many of whom were non-Cypriot. There is no official figure on what fraction of bailed-in deposits was owned by non-residents. The closest thing is a verbal statement by Demetriades that the figure was about 70 percent.[17] If this is accurate, it means that non-residents took a hit of about 5.5 billion euros that would otherwise be borne by Cypriot taxpayers. From the standpoint of the people of Cyprus, this is a substantial benefit of the bail-in over a bailout. This point is often overlooked in Cyprus.

The rejection of the original solidarity levy by parliament had massive distributional implications. The levy was to be paid by depositors in all banks, regardless of each institution's financial health. Banks that did not need recapitalization naturally opposed it. This had international implications, as some were foreign banks.[18]

There is a valid argument that the levy would have been unfair to depositors in banks that had followed more prudent practices. On the other hand, it could be reasonably argued that the large majority of BoC and Laiki depositors had no knowledge of the banks' financial position and did not knowingly take on risk. Deposit rates in Cyprus had always been relatively high and all domestic banks were paying similar rates. Yet the bail-in as implemented meant that an individual with a one million euro in the bank would have lost 900,000 euros if it was in Laiki, 427,500 euros if it was in BoC, and nothing at all if it was in a co-op.

The co-op sector avoided being bailed in and was recapitalized with programme money. This was probably for two reasons. One is that that the sector had relatively few big depositors and a bail-in of uninsured deposits would not have raised enough capital. The other reason is that the sector was protected because it traditionally had close links to the political system and its depositors were overwhelmingly Cypriot.

9.3.2 Ring-fencing Greece

The Troika insisted that Greek operations of Cypriot banks be sold off to Greek banks prior to any agreement. The rationale is clear. After a long and painful slog, Greece was finally feeling the beginning of a turnaround in 2013. The last thing anyone wanted was to see the Greek banking system implode as a result of the bail-in of Cypriot banks. A confidential ECB document dated January 27, 2013 (but leaked in 2015) states that ring-fencing banking activities performed in Greece by Cypriot banks is 'crucial to maintain financial stability in Greece's fragile banking market.'[19]

The deal was negotiated and completed in the frantic days between the two Eurogroup meetings of March 15 and March 24. Cyprus was in a very weak bargaining position as a deal was a precondition for a programme. As a result, the buyer – the Bank of Piraeus – secured a very good price and its shares shot up by 20 percent when the deal was announced. Dixon (2013) estimates the purchase price of 524 million euros to be just 19 percent of the net asset value of the transaction, implying a transfer of about 2 billion euros from Cyprus to Greece. An alternative calculation suggests that approximately 2.3 billion euros was paid by BoC depositors in Cyprus in order to save depositors in Greece and protect the Greek banking system.[20] The deal was signed by the CBC as bank executives did not agree to it.

It is somewhat ironic that great effort went into saving Greek depositors and banks even though Laiki's problems stemmed primarily from Greece. Between 2008 and 2010, Laiki lost 1.9 billion euros of deposits in Greece while it gained 1.8 billion euros in Cyprus. At end-2011 its loan portfolio in Greece stood at 13.4 billion euros against deposits of 9.7 billion euros; the shortfall was financed with deposits from Cyprus. Its loan portfolio in 2006 was just 6.0 billion euros, meaning that it more than doubled (a 123 percent increase to be exact) in just 5 years.[21] There have been reports of loans given to affiliated parties without sufficient collateral, and of loans to purchase MIG shares with the shares themselves as collateral. Ex-Laiki chairman Sarris has put the figure at 4 billion euros worth of questionable loans.[22] All in all, Cypriot banks took a huge hit from their Greek operations but when the time came for the bill to be paid, the Cypriot economy picked up the entire tab.[23]

9.4 Political economy and beyond

Political economy considerations played an important role in the escalation and resolution of the Cyprus crisis. The Christofias government's expansion of social spending while the economy was in recession in 2009–10 is a clear case of a newly elected government pandering to its constituents. The same government's decision to ask for help from Russia rather than the Troika (a Russian word, ironically) was driven by its aversion to the conditionality that would come with the latter. Even after it eventually did seek help from the Troika, it delayed the conclusion of an agreement for several months as it sought to avoid unwanted reforms such as privatizations and the abolition of wage indexation.

Ideology and personal convictions were also in play. AKEL maintains historical ties to Russia and many of its leaders – including Christofias – were educated in the former Soviet Union or other eastern bloc countries. As a 'communist' party, it holds a deep mistrust of the capitalist west and its institutions. Katsikas (this volume) discusses the significance of the 'external constraint' – typically the IMF – in the design and implementation of structural reforms. The conditionality imposed by the IMF often has far-reaching distributional implications that put it at odds with governments and interest groups in countries it seeks to help. In the case of Cyprus this tension was magnified by the ideological factor.

The Anastasiades government came to power on a platform of reform. Taking over a country on the verge of collapse, it had a clear mandate and the benefit of a honeymoon period to implement its policies (Terzi, this volume). But within a matter of days Anastasiades had to renege on one of his main campaign promises of no haircut, perhaps exemplifying what Terzi (this volume) calls Voodoo politics. But it is also likely that Anastasiades did not intentionally mislead voters but was himself blindsided by the turn of events. Despite this setback, he did press on with reforms that were successful in stabilizing government finances and the financial sector. There was markedly less success on the structural reform agenda which stalled after the informal alliance between DISY and DIKO withered.

In considering the distribution of the cost of reform, it is useful to separately consider its two major components: the cost of recapitalizing the banking sector and the cost of stabilizing government finances. Cyprus is likely unique in that the first component is significantly larger than the second, hence any discussion of the distributional burden of the crisis must necessarily focus on that. The bail-in was a massive destruction of wealth, most of which belonged to non-Cypriot nationals. In that sense, it was preferable to Cypriots to a taxpayer funded bailout. Despite this, the Cypriot government and all political parties vehemently opposed the bail-in. They feared that the loss of credibility of the banking system would be difficult to restore, and that Cyprus's reputation as a financial centre would be irreparably damaged. The Anastasiades government was particularly sensitive to this due to its close ties to the business services community that was heavily dependent on foreign – mostly Russian – clientele.

The impact of the economy's adjustment on different groups varied significantly. Private sector employees were hit the most, with pay cuts of the order of 30–50 percent in some sectors. Civil servants suffered smaller but non-trivial pay cuts and increases in pension scheme contributions. Remarkably, bank employees were among the least affected. Even though the banking system collapsed, pay cuts were modest and there was not a single layoff. The banks reduced their payrolls by offering several rounds of increasingly generous packages for voluntary retirement. All this happened against expectations that the new owners of BoC and Hellenic Bank – which include US hedge funds – would squeeze employees, and it speaks volumes for the power of the bank employees' union ETYK.

Although the focus of this chapter is on political economy, it must be emphasized that ideological bias, egotism, personal vendettas and sheer incompetence played a very significant role in this episode, particularly in the handling of the crisis before its culmination in March 2103. The significance of these factors is exemplified in the decision of the Christofias government to agree to the restructuring of GGBs without first seeking to secure support for Cyprus's own banks that were to be badly hit by that decision. It is hard to rationalize this decision using political calculus, unless one agrees with Orphanides (2016) that this was part of a deliberate assault on the banks. This claim seems extreme; inability to understand the implications of that decision – in large part due to the sour relations between Christofias and Orphanides – seems like a more likely explanation.

9.4.1 A tale of two governors

The contrasting stance of Orphanides and Demetriades towards the banking system and their clashes with the government is one of the most interesting subplots of the Cyprus crisis. The two governors have a lot in common. They are both professional economists who were living and working outside Cyprus when they were appointed. Both were appointed by presidents who were voted out of office a few months later and therefore had to serve most of their term under a different president. This president would also get to decide whether to re-appoint them for a second term. Self-serving individuals might have opted to co-operate with the new president in order to maximize the chances of re-appointment. On the contrary, both Orphanides and Demetriades followed their own course and collided openly and forcefully with the presidents. In Demetriades's case, the collision ended with his resignation less than 2 years into his term.

The two governors' attitudes towards the banks could not have been more different. Orphanides was protective of the banking system and consistently downplayed its problems in public. This is perhaps to be expected of a governor, though Orphanides has been criticized for not being aggressive enough with regard to some of the banks' questionable practices like the large exposure to the real estate sector, the purchase of GGBs, the forays into high-risk foreign markets and the selling of capital securities to unsuspecting retail investors who later got bailed in. He continues to maintain that the banks' problems were manageable if only the government would have acted on time (Orphanides 2016).

Demetriades' approach was the mirror opposite. The main themes in his public messages were transparency and the need to cleanse the system.[24] He was accused by the media and political parties (and Orphanides) for working to inflate capital needs in order to provide political support for the Christofias government. Although this cannot be ruled out, it is clear that he was also acting out of personal conviction. He shared the government's view that the commercial banks were responsible for the crisis and had a soft spot for the co-operative sector. For Demetriades, this was an opportunity to air out all the dirty banking laundry and start the banks fresh with healthy balance sheets and new management.

There is some basis in the claim that PIMCO's estimates of capital needs were *ex ante* too conservative.[25] Demetriades himself called on Blackrock to evaluate PIMCO's estimates; Blackrock concluded that PIMCO's numbers could be trimmed by 1 billion euros. Ex post, however, total capital injections into the banking system significantly exceeded even PIMCO's adverse scenario.[26] Was this self-fulfilling prophecy? Perhaps to some extent, but more than anything this outcome shows that the problems with bank balance sheets were much worse than anyone – probably including both governors – had realized at the time. Non-performing loans at BoC, the co-op sector and the smaller Hellenic Bank still stand at close to 50 percent of all loans in 2017.

9.5 Concluding remarks

The cost of rehabilitating Cyprus's financial sector was enormous. This chapter analyzes the forces that determined (a) the size of the losses and (b) the distribution of the burden across different groups. The magnitude of the losses was decided by two main factors. The first was the combination of bad banking practices, complacent supervision, and misguided government policies that created the excess build-up of credit in the years leading up to the crisis. The second factor was government paralysis in the face of mounting and widely recognized problems, which allowed them to fester to the point that conventional remedies for bank crises were no longer sufficient.

The distribution of the burden was the outcome of a much more complex set of actions and constraints involving not just Cypriot stakeholders but also European states and institutions and international organizations. The IMF maintained a hard line after having been burned in Greece. Bailout-weary European governments and citizenry were not willing to contribute to what they perceived to be a bailout of profligate southerners and Russian oligarchs. The desire to protect Greece ensured that Greek depositors were spared and the tab for losses incurred in Greece was paid by depositors in Cyprus. The decision to bail in rather than to bailout meant that non-Cypriots paid a very large part of the bank recapitalization bill that would otherwise have fallen on the shoulders of Cypriot taxpayers. Rejection of the solidarity levy meant that depositors in the two major banks paid for their institutions' failures, while everyone else, including depositors in the perhaps equally problematic co-operative sector, was spared.

The sums of money involved in each of these decisions are astronomical relative to the size of the country, and political economy considerations affected every one of them. It is hard to overestimate the importance of understanding the complex web of interests underlying every decision when the stakes are so high. But a pure political economy analysis does not provide a complete picture, for it cannot explain every action by every individual. The analysis here has shown that behavioural factors such as ideology, personal convictions, character traits and personality clashes played an important role in shaping the outcome of the Cyprus crisis. Any attempt to understand individual decision making must take these human traits into serious consideration.

Notes

1 See Clerides (2014, 2016), Demetriades (2017), Michaelides (2014), Orphanides (2016), Phylaktis (2016), Theodore and Theodore (2015), and Zenios (2013, 2015).
2 Of the 9.4 billion euros, 7.8 billion was deposits and 1.6 billion was junior bonds (International Monetary Fund 2013b). The 12.9 billion euros total includes in addition 1.675 billion used to recapitalize the co-operative banking sector and 1.8 billion that had been put into Laiki bank a year before these events. The percentages are calculated using 18.1 billion euros; using the 2014 estimate of 2013 GDP (16.5 billion euros), the bail-in would amount to 57 percent and the total recapitalization bill to 78.2 percent.
3 The governor's public and private warnings to the government are documented in Orphanides (2016).
4 The figures have since been revised downward (to −5.5, −4.8 and −5.8 for 2009–11) as a result of changes in Eurostat's methodology. We report the old figures because that is what was known at the time.
5 Results obtained from CBC website, www.centralbank.cy/en/licencing-supervision/european-banking-authority-eba-recapitalization-exercise-announced-on-8-december-2011.
6 Bouloutas is currently on trial in Cyprus (along with three other former Laiki executives) on charges of misconduct during his time at the bank. Vgenopoulos was also charged but his prosecution was cut short by his sudden death in November 2016.
7 Sarris was finance minister during the Papadopoulos presidency and is credited for successfully bringing the economy into line with the Maastricht criteria, thus enabling accession to the Eurozone. He was unable to secure investors and was removed from Laiki by the CBC in August 2012.
8 Demetriades wrote regularly between February 2011 and February 2012. All of his columns were published at the financial news site Stockwatch (www.stockwatch.com.cy), while several also appeared in mainstream newspapers.
9 Speech delivered at Nicosia Chamber of Commerce, June 13, 2012. Available from: www.centralbank.cy/el/the-governor/previous-governors/previous-governors-speeches-panicos-o.-demetriades/13962012 (in Greek).
10 Speech delivered at discussion organized by the Hellenic American Bankers Association and the Cyprus-US Chamber of Commerce, December 11, 2012; Available from www.centralbank.cy/en/the-governor/previous-governors/previous-governors-speeches-panicos-o.-demetriades/11122012.

11 A characteristic statement by Schäuble was made in an interview with German public broadcaster ARD, 17 March 2013; Available at the German Ministry of Finance website: www.bundesfinanzministerium.de/Content/EN/Interviews/2013/2013-03-17-ard-tagesthemen.html.
12 'Statement by the Eurogroup President on Cyprus,' March 18, 2013.
13 Spiegel et al. (2013) is an authoritative account of events at the Eurogroup meeting.
14 For example Spiegel et al. (2013) for *The Financial Times*, Traynor and Smith (2013) for *The Guardian* and Breidthardt and O'Donnell (2013) for *Reuters*.
15 The idea of a bad bank was quickly abandoned. Instead, Laiki's problem assets came under the management of the resolution authority (the Central Bank).
16 International Monetary Fund (2013b, p. 13).
17 The fraction of *total* deposits owned by foreigners was 37 percent, with 60 percent of that belonging to Russians, according to Fontevecchia (2013).
18 In a radio interview in October 2014, former speaker of the House of Representatives Marios Karoyian claimed that one of the main reasons the solidarity level was rejected was heavy pressure from Russia, which was protecting the interests of the Russian Commercial Bank (see http://cyprusnews.eu/deltia-typou/2543171-2014-10-09-09-45-42.html). Remarkably, the claim received very little attention in Cyprus. It was recently given additional credence in a Guardian newspaper report on the Panama Papers (Harding 2016).
19 'Ring-fencing of Cypriot Bank's Branches in Greece' (Schumann and Leontopoulos 2015).
20 The ECB document puts the deposits of Cypriot banks in Greece at 12.7 billion euros, 3.7 billion of which is uninsured (above 100,000 euros). Assuming the fraction of uninsured deposits in the two banks was the same, the required 7.8 billion euros could have been obtained by bailing in all 5.8 billion of Laiki's uninsured deposits (4.0 billion euros from Cyprus and 1.8 billion euros from Greece) and another 2 billion euros from BoC. This 2 billion could have been collected by applying a 20 percent haircut on the 9.9 billion euros of uninsured BoC deposits (yielding 1.6 billion euros from Cyprus and 0.4 billion euros from Greece). Instead, BoC depositors in Cyprus contributed 3.9 billion euros, 2.3 billion euros more than they would have paid if depositors in Greece had not been spared.
21 All figures from Laiki annual reports, 2006–11.
22 Statement made before the parliamentary committee on institutions on May 20, 2013; see www.stockwatch.com.cy/nqcontent.cfm?a_name=news_view&ann_id=174534 (in Greek). The New York Times have also reported on questionable deals during Vgenopoulos' time at Laiki (Thomas 2013a), as well as the close relationship between Bank of Piraeus chief Michalis Sallas and Bank of Greece governor George Provopoulos (Thomas 2013b). Some of these are under investigation in both Cyprus and Greece.
23 Xiouros (2016) examines several liquidation scenarios at different points in time that would have been better outcomes for Laiki's uninsured depositors.
24 His interview with *Stockwatch* on June 25, 2012 provides an insight to his thinking; available from: www.centralbank.gov.cy/nqcontent.cfm?a_id=13531. Bank governance problems that contributed to the crisis are highlighted in the report by the Independent Commission on the Future of the Cyprus Banking Sector (2013), which was commissioned by Demetriades.
25 See Michaelides (2014) and Zenios (2015). Even voices within the IMF considered PIMCO's methodology conservative. A May 15, 2013 statement by IMF Executive Director Menno Snel states that 'PIMCO has used a more conservative methodology in arriving to the final numbers' and 'very conservative assumptions were used for estimating the recovery amounts' (International Monetary Fund 2013a).
26 9.4 billion euros for the combined BoC-Laiki plus 1.5 billion euros for the co-op sector, for a total of 10.9 billion euros. BoC raised an additional 1billion euros from private investors a year later, and the CCB received another 175 million euros from the state in December 2015.

Bibliography

Breidthardt, A., and O'Donnell, J. (2013) Insight: How Europe Stumbled into Scheme to Punish Cyprus Savers. *Reuters*. [Online]. Available from: www.reuters.com/article/us-eurozone-cyprus-stumbled-insight-idUSBRE92H0RH20130318.

Clerides, S. (2014) The Collapse of the Cypriot Banking System: A Bird's Eye View. *Cyprus Economic Policy Review*, 8(2), 3–35.

Clerides, S. (2016) The Cyprus Crisis: Lessons, Challenges, Opportunities. In: Michaelides, A. and Orphanides, A. (eds.) *The Cyprus Bail-in: Policy Lessons From the Cyprus Economic Crisis*, London, Imperial College Press.

Demetriades, P. O. (2017) Political Economy of a Euro Area Banking Crisis. *Cambridge Journal of Economics*, 41(4), 1249–1264.

Dettmer, M., and Reiermann, C. (2012) German Intelligence Report Warns Cyprus Not Combating Money Laundering. *Spiegel Online* [Online]. Available from: www.spiegel.de/international/europe/german-intelligence-report-warns-cyprus-not-combating-money-laundering-a-865451.html.

Dixon, H. (2013) Cyprus Bank 'Resolution' a Bad Joke. *Reuters*. [Online]. Available from: http://blogs.reuters.com/hugo-dixon/2013/04/03/cyprus-bank-resolution-a-bad-joke/.

Fontevecchia, A. (2013) EU Takes Shot at Moscow With Cyprus Bailout as Russians Own 22% of Deposits. *Forbes*. [Online]. Available from: www.forbes.com/sites/afontevecchia/2013/03/18/eu-takes-shot-at-moscow-with-cyprian-haircut-as-russians-own-22-of-deposits/#2dacbff67069.

Harding, L. (2016) Sergei Roldugin, the Cellist Who Holds the Key to Tracing Putin's Hidden Fortune. *The Guardian*. [Online]. Available from: www.theguardian.com/news/2016/apr/03/sergei-roldugin-the-cellist-who-holds-the-key-to-tracing-putins-hidden-fortune.

Hewitt, G. (2013) Few Winners in Cyprus deal. *BBC*. [Online]. Available from: www.bbc.com/news/world-europe-21921874.

IMF (2009) *Cyprus: Staff Report for the 2009 Article IV Consultation*. IMF. Country Report No. 09/255.

IMF (2013a) *Cyprus: Request for Arrangement Under the Extended Fund Facility*. IMF. Country Report No. 13/125.

IMF (2013b) *Cyprus: First Review Under the Extended Arrangement Under the Extended Fund Facility and Request for Modification of Performance Criteria*. IMF. Country Report No. 13/293.

Independent Commission on the Future of the Cyprus Banking Sector (2013) *Final Report and Recommendations*. Available from: https://www.centralbank.cy/en//independent-commission-on-the-future-of-the-cyprus-banking-sector.

Katsikas, D. (2017) Designing Structural Reforms in Times of Crisis: Lessons From the Past. In: Manasse, P. and Katsikas, D. (eds.) *Structural Reforms in Southern Europe*, Abingdon, UK, Routledge.

Laeven, L., and Valencia, F. (2013) Systemic Banking Crises Database. *IMF Economic Review*, 61(2), 225–270.

Michaelides, A. (2014) Cyprus: From Boom to Bail-in. *Economic Policy*, 29(80), 639–689, reprinted in: Michaelides, A. and Orphanides, A. (eds.) *The Cyprus Bail-in: Policy Lessons From the Cyprus Economic Crisis*, London, Imperial College Press.

Orphanides, A. (2016) What Happened in Cyprus? The Economic Consequences of the Last Communist Government in Europe. In: Michaelides, A. and Orphanides, A. (eds.) *The Cyprus Bail-in: Policy Lessons From the Cyprus Economic Crisis*, London, Imperial College Press, pp. 163–207.

Parkin, B. (2013) *Russia-Cyprus Money Flows Imply Laundering, Schaeuble Says.* [Online]. Available from: www.bloomberg.com/news/articles/2013-01-21/russia-cyprus-money-flows-imply-laundering-schaeuble-says.

Phylaktis, K. (2016) The Cyprus Debacle: Implications for the European Banking Union. In: Castañeda, J. E., Mayes, D. G. and Wood, G. (eds.) *European Banking Union: Prospects and Challenges*, Abingdon, UK, Routledge.

Reinhart, C. M., and Rogoff, K. S. (2009) *This Time Is Different: Eight Centuries of Financial Folly*, Princeton, NJ, Princeton University Press.

Schumann, H., and Leontopoulos, N. (2015) How the Troika and Piraeus Bank Sealed Cyprus's fate. *The Press Project*. [Online]. Available from: www.thepressproject.gr/details_en.php?aid=73470.

Spiegel, P. (2013) The Cyprus Bailout Blame Game Begins. *Financial Times*. [Online]. Available from: www.ft.com/content/d83af1f7-fede-360e-bb60-59f40e709adc.

Spiegel, P., Hope, K., and Peel, Q. (2013) Cyprus: A Poor Diagnosis, a Bitter Pill. *Financial Times*. [Online]. Available from: www.ft.com/content/a8c52cc6-92e6-11e2-b3be-00144feabdc0.

Stephanou, C. (2011) The Banking System in Cyprus: Time to Rethink the Business Model? *Cyprus Economic Policy Review*, 5(2), 123–130.

Terzi, A. (2017) The Political Conditions for Economic Reform in Europe's South. In: Manasse, P. and Katsikas, D. (eds.) *Structural Reforms in Southern Europe*, Abingdon, UK, Routledge.

Theodore, J., and Theodore, J. (2015) *Cyprus and the Financial Crisis: The Controversial Bailout and What It Means for the Eurozone*, UK, Palgrave McMillan.

Thomas, L. Jr. (2013a) A Wily Banker Reaches the Top. *The New York Times*. [Online]. Available from: www.nytimes.com/2013/06/11/business/global/a-wily-banker-reaches-the-top-in-greece.html.

Thomas, L. Jr. (2013b) In Greece, the Banking Chief Draws Scrutiny. *The New York Times*. [Online]. Available from: www.nytimes.com/2013/10/17/business/international/in-greece-the-banking-chief-draws-scrutiny.html.

Traynor, I., and Smith, H. (2013) Cyprus Bailout: How Nicos Walked Straight Into a German Sucker Punch. *The Guardian*. [Online]. Available from: www.theguardian.com/world/2013/mar/18/cyprus-bank-bailout-nicos-germany.

Xiouros, C. (2016) Handling of the Laiki Bank ELA and the Cyprus Bail-In Package. In: Michaelides, A. and Orphanides, A. (eds.) *The Cyprus Bail-in: Policy Lessons From the Cyprus Economic Crisis*, London, Imperial College Press.

Zenios, S. A. (2013) The Cyprus Debt: Perfect Crisis and a Way Forward. *Cyprus Economic Policy Review*, 7(1), 3–45.

Zenios, S. A. (2015) Fairness and Reflexivity in the Cyprus Bail-In. *Empirica*, 43(3), 579–606.

10 Non-performing loans in the European periphery

The political economy of reform

Eleni Panagiotarea

10.1 Introduction

Structural adjustment in the financial sector of many crisis stricken European countries remains work in progress. At the Eurozone level, the Single Supervisory Mechanism (SSM) has used its authority to conduct comprehensive assessments of the banking system which, in principle should help ensure that banks are adequately capitalized and in a position to withstand possible financial shocks. Keeping a watchful eye further supports the repair of bank lending and the monetary policy transmission mechanism. Reforms aimed at bringing about a reduction in the banks' bad debt overhang, however, have been far from systematic or systemic, aiming to address contagion effects or future unforeseen external developments that could disrupt financial stability. As a result, bank lending in the Eurozone remains anaemic, weighed down by high levels of non-performing loans (NPLs).[1] In fact, the highest ratios of NPLs relative to total loans systematically show up in the financially stressed member states, Cyprus, Greece, Portugal, Italy and Ireland (EBA 2016), those most in need to finance their recovery and return to sustainable growth.

Of all the stressed members, Greece and Portugal make for an interesting 'odd couple'. Portugal has been almost invariably portrayed as a 'success story'. It exited its programme in May 2014 and has already concluded its fifth post-programme monitoring. Greece constitutes the perennial 'special case'. It is currently implementing its third bailout programme, agreed with its creditors in August 2015; the first programme was derailed and the second was never completed. Portugal has picked up on economic performance, buoyed by consumption, strong exports and improved investment. Greece, on the other hand,[2] has grappled with recession, remaining a laggard at a time when Eurozone growth has held steady. Beneath easy narratives however, financial stability, a central pillar in the countries' respective adjustment and post-adjustment paths, has been eluding both countries.

In Portugal, the ratio of non-performing to total corporate loans remains a serious burden on banks' balance sheets, having risen from under 2 percent in 2008 to 12.7 percent in mid-June 2016. Servicing and/or workout platforms (intended to aid in the management of NPLs) have been redesigned and new institutions to provide financing alternatives have been created, yet significant risks remain: thin capital buffers, large amounts of foreclosed real estate assets and elevated exposures to the Portuguese sovereign debt, besides banks' weak business models and profit rates (European Commission 2017a). In Greece, non-performing exposures at the end of the first quarter of 2016 reached 45 percent of total exposures or, in absolute terms, EUR 108.6 billion (Bank of Greece 2016). Greece's non-performing exposure ratio is the second highest in Europe, primarily linked to 'the unprecedented contraction of domestic economic activity in recent years' (Monokroussos et al. 2016, p. 53). Despite legislative efforts to strengthen the NPL framework and successive bank recapitalizations, progress has been limited and significant issues which impede a wider restructuring of the economy in favour of tradable goods and services remain.

This chapter aims to compare the political economy factors that have conditioned the policy reforms related to NPLs resolution in Portugal and Greece. In principle, governments could overcome the political costs and distributional conflicts that inevitably arise in a difficult reform process by 'embracing' the external constraints imposed by creditors. Conditionality, an organizing principle of EU-IMF programmes, could add on to the pressure, reducing perceived or real margins for noncompliance. It could even relieve domestic pressure exercised by veto players[3] and others, with national authorities using the Troika/Institutions[3] as a scapegoat. The chapter concentrates on the NPLs reform experience of Greece and Portugal, which remains central to the stabilization and effective operation of the two banking systems and a prerequisite for a return to sustainable growth.

Comparisons of national strategies are, by definition, difficult. Initial conditions and the magnitude of the problem vary. Different time frames and different institutional set-ups affect design and outcomes. More than half of Portugal's NPL resolution strategies have been devised in post-programme surveillance. In Greece, reform design has been bogged down by politics, weak institutional capacity and an adverse economic environment. Still, as outcomes are evaluated against stated goals and appraised in the context of quantitative targets, the reform processes in the two countries offer a number of important lessons in managing political economy risks, including garnering political support and fine-tuning the reform design.

10.2 The political economy of NPLs resolution

The presence of NPLs on banks' balance sheets has damaging effects on the economy: it dampens the credit supply, impairing banks' ability to lend to the real economy; NPLs reduce bank profitability; they entail higher provisioning, which lowers banks' net-operating income and constrains operational capacity; being classified as risky assets, NPLs consequently tie up substantial amounts of precautionary capital and hence crowd out new credit; finally, NPLs burden banks with higher funding costs and affect their capacity to generate profits, because they entail low expected revenues and, thus, heighten risk perceptions on the part of investors. According to the IMF, deteriorating balance sheets lead to a combination of higher lending rates, reduced lending volumes and increased risk aversion of market participants who become weary of banks' bill of health (IMF 2015).

For countries like Greece and Portugal, timid or slow resolution of banks' balance sheets does not allow the swift debt reduction of viable firms or the winding down of unviable firms, thus impeding the process of corporate restructuring and reduction of the private sector debt overhang. Governments keen to restore the productive pillars of the economy destroyed during the crisis, or even before, must create the conditions for a rapid and effective workout of NPLs. A growing literature on the macro-financial effects of NPLs finds a robust correlation between high NPLs and weak credit and GDP growth, with causality going both ways (e.g. Klein 2013; Nkusu 2011; Espinoza and Prasad 2010).

The successes and more notably the failures of recent NPLs resolution strategies – the ratio of NPLs is still at two-digit levels in six Euro area countries, Cyprus, Greece, Italy, Ireland, Portugal and Slovenia[4] – suggest that there is no quick fix. Examining the causes and consequences of such persistently high NPLs in *both* Euro area and non-Euro area countries, Aiyar et al. (2015) claim that weak cyclical conditions constitute a serious impediment, exacerbated by obstacles related to information availability, deficiencies in the insolvency and debt enforcement systems, challenges faced by supervision authorities, bank's capacity to manage NPLs and difficulties in developing a distressed debt market. The main stakeholders, regulators, elected politicians, bankers and investors are embedded in NPLs resolutions strategies which are formulated 'behind closed doors', away from serious parliamentary scrutiny or public debate, yet determine whose loans will be affected, which companies will be wound up and which supported in their turnaround; which organizations will manage or sell distressed debt and the conditions under which the relevant market will evolve. Such strategies are thus open to political entrepreneurship, as governments seek to shield their clienteles from adverse outcomes, whereas special interests seek to capture resolution design and implementation.

10.3 Portugal

10.3.1 A clean bill of health?

Financial stability, a central pillar in the country's programme, has not yet been restored in the Portuguese financial sector. Financing conditions in the economy have remained difficult. Following the end of the programme, Portugal had to grapple with the failures of Banco Espirito Santo (the bank's resolution was completed in August 2014) and of Banco Internacional do Funchal (its resolution was finalized in December 2015). These state rescues pushed the country's 2014 and 2015 budget deficits above the targets agreed with Brussels, and damaged the credibility of the consolidation effort, highlighting how the bank-sovereign nexus continues to pose a risk to the sovereign's creditworthiness. The stability of the banking system was questioned by the uncertainty plaguing the sale of Novo Banco (the 'good bank' formed when Banco Espirito Santo was wound up[5]) and by the weak capital position of state-owned Caixa General de Depositos. In a bid to stave off a sell-off of shares of the banks involved, the European Commission and Portugal agreed in August 2016 to recapitalize Caixa at market terms.[6] Because of concerns about the effect of the public capital injection on the fiscal deficit for 2016, the recapitalization was postponed to 2017. In this way, Lisbon is expected to reduce its budget deficit to 2.0 percent of GDP in 2016 (from 4.5 percent), according to the Commission's 2017 spring forecast (European Commission 2017b), maximizing its chances to leave the Excessive Deficit Procedure in 2017.

In post-programme surveillance, the major sources of weakness were identified in the banks' weak asset quality, low interest margins and in the economy's sluggish growth. Balance sheet repair has dragged on, impeding the flow of liquidity to high-productivity firms and constraining economic activity. The share of banking assets tied up in low-productivity firms has remained large. Numbers paint a bleak picture: the country's corporate sector is heavily indebted with NPL ratios having reached 20 percent in April 2016. Household indebtedness levels have risen to 141 percent of disposable income (the EU average stands at 120 percent). These trends signal serious difficulties ahead both for unsecured consumer lending (14 percent NPL ratio) and retail housing loans (6 percent NPL ratio). The banks' cover ratios for loan losses in the corporate (65 percent), consumer (75 percent) and housing sectors (25 percent), suggest that banks still need to refinance large stocks of uncovered NPLs, exposing their capital to complex collateral valuations and recovery procedures. Banks are also exposed to real-estate assets and investments in loan recovery funds, estimated at EUR 12.5 billion at the six largest banks (Moody's 2016).

10.3.2   The political economy of NPL management in Portugal

In Portugal, agreement on a 78 billion bailout with the trio of Institutions, the European Commission, the ECB, and the IMF in April 2011, *preceded* parliamentary elections. The minority government of the Socialist Party (PS) had resigned a month earlier, after a package of cuts targeting healthcare, pensions and welfare was rejected by the Portuguese parliament. The programme agreed by Socialist Socrates's caretaker government, in return for financial assistance, was eventually 'harder and more comprehensive than the one the parliament voted against'.[7]

The Troika struggled to ensure that the programme would not be reversed, by successfully turning the participants to negotiations into stakeholders, and creating the conditions for 'national' rather than 'partisan' programme ownership.[8] Embedding the main opposition parties in the process and acquiring their approval paved the way for garnering social consensus. It also provided political leaders with the incentive to support difficult reforms on the financial front, including measures to foster a gradual and orderly de-leveraging of bank balance sheets, reinforced capitalization of banks and improved banking supervision and the sale or unwinding of the BNP bank, while also providing adequate financing of the economy. Policy design followed the IMF's template of fiscal consolidation-structural adjustment reform-financial stability; the 'model' that was imposed involved, as in Greece and in Ireland, a significant dilution of sovereign control over economic decision making. The coalition government that emerged from the June 2011 parliamentary elections had one 'mandate': to implement the programme. A strong parliamentary support, reflecting broad political consensus and the absence of electoral challenges, allowed the new Prime Minister Passos Coelho, to strive 'to go beyond the Troika'[9] to swiftly reconquer investor confidence.

The government was able to exploit favourable 'initial conditions' (Katsikas, this volume), as Portuguese banks, which operated a rather traditional financial intermediation business model, weathered the first phase of the crisis relatively well; they were not exposed to toxic assets and had not experienced a property boom and bust episode. Technical capacity was provided by the Institutions in the form of consultation, while structural conditionality matched political resolve: by June 2012, authorities had amended legislation to strengthen the early intervention framework, amended the Insolvency Law to better facilitate effective rescue of viable firms, amended the framework for bank access to public capital and had made effective the amendments to the Corporate Insolvency Law to better support the rescue of viable firms.

The government grasped the importance of timing, but was also able to front-load reforms on account of its cohesion – evident in the absence of rivalry among parties in the coalition, or of differences within the government regarding the various measures – and a largely 'neutralized' opposition. 'Shocks' still interfered with programme design: these included the Constitutional Court rulings that reduced the government's ability to cut public spending, the fiscal devaluation plan to reduce social security taxes and compensate the loss in fiscal revenues through an increase in consumption taxes (VAT taxes) which failed to gain political support and the Eurozone-wide recession which severely affected Spain, Portugal's largest trading partner. At the same time, the Institutions underestimated, as in other countries, (notably Greece where the IMF staff used a conventional value of the fiscal multiplier (0.5) in programme design), the negative effects of fiscal consolidation on output and employment.

Asset quality worsened during the programme period, the rising amount of NPLs reflecting the challenging economic and financial environment. The high level of NPLs however remained a significant problem, even after Portugal exited the programme and posted positive GDP growth. Policy makers stuck to the strategy of the orderly de-leveraging of the private sector and mitigating the social and economic costs associated with insolvencies (European Economy 2014). In-court, out-of-court and hybrid mechanisms[10]were created to provide banks and debtors with incentives to move to swifter resolution. The institutional framework was further strengthened with the implementation of an early warning system for over-indebted firms in banks' loan books and a special assessment programme of banks' policies to deal with distressed debt. To maintain a more balanced capital structure, companies were provided with recapitalization instruments, alternatives to bank debt financing and fiscal incentives; introducing stakeholder involvement in the process revised the legal framework for preferred equity and dividends (Bouveret et al. 2016).

Staying the course remained central, even at post-programme surveillance stage and even when there was a government turnover. The legislative elections of 2015 saw the *Portugal à Frente*/Portugal Ahead coalition, formed by the PSD and CDS-PP[11] win the largest share of votes yet fall short of a parliamentary majority, raising again the perennial question of whether electorates discriminate between reformist and non-reformist governments (Buti et al. 2014); the electoral outcome provided no clear answer, and allowed significant space for policy entrepreneurship.

President Cavaco Silva appointed a PSD-CDS minority government, expected to comply with Eurozone rules and uphold financial stability. The government was short-lived, following a vote of no confidence in the legislature. A long process of government formation ensued, resulting in the Socialists (PS) forming a minority government with the support of the Left Bloc (B.E), the Portuguese Communist Party (PCP) and the Ecologist Party 'The Greens' (PEV), despite years of rivalry among the groups. As new Prime Minister António Costa broke with party tradition and departed from the Socialists' 40-year policy not to negotiate to their left (Fernandes 2016), he created the conditions for a stable post-austerity order, where years of hardship would end, families' disposable incomes raised and benefits for poor households introduced. He was also quick to assure that a government led by the PS would not put at risk the commitments to the European institutions undertaken by the Portuguese state. Echoing the PSD-CSD 2011–15 government, he set the stage for a national rather than conflictual approach to implementation, where preserving the 'clean-exit' environment was key.

10.3.3 Implementation vs technical capacity

Portugal exited a 3-year recession in 2014, but growth has not been sufficiently robust to stimulate strong demand for loans, or to allow NPL resolution strategies to produce meaningful results on banks' balance sheets. Investors willing to support individual lenders have been deterred by the complexities of resolution procedures.[12] On the NPLs resolution front, authorities have been struggling with the high stock of problematic assets. Loss-absorption capacity has improved, yet Portuguese banks remain among the most poorly capitalized institutions in the Euro area, partly owing to a large volume of Deferred Tax Assets (DTAs),[13] which make up about 30 percent of the system's regulatory core capital (Moody's 2016). The strategy of aggressive write-downs or sales of non-performing loans to help clean up balance sheets and spur loan supply is thus not really available, as any material losses incurred would require capital injections; the capacity of Portuguese banks to plug in new capital however remains limited. At the same time, state support would have to be in line with EU state aid rules and the Bank Recovery and Resolution Directive (BRRD) established to deal with banks that are failing or likely to fail. Even if 'cleared', bailout money provided by the sovereign could push up Portugal's public debt-to-GDP ratio, which at about 130 percent of GDP is the third highest in the EU, after Greece and Italy. One-off fiscal costs, arising from further stress in the banking sector, could produce 'permanent effects on debt' (OECD 2017).

Seeking to contain the fragility of a system that remains vulnerable to external shocks and to high levels of public and private debt, the government has kept policy disagreements among its coalition partners to manageable levels, has reiterated its commitment to Eurozone imperatives, and has succeeded not to antagonize the markets – even after a restoration of public-sector pay increase, income tax cuts and an increase in the national minimum wage in the first three months of 2016. Building up technical capacity, however, by addressing regulatory impediments or improving features of the judicial system, such as structural inefficiencies in debt and collateral enforcement, has proven more elusive. In spite of the framework that has been set up, the Institutions consider that 'a comprehensive plan' is 'urgently needed' (European Commission 2016). Firms' options for restructuring have been bogged down by the system's limited capacity to deal with the number of cases that seek access, particularly SMEs. Firms have also been slow to understand the procedures, frequently opting to access the pre-insolvency provisions, when they are already too close to insolvency (Bouveret et al. 2016). The complexities of the legal framework create further counter-incentives; some provisions, including, for example, no principal write-off, or a ceiling of 150 instalments, have inhibited the meaningful participation of public creditors, such as tax and social security authorities. At the same time, the significant increase of insolvency cases has led to a growing backlog of applications, due to the limited number of specialized judges, the small number of qualified insolvency administrators and the limitations of the new designed body, the Institute of Support to Small and Medium Enterprises and Innovation in promoting entrepreneurship and facilitating business financing.

10.4 Greece

10.4.1 Three recapitalizations: the good, the bad, and the ugly

The Greek case is one of the most painful examples of how the sovereign-bank loop can wreak havoc, with Greek banks' fundamentals, asset quality ratios and profitability deteriorating substantially during the crisis. The successive downgrades of the credit ratings of the Hellenic Republic and rising sovereign spreads in 2010 effectively precluded banks' access to international capital and money markets. The restructuring of Greek government bonds held by the private sector in 2012 led to banks suffering losses of about EUR 38 billion, equal to about 170 percent of their total Core Tier I (CT1) capital at the time (Bank of Greece 2017). The ensuing liquidity squeeze restricted the ability of banks to finance the real economy. Deposits declined by EUR 117 billion between September 2009 and December 2015, a 44 percent drop (Bank of Greece 2017). This reflected both growing uncertainty regarding Greece's continued participation in the Eurozone and the reduction of loans throughout the period.

With the stability of the banking sector under threat, the Bank of Greece (BoG) and the government proceeded, in the context of the first bailout programme, to secure public resources to cover the recapitalization needs and restructuring costs for the period 2012–14. In March 2012, the BoG conducted a strategic assessment of the banking sector which identified four 'core banks', namely National Bank of Greece, Eurobank, Alpha Bank and Piraeus Bank, deemed suitable to be recapitalized with programme funds (Bank of Greece 2012). Under the provisions of the Greek Recapitalization Law (law 3864/2010), the Hellenic Financial Stability Fund (HFSF) was established and funded with EUR 50billion; its role was to facilitate and supervise the recapitalization and consolidation of the banking sector and manage the holding of the banking shares that it acquired. The first banking recapitalization took place in the period April to July 2013. The HFSF contributed EUR 25.5billion and ended up holding 81 to 95 percent of the total capital of all four systemic banks while the private sector contributed EUR 3.1billion.

Yet, challenges remained, since net interest margin remained low and NPLs kept rising. Thus, a reassessment of banks' capital needs was deemed necessary. In the second half of 2013 BlackRock and the BoG conducted a troubled assets review, and a diagnostic study for the domestic loan book together with an assessment of loans in foreign branches/subsidiaries. This led to a second recapitalization in the period April to May 2014. All banks opted for a share capital increase to the tune of EUR 8.3 billion with cancellation of pre-emption rights; the HFSF which agreed not to participate in the capital increases, and acted as a backstop (its funds were not utilized), saw a significant dilution of its holdings: a large number of international and domestic investors participated in the banks' capital increases. At the end of 2014, the HFSF's participation in Alpha was trimmed to 66.2 percent (from 81.7 percent), in Eurobank to 35.4 percent (from 95.2 percent), in NBG to 57.2 percent (from 84.4 percent) and in Piraeus to 66.9 percent (from 81 percent).

In 2015, the six-month long negotiations of the new Syriza-Anel 'anti-austerity' government with the Institutions stalled and the programme expired; growing political uncertainty saw an acceleration in the outflow of deposits which triggered the imposition of capital controls, followed by a 5-week banking holiday. Banks had to resort to emergency liquidity assistance (ELA) provided by the BoG, and authorized by the ECB, which kept Greece on a tight leash. It was clear then that the Greek banking system, facing a persistently increasing ratio of NPLs, would require a new recapitalization. Against the backdrop of an adverse economic environment, the SSM conducted, as part of the third programme, a comprehensive assessment and a stress test of the four banks; this identified an aggregate capital shortfall of EUR 4.4 billion under the baseline scenario and of EUR 14.4 billion under the adverse scenario. The banks subsequently laid out their respective plans to the ECB, specifying how they would address the capital requirements.

With the adoption of the relevant recapitalization law by Parliament (Law 4340/2015), the Act of the Ministerial Council (36/2.11.2015), and the ECB's approval of capital mitigating actions, which amounted to EUR 0.6 billion, the recapitalization process was completed: foreign investors participated with around EUR 5.3 billion, while banks covered an additional EUR 2.7 billion through liability management exercises (voluntary bond swap offers to bank holders). Of the four banks, Piraeus Bank and the National Bank of Greece required additional funds of EUR 5.4 billion, far less than the EUR 25 billion that had been set aside for banking recapitalization in the new Financial Assistance Facility Agreement, signed by the ESM, the Greek government, the BoG and the HFSF. Domestically, the fact that only approximately a fifth of the funds that was set aside was tapped, was hailed as a vote of confidence by private investors in the resilience of the Greek banking sector.

The ESM Board of Directors authorized two disbursements on 1 and 8 December 2015 (EUR 2.72 billion for the capital needs of Piraeus Bank and EUR 2.71 billion for National Bank of Greece respectively; European Commission 2015a, 2015b) on the basis of a Commission report which confirmed that the capital injection could be granted as a precautionary recapitalization within the meaning of the BRRD.[14] The government transferred the ESM notes to the HFSF, which received common shares and other securities in the recapitalized banks in exchange for the assistance. The third round of capital raising resulted in a further significant dilution of HFSF participation in the systemic banks, since its shareholding was reduced to 11 percent in Alpha, 2.4 percent in Eurobank, 40.4 percent in NBG and 26.4 percent in Piraeus.

10.4.2 The external constraint and the domestic setting

Greece's NPLs problem meanwhile continued to grow; the economy deteriorated under the strains of austerity, uncertainty set in and deposit withdrawals continued apace. The political system's extreme polarization and the electoral pressures it generated allowed bank owners/stakeholders/major over-indebted companies to retain their crony links with successive governments and seek to dilute proposed change. It also fuelled debtors' resistance to settling their debts, as reforms that had been undertaken, for example, the personal insolvency law (established in 2010, and later reformed in 2013 and 2015) provided blanket protection to all, failing to draw a distinction between truly distressed borrowers and strategic defaulters. Weak institutional capacity – evidenced in the quality of lengthy legal procedures, insufficient court capacity and poor administrative performance – further encouraged debtors' hopes that they could forego payments in the expectation of more favourable settlements in the future. Against this background, corporate and household strategic defaulters have ended up constituting 20 percent of the country's NPLs (Bank of Greece 2016).

Creating a credible and effective framework has thus, following the third recapitalization round, become a central priority for Greece's creditors. Law 4354/2015 mentioned above laid the groundwork for the management of NPLs and the transfer of NPL portfolios to special purpose entities. It provided for NPL management companies to co-operate with Greek banks in order to effectively manage NPLs and achieve significant recovery rates and for the creation of a secondary market for NPLs. The Syriza-Anel government was still able to protect from sale those NPLs that were linked to primary residences with a taxable value under EUR 140,000 until June 2016. The government also extended, for a 3-year period, the application of law 4307/2014 (so-called 'Dendias law'), which provided incentives for SMEs to reach settlement agreements with their creditors. It introduced amendments that would enable the existing law to operate as the main framework for NPLs resolution (Parliamentary Budget Office 2016), thus overriding the Memorandum commitment to develop a market for NPLs.

The Institutions however asked Greece to sign a Supplemental Memorandum of Understanding on 16 June 2016. This was required in the context of the government's poor record in implementing the recently agreed programme. On the NPLs front, amendments to Law 4354/2015 set the stage for a radically new regime. The liberalization of the sale and management of all performing and non-performing loans, except those secured by primary residences with an objective value of the property below 140,000 euros exempted until 1 January 2018, was to be 'immediate'[15] (Supplemental MoU 2016, p. 21), paving the path for a Greek NPLs market. Other 'prior actions' required were: a reform of the out-of-court procedure; the improvement of the judicial infrastructure in terms of legislation, the judiciary system and law enforcement; and a reform of the tax treatment of loan write-offs and the adoption of a new corporate insolvency law. In this context, the Bank of Greece was to implement a framework of operational targets and monitoring of NPL resolution strategies for all Greek banks.[16]

The issue of Greece's weak institutional capacity, and how it translated into longer periods of implementation, remained largely unaddressed. The effectiveness of the insolvency and enforcement regimes has been undermined by the judicial system's backward technology and data systems, as well as inefficient bureaucracy. Litigation has been exceedingly time-consuming, providing creditors with very low returns; debtors on the other hand have not considered bankruptcy a credible option and have thus tended to resist reasonable restructuring offers by creditors (Potamitis 2015). Inadequate insolvency administrators have slowed down system operations, while out-of-court debt restructuring has been bogged down by complicated procedures that discourage parties to negotiate enforceable solutions to corporate indebtedness. In effect, in the presence of half-baked new procedures, the country's prior experience of moratoria and absence of sanctions suggested that bad debtors would end up with better deals if they forewent the new mediation channels, in court and out of court.

Meanwhile, the Bank of Greece, together with the SSM, has introduced a framework to monitor banks' strategies and performance against so-called 'Key Performance Indicators' (KPIs) (Supplemental MoU 2016, p. 22). These indicators require banks to reduce their NPLs by around 40 percent by 2019. The idea of KPIs first surfaced in June 2014, when banks were supposed to begin 'gradual reporting under these KPIs by June 2014, with full reporting to commence from end-2014' (IMF 2014, p. 178). No such reporting has been documented to date. Bringing in the SSM and putting on the table penalties, both regulatory and administrative that would occur in the case of missed targets, is expected to overcome previous reform resistance.

10.4.3 *The political economy of NPL management in Greece*

Three rounds of recapitalizations and substantive liquidity support from the ECB have yet to imbue confidence in the banking sector. Although the 2015 recapitalization helped bring banks' capital ratios from 8 percent Common Equity Tier 1 (CET1) in mid-2015 to around 18 percent at end-September 2016, the quality of capital is weak, half of which comprised of deferred tax assets (DTAs), representing contingent liabilities of the state. Capital controls have been loosened, yet they remain in force on a number of cash transactions, including withdrawal ceilings or the transfer of funds abroad. Governance issues persist unresolved; political interference in the HFSF has not been contained, as evidenced in the way a number of appointments and dismissals have been handled by the Ministry of Finance, and recent legislation tightening eligibility for bank boards has not been fully implemented. The ECB has restored Greek banks' eligibility for monetary policy operations but has not added Greece to its Quantitative Easing (QE) programme. Non-performing loans have continued to rise reaching the second highest level in the Eurozone, just behind Cyprus. NPLs constitute 45 percent of total loans in the third quarter of 2016, almost four times as high as in 2010. Provisioning stands at 50 percent of total NPLs (IMF 2017).

While in Portugal strengthened government capacity together with broad cross-party cooperation allowed for the development of a NPLs resolution framework – however rudimentary, in Greece collateral liquidation was discouraged, the household insolvency law was inefficiently implemented, blanket moratoria on residential property debt were extended, no secondary market for NPLs was created and the tax regime and the large volume of arrears to the public sector gave little incentive to banks to proceed with restructuring (ECB 2016). The high government turnover of the period contributed to inaction or even mismanagement of 'reforms' that emanated 'from above'. Since 2009, Greece has had seven governments, their ideological profile ranging from the centre right and the centre left, to the far left and nationalist right; a technocratic and two caretaker governments have also held power.

A 'rapid and decisive reduction of NPLs' was a key objective in the three Memoranda, yet it never made it into any party platform or programme. Regardless of political orientation, governments failed to make the case for NPLs resolution on the grounds of resuming credit and growth. Interestingly, in Greek public discourse, democratic politics was described as having bowed down to the diktats of external strategies and democratic 'decisions' were reduced to attempts to acquiesce financial markets. In reality, governments were both able to maintain a suboptimal status quo and to over-ride conditionality, protecting the debtors that stood to lose from a faster NPLs resolution process. With few variations, they signalled that the emerging framework was malleable to political 'fine-tuning' and that the protection of the broadest range of debtors possible remained paramount, even if it included strategic defaulters. It could be argued that the more national politicians discarded programme ownership, the more democratic politics usurped itself.

Elections brought to power a coalition government, 'Syriza (Coalition of the Radical Left) – and Anel (Independent Greeks) which, as in the Portuguese case, promised the end of austerity. Syriza, the senior partner, had actively campaigned against the MoU, and had promised to 'tear it up with one law and one article' once in power. Capitalizing on popular discontent, the protest movement that benefited most from the destruction of the Socialist Party quickly cemented its electoral appeal as the alternative pole to the two-party system. While in Portugal the Socialist Party co-operated with parties to its Left, Syriza's bid to become the first Left government of Greece led it to forge an 'unholy alliance' with the far-right Anel party. The two parties shared a background of anti-liberalism and Euroscepticism, thrived on anti-establishment rhetoric and capitalized on the pre-existing discourse of national populism (Petsinis 2017).

Elected as an outsider, the Syriza party quickly became an insider. It was more politically rentable to continue along the set path, where pay-offs were known, and the incentives to change the *status quo* were limited. It took another crisis, Greece's near exit from the Euro in August 2015, before a renewed attempt was made to tackle the NPL problem. The Institutions however *also* stuck to their set path of building up the institutional framework and creating the incentives for it to be employed by public and private creditors. Even if a clear sequencing of reforms was not really available, performance goals goaded relevant legislation, and compensated for the fact that Greece remained a laggard in upgrading its technical capacity – in spite of the technical assistance that it received from the IMF and from Eurozone countries facing similar issues (ECB 2016).

Today, secondary legislation is pending on a number of reforms, including electronic auctions under the Code of Civil Procedure (CCP); the out-of-court procedure and pre-bankruptcy process lack institutional traction, discouraging affected parties to engage with them; strategic defaults, which are estimated to account for 20 percent of delinquent loans, have not been addressed. The Government Council on Private Debt, which was created in 2013 as a comprehensive mechanism for the effective management of NPLs, has been dormant. Changes to its composition and support structures induced by programme conditions remain cosmetic.[17] The Council has limited itself to rubber-stamping ministerial decisions.

On the positive side, the implementation of even partial reforms induced further reforms (Abiad and Mody 2003). The enhanced supervisory framework for NPL management, for example, materialized, following the BOG's decision in 2014 to introduce a rulebook for the management of loans in arrears and NPLs, together with a guideline that required banks to define resolution procedures with distressed borrowers in order to standardize the loan workout process. In turn, the third MoU has been instrumental in producing a large number of improvements, including quantifiable targets and a NPLs market to complement the restructuring efforts of banks.

10.5 Conclusion: Portugal, Greece and lessons for policy design

High and rising levels of NPLs have become a source of systemic risk, both in Greece and in Portugal. While at different stages of NPLs accumulation, both countries have been provided with a road map for reform. Whether this is credible and whether it can deliver, depends heavily on the broader institutional context – the integrity of the legal and judicial process, and the effectiveness of the enforcement regimes – the emergence and actual operation of a secondary market for NPLs, the supervision of the SSM *and* economic conditions on the ground. Political stability is obviously critical to enhance reform progress and help increase confidence in the resolution path taken.

As suggested in this chapter, the Portuguese and Greek cases differ along a number of dimensions. First, in Greece, the crisis and the external intervention served to speed up reform legislation (after long periods of inertia), but failed to trigger an equivalent fast pace implementation effect. In Portugal it was the prevention of a future crisis that acted as a sufficient incentive/constraint on policy makers' actions.

Second, Portugal offered a good example of the fact that the Troika is not necessary for the implementation of reforms. Most relevant reforms were undertaken following the country's exit from the programme and during post-surveillance. Conversely, in Greece, the bailout programmes and in particular the third programme created a critical layer of pressures, as they linked NPLs resolution strategies with timetables, key performance indicators, and prior actions that determined the country's access to bailout funding.

Third, the two countries also differed in terms of the key issue of 'ownership'. Portuguese governments of the period, including the PS anti-austerity minority one, could achieve a political consensus behind a platform of reforms. In Greece, the absence of political consensus and governments' near universal stance of protecting all debtors including strategic defaulters, regardless of income or other criteria, contributed to the banks' very slow pace of balance sheet repair.

Fourth, technical capacity was a crucial constraint for Greece, but less so for Portugal, which had a previous history of reforms. The haphazard approach to insolvency and enforcement issues, combined with the low efficiency of the public administration and the legal system significantly inhibited banks' ability to reduce their NPL stock.

Overall, strategies to reduce NPLs in Portugal and Greece provide a number of lessons for policy design.

(1) Initial conditions, including fiscal constraints or a substantial private debt overhang, do affect policy design and, in fact, may preclude the appropriate sequencing and pacing that would theoretically make adjustment smoother and fairer. To temper their effect, front-loaded reforms (for example, in Portugal the early intervention framework was strengthened and the insolvency law amended), can help restore confidence and contain the cost of failure where it is predicted to be high (Dornbusch 1991). Back-loading reforms (for example, the creation of a NPLs market in Greece) make for a smoother adjustment path but run the risk of reform fatigue, inertia setting in or the re-empowerment of bad debtors.

(2) Even if a 'one size fits all' approach (Rodrik 2007) constitutes the only available option (in both Portugal and Greece 'a comprehensive strategy to address NPLs' was to expedite the very slow NPLs resolution processes), the Institutions should calibrate it, once basic reforms have taken off.

Otherwise, there is a danger that, as in the case of Portugal, 'the most effective policies' are left undefined (European Commission 2016). The correct approach should involve a strategy for upgrading technical capacity, bringing in the widest range possible of public and private debt holders, catering for the large universe of SMEs and creating pro-reform constituencies that have a stake in out of court and in court structures working.

(3) The distribution of benefits that arise from reform should be made clear and transparent. In both Portugal and Greece, policy makers failed to explain that timely NPLs resolution would be beneficial for society as a whole, yielding positive distributional dividends by favouring small enterprises and households. While in Portugal politicians paid lip service to 'efficiency' and 'performance' targets in the hope that expected spillovers would acquiesce financial markets, in Greece, strategic defaulters and zombie firms were protected at the expense of consistent borrowers and healthy firms.

(4) The Institutions' 'external constraint' dimension was at its most effective during crisis episodes (for example, Greece's near exit from the euro in the summer of 2015), during financing gaps (when repayment of loans was not available without the disbursement of bailout funds) and when reform objectives clearly required the design of a new framework, such as a secondary market for NPLs. Allowing for Greece's special circumstances, conditionality would have yielded better results if it had been applied across a set of clear and visible targets that would garner, in turn, the support of interested stakeholders and provide policy makers with a positive reform narrative in public debate.

(5) Addressing democratic legitimacy concerns and ascertaining the appropriate role of governing majorities/parliaments should be analyzed on a case by case basis. In Greece, for example, maintaining the status quo, including loopholes to undermine passed legislation on enforcement and bankruptcy regimes, was a consistent government preference, hence, one would assume, in line with democratic rule. In Portugal, the entire political class had 'internalized' the constraints associated with membership in a Union that remained vulnerable to changing market sentiments and where self-fulfilling multiple equilibria arose (De Grauwe 2011). NPLs strategies were thus viewed from the perspective of reducing the fragility of the banking sector and the unwelcome attention of the markets.

(6) Ownership is critical for sustaining the reform drive. Although in Portugal the current resolution framework continues to miss an unambiguous mandate to maximize value – by selling assets or guaranteeing that foreclosure and bankruptcy processes are functioning (European Commission 2016), the political consensus that has formed regarding the necessity of banks to manage the NPLs on their balance sheets has prodded the process forward. Greece's entire political class, on the other hand, has yet to acknowledge the link between high NPLs and weak credit and GDP growth, shying away from a national platform that would have produced a better implementation schedule, dispensed with moratoria early on and penalized strategic defaulters.

Notes

1 Non-performing loans are defined as loans that are 90 days or more past due, unlikely to be repaid in full without using collateral and impaired according to accounting rules, as well loans that have been restructured for less than a year.

2 In Portugal, GDP increased by 1.4 percent in 2016 and the positive carryover is expected to improve the growth rate to 1.8 percent in 2017 before slowing to 1.6 percent in 2018. Greece, on the other hand, fell back into recession. European Commission, *spring 2017 Economic Forecast*.

3 The trio of institutions, the European Commission, the European Central Bank and the International Monetary Fund, that laid down stringent austerity measures in exchange for bail-outs in Greece and Portugal. Following Greece's third bailout programme, the ESM was added to the group of international lenders, with the Troika renamed as 'quartet', 'quadriga' or 'Institutions'.

4 According to the ECB Supervisory Banking Statistics.

5 This is the bridge bank that was formed when Banco Espirito Santo was wound up. Portugal's Resolution Fund provided 4.9 million euros for its capitalization, which was paid out by the Portuguese state. The loan is to be primarily reimbursed by the proceeds of the sale of assets of the Novo Banco.

6 The agreement envisages an injection of up to 2.7 billion euros in state funds and nearly as much in debt and equity.

7 Statement by then Finnish finance minister Jyrki Katainen in Leigh, P. (2011), *EU: All Portuguese Parties Must Back Bailout-austerity Package* [Online]; available from: https://euobserver.com/economic/32149 [Accessed 18 January 2017].

8 According to the IMF, 'National ownership refers to a commitment to a program of policies, by country officials who have the responsibility to formulate and carry out those policies, based on their understanding that the program is achievable and is in the country's best interest', Statement of the IMF Staff Principles Underlying the Guidelines on Conditionality, Revised, January 9, 2006.

9 *Profile-Portuguese PM and Candidate for Reelection Pedro Passos Coelho* [Online]; available from: www.reuters.com/article/portugal-leader-profile-idUSL 5N11V2PY20150930 [Accessed 18 January 2017].

10 An in-court fast-track mechanism to tackle insolvency was created in September 2012. The out-of-court tools, the Extrajudicial Company Recovery System (SIREVE) and the Special Revitalisation Procedure (PER, which involved little intervention of the judicial system) were expected to work on the basis of voluntary negotiated procedures between debtors and creditors.

11 It was formed for the parliamentary elections. It had previously fought the 2014 European Parliament elections as *Aliança Portugal (Portugal Alliance)*.

12 On December 29, 2015 the central bank, Bank of Portugal (BoP), decided to transfer five senior bonds totalling 1.985 billion euros owed by Novo Banco to Banco Espirito Santo, the bad bank holding the failed group's weak assets. When BES failed in August 2014, all shareholder and junior creditor holdings were bailed-in, while senior debt ended up with Novo. The issue became contentious due to the fact that only five select bonds were transferred to the BES bad bank out of the 52 pari passu (equal seniority and status). These were sold to institutional, as opposed to retail, investors, and were issued under Portuguese law.

13 The creation of deferred tax assets is an accounting practice allowing companies to postpone the payment of tax to the state from a loss-making year to a profit-making one, in effect offsetting losses with profits. The ECB has accepted and acknowledged that part of banks' deferred tax obligations can be used as capital that can be added to the sum used for the calculation of capital adequacy indices.

14 Under the Bank Resolution and Recovery Directive, a bank in need of state aid has to be put in resolution. Only in narrowly defined exceptional conditions can state aid be

provided to a bank outside resolution. Such an exception is defined in Article 32(4)(d)(iii) BRRD and is referred to as 'precautionary recapitalization'.
15 The only loans that were temporarily exempted were those secured by primary residences with an objective value of the property below EUR 140.000; liberalization for these categories of loans would enter into force on 1 January 2018. The authorities were also to adjust related secondary legislation to the amended Law 4354/2015 and set up the related consultative committee by the Government to fully operationalize the licensing framework of credit servicing firms; they would also amend, as part of the tax policy reforms, the income tax law to ensure that for a specified period of time debt write-offs as result of restructuring agreements are not considered as taxable income of the borrower.
16 The Bank of Greece had introduced a number of Executive Committee Acts: 42/2014 on the supervisory framework for non-performing exposures, introducing a harmonized framework and accelerating banks' efforts regarding efficient NPE management; ECA 47/2015, establishing a comprehensive prudential reporting framework for NPEs; the Code of Conduct on NPL management by virtue of Decision 116/25.8.2014, issued by the Bank's Credit and Insurance Committee, in the context of Law 4224/2013.
17 The Council was created with law 4224/2013. The 6/17.2.2014 Ministerial Decision established it; a new Ministerial Decision of 20/14.8.2015 changed the composition of the Council's members. The BoG set up a project management office in December 2015 to support the Council (Report on Greece's compliance with the second set of milestones of December 2015'; available from: http://ec.europa.eu/economy_finance/assistance_eu_ms/greek_loan_facility/pdf/2nd_set_milestones_note_to_ewg_en.pdf, December 2015). A year and a half later, the Supplemental Memorandum called for a Secretariat to support the Government Council on Private Debt.

Bibliography

Abdul, A., and Ashoka, M. (2003), Financial Reform: *What Shakes it? What Shapes it?* IMF Working Paper. WP/03/70. [Online]. Available from: http://voxeu.org/article/reform-and-be-re-elected [Accessed 17 January 2017].

Aiyar, S., Bergthaler, W., Garrido, J. M., Ilyina, A., Jobst, A., Kang, K. D., Kovtun, D., Liu, Y., Monaghan, M., and Moretti, M. (2015) *A Strategy for Resolving Europe's Problem Loans*. IMF. Staff Discussion Note No. 15/19.

Alesina, A., and Drazen, A. (1991) Why Are Stabilizations Delayed? *American Economic Review*, 81(5), 1170–1189.

Bale, T., and Bergman, T. (2006) Captives No Longer, But Servants Still? Contract Parliamentarism and the New Minority Governance in Sweden and New Zealand. *Government and Opposition*, 41(3), 422–449.

Bank of Greece (2012) *Report on the Recapitalisation and Restructuring of the Greek Banking Sector*, December 2012. [Online]. Available from: http://www.bankofgreece.gr/BogEkdoseis/Report_on_the_recapitalisation_and_restructuring.pdf [Accessed 19 February 2017].

Bank of Greece (2016) *Monetary Policy Report 2015–2016*. [Online]. Available from: http://www.bankofgreece.gr/Pages/en/Bank/News/PressReleases/DispItem.aspx?Item_ID=5365&List_ID=1af869f3-57fb-4de6-b9ae-bdfd83c66c95&Filter_by=DT [Accessed 21 February 2017].

Bank of Greece (2017) *Speech by the Governor of the Bank of Greece Yannis Stournaras at the International Forum of Independent Audit Regulators (IFIAR)*, 8 February. [Online]. Available from: http://www.bankofgreece.gr/Pages/en/Bank/News/Speeches/

DispItem.aspx?Item_ID=408&List_ID=b2e9402e-db05-4166-9f09-e1b26a1c6f1b [Accessed 21 February 2017].

Boughton, J. (2003) *Who's in Charge? Ownership and Conditionality in IMF-Supported Programmes*. IMF. Working Paper No. 03/91.

Bouis, R., Causa, O., Demmou, L., Duval, R., and Zdzienicka, A. (2012) *The Short-Term Effects of Structural Reforms: An Empirical Analysis*. OECD Economics Department. Working Paper No. 949.

Bouveret, A., Yackovlev, I., Bergthaler, W., and Queyranne, M. (2016) Dealing With Private Debt Overhang: Corporate Debt Restructuring. In: Gershenson D., Jaeger, A. and Lall, S. (eds.) *From Crisis to Convergence: Charting a Course for Portugal*. IMF. European Departmental Paper No. 16/02.

Buti, M., Turrini, A., and van den Noord, P. (2014) *Reform and Be Re-elected: Evidence From the Post-crisis Period*. VoxEU. [Online]. Available from: http://voxeu.org/article/reform-and-be-re-elected [Accessed 17 January 2017].

De Grauwe, P. (2011) *The Governance of a Fragile Eurozone*. CEPS. Working Document No. 346.

Dornbusch, R. (1991) Credibility and Stabilisation. *Quarterly Journal of Economics*, 106(August), pp. 837–850.

Drazen, A. (2002) *Conditionality and Ownership in IMF Lending: A Political Economy Approach*. IMF. Staff Papers No. 49 Special Issue.

Duval, R., and Furceri, D. (2016) *IMF Survey: Structural Reforms in Advanced Economies: Pressing Ahead and Doing them Right*. IMF Research. [Online]. Available from: www.imf.org/external/pubs/ft/survey/so/2016/res040616a.htm [Accessed 10 July 2016].

Dyson, K., and Featherstone, K. (1996) Italy and EMU as a 'Vincolo Esterno': Empowering the Technocrats, Transforming the State. *South European Society and Politics*, 1(2), 272–299.

EBA (2016) *EBA Report on the Dynamics and Drivers of Non-Performing Exposures in the EU Banking Sector*. London, EBA.

ECB (2016) *Stocktake of National Supervisory Practices and Legal Frameworks Related to NPLs*. ECB. [Online]. Available from: www.bankingsupervision.europa.eu/legal-framework/publiccons/pdf/npl/stock_taking.en.pdf [Accessed 15 October 2016].

Eichenblaum, M., Rebelo, S., and de Resende, C. *The Portuguese Crisis and the IMF*. IMF Independent Evaluation Office. BP/16–02/05.

Espinoza, R., and Prasad, A. (2010) *Nonperforming Loans in the GCC Banking System and their Macroeconomic Effects*. IMF. Working Paper No. 10/244.

European Commission (2016) *Post-Programme Surveillance Report*, Portugal, Summer 2016, Institutional Paper 36, September 2016

European Commission (2017a) *Staff Working Document, Country Report Portugal 2017 including an In-depth Review on the Prevention and Correction of Macroeconomic Imbalances*. Accompanying the document COMMUNICATION FROM THE COMMISSION TO THE EUROPEAN PARLIAMENT, THE COUNCIL, THE EUROPEAN CENTRAL BANK AND THE EUROGROUP 2017 European Semester: Assessment of progress on structural reforms, prevention and correction of macroeconomic imbalances, and results of in-depth reviews under Regulation (EU) No 1176/2011 {COM(2017) 90 final} {SWD(2017) 67 final to SWD(2017) 93 final}. European Commission. SWD/2017/087 final.

European Commission (2017b) *2017 European Economic Forecast-Spring 2017*. European Commission. Institutional Paper No. 53.

European Commission (2017c) *Country Report Portugal 2017, Including an In-Depth Review on the Prevention and Correction of Macroeconomic Imbalances*. European Commission. Commission Staff Working Document SWD 87 final.

Fernandes, J. (2016) The Seeds for Party System Change? The 2015 Portuguese General Election. *West European Politics*, 39(4), 890–900.

Fernandes, J., and Jalali, C. (2016) A Resurgent Presidency? Portuguese Semi-Presidentialism and the 2016 Elections. *South European Society and Politics*, 22(1), 121–138.

Fernandez, R., and Rodrik, D. (1991) Resistance to Reform: Status Quo Bias in the Presence of Individual-specific Uncertainty. *The American Economic Review*, 81(5), 1146–1155.

IMF (2014) *Greece Fifth Review Under the Extended Arrangement Under the Extended Fund Facility, and Request for Waiver of Nonobservance of Performance Criterion and Rephasing of Access*. IMF. Country Report No. 14/151.

IMF (2016) *Portugal: Concluding Statement of the Fourth Post-Programme Monitoring and 2016 Article IV Consultations Discussions*. IMF. [Online]. Available from: https://www.imf.org/external/np/ms/2016/063016a.htm [Accessed 7 July 2016].

IMF (2017) *Greece Article IV Consultation-Press Release; Staff Report; And Statement By the Executive Director for Greece*. IMF. Country Report No. 17/40.

IMF European Department (2015) *Euro Area Policies: Selected Issues*. IMF. Country Report No. 16/220.

Katsikas, D. (2017) Designing Structural Reforms in Times of Crisis: Lessons From the Past. In: Manasse, P. and Katsikas, D. (eds.) *Structural Reforms in Southern Europe*, London, Routledge.

Klein, N. (2013) *Non-performing Loans in CESEE: Determinants and Impact on Macroeconomic Performance*. IMF. Working Paper No. 13/72.

Monokroussos, P., Thomakos, D., and Alexopoulos, T. A. (2016) *Explaining Non-Performance Loans in Greece: A Comparative Study on the Effects of Recession and Banking Practices*. Hellenic Observatory Papers on Greece and Southeast Europe. GreeSE Paper No. 101.

Moody's (2016) *Banking System Outlook-Portugal*. October. [Online]. Available from: https://www.moodys.com/viewresearchdoc.aspx?docid=PBC_1042052 [Accessed 21 January 2017].

Moravcsik, A. (1994) *Why the European Community Strengthens the State: Domestic Politics and International Cooperation*. Center for European Studies. Working Paper No. 52.

Nkusu, M. (2011) *Nonperforming Loans and Macrofinancial Vulnerabilities in Advanced Economies*. IMF. Working Paper No. 11/161.

Nsouli, M. S. M., Rached, M. M., and Funke, M. N. (2002) *The Speed of Adjustment and the Sequencing of Economic Reforms: Issues and Guidelines for Policymakers*. IMF. Working Paper No. 02/132.

Parliamentary Budget Office (2016) *Quarterly Report January-March 2016*, Athens, Greece, June.

Petsinis (2017) *Syriza and ANEL: A Match Made in Greece*. [Online]. Available from: www.opendemocracy.net/can-europe-make-it/vassilis-petsinis/syriza-and-anel-match-made-in-greece [Accessed January 2017].

Potamitis, S. (2015) *The Mounting 'Non-Performing Loan' Problem in Greece*. Eurofenix, Spring 2015. [Online]. Available from: http://globalinsolvency.com/sites/all/files/greece_2_article_eurofenix_spring_2015.pdf [Accessed 21 January 2017].

Rodrik, D. (2007) World Too Complex for One-Size-Fits-All Models. *Post-Autistic Economics Review*, issue no. 44, 9 December 2007, pp. 73–74 [Online]. Available from: http://www.paecon.net/PAEReview/issue44/Rodrik44.pdf [Accessed 2 March 2017].

Supplemental Memorandum of Understanding (2016). [Online]. Available from: http://ec.europa.eu/economy_finance/assistance_eu_ms/greek_loan_facility/pdf/smou_en.pdf [Accessed 17 July 2016].

11 The restructuring of Spain's banking system

A political economy approach

Miguel Otero-Iglesias and Federico Steinberg

11.1 Introduction

This chapter examines the political economy of the restructuring of Spain's banking sector, which took place between 2007 and 2014, from the beginning of the global financial crisis to the completion of the Spanish bailout programme.

In the first years of the international financial crisis (2007–09), Spanish financial institutions were not as severely affected as in other advanced countries. However, their apparent success was short-lived. The implosion of the real estate bubble, the depth of the double-dip recession that the Spanish economy experienced between 2009 and 2012, the slow reaction and misdiagnoses by the political authorities in the early and medium stages of the crisis, the weaknesses in the regulatory and supervisory frameworks and the bad practices for lending (especially in the savings banks, known as *Cajas de Ahorro*, or in short: *Cajas*), all help to explain this reversal. In addition, institutional design failures of the Economic and Monetary Union (EMU) aggravated the consequences of the crisis as Spain experienced intense capital outflows as a result of contagion from Greece.

While there were elements of the crisis that were particular to Spain (for instance a specific regulatory and supervisory framework for the *Cajas*), the Spanish banking crisis was in many ways a traditional one, driven by excessive leverage due to a real-estate bubble, and by banks' over-reliance on funding from the wholesale international markets. Indeed, paraphrasing Reinhart and Rogoff (2009), this crisis 'was not different'.

As we will explain in this chapter, the crisis was however particularly intense and had unique features. Spanish financial institutions eventually required over 150 billion euros in public support (42 billion euros of which came from the bailout), the financial sector was completely restructured and most of the centennial *Cajas* disappeared.

The chapter starts with an analysis of the Spanish financial sector before and during the crisis. It then explores the political economy of the banking reform by focusing on how different actors with divergent objectives worsened the crisis and delayed reform, at a huge cost for society. The final section extracts the main lessons.

11.2 The evolution of the Spanish financial sector in the context of the crisis

In the run up to the global financial crisis, Spanish banks had a 'traditional' business model. This however, did not prevent a securitization frenzy during the years that preceded the crisis, nor a significant expansion of the number of branches (particularly among the *Cajas*) and an expansion of credit, largely financed through tapping the wholesale market for funding. These elements made this 'traditional' business model vulnerable.

In Spain, around 65 percent of banks' assets were loans to customers and government securities, which at that time were considered among the safest possible investments. More than 50 percent of the lending to non-financial corporations was loans to property developers, especially by the *Cajas*. Moreover, loans made to consumers for the purpose of house purchases were over 70 percent of the total loans to consumers. This led to an increase in house prices of over 180 percent between 1997 and 2007 (Royo 2013).

Another important development in the decade prior to the crisis was the growth of securitization (Losada López 2006). According to data from the *European Securitization Forum*, by 2005 securitization in Spain represented 13.3 percent of the European total (the second largest after the UK's 45.5 percent), and the total value of securitized assets multiplied almost by six between 2001 and 2005, reaching €71.75 billion. Securitization weakened credit risk controls in the years leading to the crisis in Spain, but also across Europe (Carbó-Valverde et al. 2011, p. 11).

Besides these general features, it is important to highlight that Spain had a dual banking system of (private) commercial banks and (public) savings banks, the *Cajas*, which were not listed on the stock market and accounted for half of the financial sector's assets. They did not have formal shareholders, did not distribute profits and were governed by a broad range of private and public stakeholders. The *Cajas* were peculiar credit institutions, a combination of a commercial bank and a foundation, which dedicated a significant portion of their profits (usually over 20 percent) to social causes.

The *Cajas* became the instrument to fund the many real-estate projects that created the prosperity that helped local government officials get re-elected (Santos 2014). They were regulated by both the national government and by regional governments, and the Bank of Spain had limited supervisory competences over them. This complicated their oversight, and interference from political stakeholders also adversely affected their financial stability. In the end, the politization of the *Cajas* was a crucial issue to explain their actions in the years prior to the crisis. The more politicized the leadership, the worst their performance (Garicano 2012).[1]

11.2.1 Enter the global financial crisis

Initially, after the bankruptcy of Lehman Brothers in September 2008, Spanish banks, unlike their counterparts in most parts of the advanced world, seemed to weather the crisis rather well. They experienced no major losses and required no state recapitalization. This positive performance can be explained by the implementation of a 'dynamic provisioning system', which established counter-cyclical capital buffers for banks (Fernández de Lis and García-Herrero 2012). The central bank also prevented banks from developing highly complex and synthetic off-balance sheet activities, which sunk banks elsewhere.

In late 2009, however, major financial problems began for many of the *Cajas*. They had financed real-estate developers that started to go bankrupt and they found increasing difficulties in accessing wholesale markets to roll over their debts. In response, in 2009 the government created the Fund for Orderly Bank Restructuring (FROB in Spanish) to recapitalize them. The *Cajas* were particularly dependent on wholesale funding, which had been central to their efforts to expand and strengthen their national presence after the 1988 Royal Decree that lifted their geographical limitations.[2] Consequently, their market share measured in terms of total assets increased from around 20 percent in the 1980s to 40 percent in 2010. Most of them did not have the financial muscle or technical expertise to undertake such an expansion (Garicano 2012).

The real-estate boom-bust cycle, which materialized in particular in the *Cajas*, exposed the weaknesses in the policy and regulatory frameworks, as well as the sector's over-reliance on wholesale funding. By the end of 2011, land prices, adjusted for inflation, had fallen around 30 percent from their 2007 peak, and home prices were down by up to 22 percent. As a result, the quality of Spanish banks' assets plummeted. At that point, Spanish financial institutions had accumulated €405 billion in loans associated with the real-estate sector given to developers and companies, and, almost half of them were classified as troubled assets by the Bank of Spain (Mars 2012). As credit dried up, it affected the liquidity of the *Cajas* and in some cases their solvency. Finally, Spain suffered intense capital outflows as contagion from the Greek crisis intensified. These outflows were mitigated by the TARGET2[3] balance of the Eurosystem, which allowed the financial sector to maintain adequate levels of liquidity.

By June 2012 the situation had become untenable and Spain, whose borrowing costs had skyrocketed, was forced to seek a rescue amid growing fears that the financial crisis could drag down its entire economy and lead to a sovereign crisis that threatened the euro.

The Eurogroup offered to bailout the financial system with up to €100 billion, of which €42 billion ended up being used. Spain had already adopted several financial reforms, but the conditionality attached to the rescue triggered the most aggressive one, which included 32 specific measures to clean up the financial system. Insolvent banks were recapitalized, a 'bad bank' was created and the process of mergers and acquisitions was completed, reducing the number of *Cajas* from 45 to nine (which by now are almost all banks). Finally, the European bailout established the bail-in of some junior creditors. It was the first time that hair-cuts to creditors were used in the crisis, and it was subsequently used in the 2013 Cyprus bailout, and latter incorporated into the rules of the European Baking Union through the Bank Resolution and Recovery Directive (BRRD).

By 2014, access to credit was largely restored. Yet, as in most other countries, the crisis led to a larger concentration in the financial sector, which will intensify further the challenge of 'too big to fail'.

11.3 The political economy of the Spanish banking crisis: explaining the delay

One of the most striking factors of the Spanish banking crisis was the delay in making the key decisions to tackle the problems. Moreover, it was only when the Spanish government requested external help that the full restructuring of the financial sector took place. Limited action from 2007 to 2012 meant that banking losses were much larger than if the authorities had intervened earlier on, and consequently, by the time the restructuring of the largest institutions took place, the country's fiscal position had severely weakened.

As Terzi and Katsikas explain in their chapters in this volume, the policies that are required to solve a crisis have redistributive consequences. Therefore, conflicting domestic interests make political decisions more difficult and, in certain contexts, block solutions and delay actions. As Frieden (2015, p. 11) highlights: 'Especially in the case of financial crises, delay can be extremely costly. Bad debts accumulate, dragging the economy further and further down and retarding a possible recovery'.

In the Spanish case, the concept of 'the power of inaction', as developed by Woll (2014), is particularly helpful. She explains that we need to take into account but go beyond the lobbying capacity and institutional centrality of the banking sector in order to understand the massive bail-outs of the financial system that happened in Europe and the United States after the global financial crisis. The institutional importance of the banking sector is key in any capitalist society and therefore it will always receive special treatment from politicians, particularly in the banking-based financial systems predominant in Continental Europe, including Spain. Thus, the financial sector has structural power because the state depends on it.

The importance of the banking sector for the society develops through a socialization process and, ironically, in moments of crisis, it is reflected not so much in the capacity of the bankers to proactively determine outcomes but rather in that they can afford to act passively because they know that the government will step in to stabilize the sector. This is essentially the power of inaction. As Woll puts it (2014, pp. 58–59):

> During a banking crisis, neither the financial industry nor the government wants to see the economy collapse. But if the financial industry knows that the government will not let this happen, their best strategy is to be uncoordinated and benefit from a bank bailout scheme financed entirely through the public budget. [In other words], because of their structural importance the capacity to be collectively inactive determines the degree of domination of a small banking minority over the general public.

After analyzing several banking bail-outs that took place after the collapse of Lehman Brothers, Woll comes to the conclusion that private participation (and therefore a fairer burden sharing) in the rescue operations was higher where the biggest banks were threatened by the crisis; this was specially the case in France and Denmark, and less so in the United States, UK and Germany. This leads her to state (Woll 2014, p. 172):

> what is pivotal is the health of the leading financial institutions. If the most significant ones are healthy or a significant portion of a country's financial industry has no need for government support, individually, this is likely to lead to collective inaction. The healthy institutions can simply walk away from the negotiation table.

We argue below that this is precisely what happened in Spain since the *Cajas* were in trouble while Banco Santander and BBVA, by far the largest two banks, were not.

11.3.1 Key actors and their objectives

Two different governments, one from the centre-left Socialist Party (PSOE) led by José Luis Rodriguez Zapatero and one from the centre-right Conservative Party (PP) led by Mariano Rajoy, were in power during the global financial crisis, its aftermath and the restructuring of the Spanish financial system. The policies implemented through the crisis aimed at minimizing the use of taxpayer's money for bailing out banks, because helping banks was expected to be very unpopular among voters. Citizens' resistance to banking rescues is a universal phenomenon, but in the case of Spain the electorate was even less prepared to accept it since the authorities had repeatedly stated that the Spanish banking system was one of the most resilient in the world. For instance, President Zapatero said in New York in September 2008, just after the collapse of Lehman Brothers, that 'Spain probably has the most solid financial system of the international community. It has an internationally celebrated model of regulation and supervision for its quality and rigor' (Expansión 2008).

Moreover, both the socialist and the conservative repeatedly emphasized that the restructuring of the Spanish financial system should not entail the use of public funds. This led them to pursue strategies that aimed at reducing capital needs (especially in the *Cajas*), for example by promoting mergers and acquisitions, and by encouraging the entry of private capital in the weak institutions. Unfortunately, as we will see, these strategies subsequently proved to be misguided.

Another important motivation that guided Zapatero's PSOE governments (in)actions at the beginning of the Spanish crisis was to maintain the credibility that the Spanish financial system had acquired during the early phases of the recession through the practices of dynamic provisioning (counter-cyclical capital buffers for banks), which was widely regarded as an example of good supervision, namely at the G-20 meetings of 2008 and 2009. Openly recognizing the vulnerabilities of the system would have generated a loss of international prestige for Spain at a time when the country was undertaking intensive diplomatic efforts to become a permanent member of the G-20, and would have possibly triggered dangerous capital outflows. Finally, few people in the government anticipated that the international financial crisis would become a European sovereign debt crisis in 2010, leading to a double-dip recession in Spain; nor that the external environment would make the rolling over of the *Cajas's* bad debt impossible. Hence the government favoured mergers and acquisitions rather than recapitalization or resolution. This strategy also resonated with the idea that the *Cajas* had a liquidity as opposed to a solvency problem, one that could be easily solved by the ECB and that did not require additional capital (De Juan et al. 2013).

Another crucial actor was the Bank of Spain. Its credibility was seriously damaged by the Spanish banking crisis, especially in its latest stages, when the Rajoy government decided that the task of calculating the recapitalization needs of the system would be assigned to the IMF and to private consultancy firms, rather than to the Bank of Spain's own staff. In Spain, the Governor of the Central Bank is appointed by the government, although the bank is independent by statute. And yet, as is the case with other formally independent Spanish institutions like the Constitutional Court or the Office for Competition Policy, the government exerts strong pressure on the Governors when it comes to key decisions. For instance, under the term of Jaime Caruana as Governor, the Bank's staff gave various alerts to the Board that a real estate bubble was in the making, due to excessive credit growth, between 2000 and 2006. However, no decisive action was taken (Bolaños 2011). To be fair, it is important to remember that monetary policy is decided by the ECB and not by the Bank of Spain, and that, as a consequence, real interest rates were negative in Spain for several years in the run up to the crisis.

The *Cajas*, another key actor, were highly politicized institutions, and although the Catalan *La Caixa* and the *Cajas* from the Basque Country were well-managed, most of them engaged in malpractices, did not provision for losses and expanded their activities both geographically and sectorally beyond their capacity. By doing so they became instruments of political parties and trade unions. Their main goal throughout the crisis was to maintain the *status quo*, and that required a variety of actions: from distorting financial statements, to hiding losses or exercising political influence vis-a-vis the central government to ensure that their activities were not under full scrutiny (Garicano 2012; De Juan et al. 2013).

Conversely, the big banks, especially Santander and BBVA, had relatively solid balance sheets and good management. Even though they were also exposed to real estate, they had lower levels of non-performing loans, and their international expansion ensured a diversified base for profits, which proved crucial for maintaining stable cash-flows throughout the crisis. Their main goal was to maintain their credibility and to show investors that their business model was distinct from that of the *Cajas*. Given their size and influence, the government considered essential to isolate them from the solvency problems of the rest of the system. This meant that the financial reforms aimed at increasing capital requirements were always done with the goal of not compromising their solvency. In addition, in order to protect their balance sheet, their involvement in the mergers and acquisitions process was limited.

Finally, the European institutions were also key players in the crisis. Although the lion's share of the recapitalization of the *Cajas* took place before European intervention and was financed mostly by the Spanish state through the FROB, created in 2009 (which injected 59 billion euros in the *Cajas*), European institutions required a full restructuring of the Spanish financial sector as a precondition for the bailout. They ended up providing almost 42 billion euros of the funds required for recapitalizing the *Cajas*. However, they only intervened once it was clear that the strategies undertaken by the Spanish government had failed and that the insolvency of some *Cajas* was threatening the solvency of the Spanish state and, with it, of the euro.

11.4 Turning points

Throughout the crisis, there were a number of key decisions (most of them mistakes) that determined the future evolution of events. We now review them through the lenses of the key actors involved.

11.4.1 Wrong diagnosis

Initially, the crisis was diagnosed as a temporary liquidity problem. The idea that injecting large quantities of liquidity would be enough to stabilize the situation was widely held (especially given that the ECB had been providing liquidity since 2007) in the expectation that the crisis was an Anglo-Saxon phenomenon that would not affect the Eurozone's financial system. In addition, since the position of the large Spanish banks was relatively sound, there was a resistance to increase provisions that could undermine their profits.

In this context, both the government and the Bank of Spain decided not to take decisive action at an early stage. The fact that there were no toxic assets in the banks and *Cajas's* balance sheets and the good reputation of the Bank of Spain as a supervisor contributed to the idea that Spain could overcome the collapse of the real estate bubble with a quiet and restricted process of simple consolidation, as had been the case in previous crises.

In addition, given that the Greek crisis had not yet fully materialized and that the July 2010 stress tests of the Spanish banking system did not reveal capital needs, it was 'rational' for the government to maintain its optimism and pursue a strategy of 'wait and see'. Needless to say, the *Cajas* were more than pleased with this strategy because it enabled them to continue with business as usual. The local and regional governments were also happy because they would remain in control, and BBVA and Santander were also content because they did not have to contribute to the solution of the problem.

However, this 'wait and see' strategy turned into a policy of 'extend and pretend'. In mid-2009, with the first symptoms of the European debt crisis, the collapse of *Caja Castilla La Mancha* and the double-dip recession, rolling over debt and betting on a rapid recovery were seen as the best alternative to avoid using large quantities of taxpayer's money for either nationalizations or the creation of a bad bank. As de Juan et al. (2013) critically emphasize, the prevalent attitude was to ignore the problem because there was no clear solution. Not all was inaction, though. Positive decisions during this period included the creation of the FROB in 2009 and the initial steps to merge the *Cajas* and transform them into banks.

11.4.2 Critical mistakes when addressing the problems of the Cajas

Only in early 2010 did the authorities finally realize that the crisis and the *Cajas's* mismanagement had led to substantial capital shortages that had been hidden for years by abundant liquidity and supervisory forbearance. At this point, the Bank of Spain and the government agreed on a series of mergers between the different *Cajas*.[4] The objective was to create larger institutions, which would result from the acquisition of the 'bad *Cajas*' by the 'solvent *Cajas*', to be accomplished with the minimum possible amount of public funds. It was expected that larger and stronger financial institutions would be able to attract more private capital at a later stage. This approach also diluted political tensions, since each *Caja* would be allowed to maintain its brand name and continue its activity (but in a context of a more efficient business model), thus preserving the political interests of regional governments. The *Cajas* had a peculiar legal status, since they were not private entities and had no shareholders. This implied that they could not access the private capital markets until they were transformed into banks. Thus, the merger required creating new legal entities into which the existing *Cajas* were absorbed.

Having been reluctant to acknowledge the *Cajas's* losses, the government and the Banks of Spain underestimated their capital needs for the mergers. The 'good *Cajas*' were not good enough, so once merged with the bad ones, they turned up to be large but weak banks, unable to appeal to private investors. As the European debt crisis worsened and the second recession deepened, non-performing loans rose in the banking sector undermining the solvency of most financial institutions.

The case of *Bankia* is emblematic of the government failure to deal effectively with the *Cajas*. *Bankia* resulted from the merger of *Caja Madrid* with six smaller *Cajas*. It was floated in the Spanish stock market in July 2011, and ended up requiring a 24 billion euros capital injection. This was the event that precipitated the European bailout in mid-2012. Despite the consolidation effort, mismanagement and misreporting at *Bankia* continued as before, giving rise to strong political tensions between Rodrigo Rato, *Bankia*'s President (and former Finance Minister and Managing Director of the IMF) and the leader of the PP government, Rajoy. *Bankia*'s losses only became evident once the government passed a law that required banks to raise their provisions. The government then planned to merge *Bankia* with *La Caixa*, the other large *caja*, which had a relatively sound financial position and could have absorbed most of the losses from *Bankia*, but the operation was torpedoed by political interference since *Bankia* was the main *caja* from Madrid and *La Caixa* the main financial institution from Catalonia (Sarriés Menéndez 2015).

Finally, less than two years after *Bankia* had gone public, its insolvency was disclosed and the Spanish authorities had to request their European partners a credit line of up to 100 billion euros.

11.4.3 Grey areas of the bailout

The complete restructuring of the Spanish financial system was only enacted when the European institutions entered the game. After the European Commission, the ECB and the European Stability Mechanism (ESM) signed a Memorandum of Understanding with the Spanish government, a transparent and independent audit of the financial institutions was finalized: the losses were fully recognized, and the damaged banks recapitalized by creating a 'bad bank'. All this happened in a relatively short time. The resolution lasted 18 months, ending in January 2014. In order to bypass the domestic political constraints and to force the adoption of the necessary measures, an external actor was needed. The bailout conditionality included 32 specific actions. Many features of the Spanish banking bailout were later used as a model for designing the architecture of the European Banking Union, especially the bail-in provisions, whose aim is to minimize the use of taxpayer's money.

The bailout can be regarded as a success (IMF 2014). It contributed to the stabilization of the European financial markets and triggered substantial reforms in Spain. However, it also contributed to undermine the credibility of the Bank of Spain: the conservative government deliberately did not involve the Bank of Spain in the task of assessing the capital needs of the Spanish banking system because its Governor was linked to the socialist party and there have been clashes between the Bank's Board and the Ministries of Economics and Finance. Such assessment was conducted first by the IMF first and later by two private consulting companies, Oliver Wyman and Roland Berger. By June 2012, they estimated the capital needs of the system between 51 and 62 billion euros (slightly over what was finally needed).

The Spanish government recapitalized the financial institutions by using ESM funds. It tried to convince its European partners that the best strategy would be for the ESM to directly inject funds in the troubled financial institutions. However, since the banking union was still a project, the ESM instrument for direct bank recapitalization had not been adopted yet (it was approved in December 2014), and Germany strongly opposed using European funds to purchase legacy assets. Hence, the ESM ended up making a loan to the Spanish Treasury. The loan of over 41 billion euros had 'concessional terms' (a variable interest rate of about 1 percent) and was used to recapitalize the banks through the FROB, increasing Spanish external liabilities by about 4 percent of GDP. Given that Mario Draghi, the ECB Governor, made his 'whatever it takes' speech in June 2012, which dramatically reduced risk premium on peripheral Eurozone sovereign debt, the sustainability of Spanish debt was not compromised by the ESM loan.

One of the most controversial issues of the intervention was the bail-in provision, by which junior creditors, especially holders of *participaciones preferentes* (preferred shares) suffered losses. Its goal was to reduce the use of public funds, and in fact this principle later became one of the pillars of the European Banking Union. Even though its logic is sound, especially in cases where a small number of financial institutions require recapitalization, in the event of a systemic crisis its implementation is problematic, since losses (and thus capital needs) may be very large. In the Spanish case, the bail-in process imposed hair-cuts of up to 60 percent to junior creditors, and precipitated complex litigations.

11.5 Conclusion

Between 2009 and 2013, Spain suffered its worst financial crisis in decades. Although successive governments implemented a number of gradual reforms of the financial system, the restauration of the solvency and credibility of Spanish banks required a 42 billion euros bailout from the European authorities, which triggered a complete restructuring of the financial sector and the disappearance of most of the centennial *Cajas*. The Troika, which attached harsh conditionality to the 2012 rescue package, only intervened when the mismanagement of the Spanish *Cajas* crisis threatened the stability of the euro. This 4-year delay in implementing the financial reform dramatically increased its cost.

Our analysis confirms a long-standing tenant. Financial systems collapse when they are allowed to take on too much risk and when they are not required to have sufficient capital on reserve to absorb the losses associated with their risky investments and loans (Calomiris and Haber 2014). Indeed, the crisis in Spain was rooted in policies that eroded underwriting standards and weak prudential regulation. In many Spanish *Cajas* – not so much in banks, most of which weathered the crisis rather well – there was a failure of risk management, which led to an increase in risky lending and to inadequate levels of capital cushions.

While many actors understood the risk that a potential collapse of the banking system would have represented to the Spanish economy, there was a strong sense of complacency because the country had navigated relatively unscathed the first phase of the international crisis. Some public officials understood the risks, but they either had little incentive to change the rules of the game or had not the courage to act. Politicians hoped that the economy would recover quickly after the 2009 global recession, a development that would have reduced the relative size of non-preforming loans and would have improved the solvency of the financial sector. Local authorities, some of which were responsible for the practices that nurtured the real estate bubble, did everything they could not to change the *status quo*. Bank supervisors and regulators did not act in advance in order to prevent the solvency problems of the *Cajas* due to both misjudgement and political pressure from the government. In other words, even if the costs of their inaction would potentially materialize in the future, the benefits of looking elsewhere were immediate. In particular, 'the power of inaction' (Woll 2014), and the fact that the large Spanish banks, like Santander and BBVA, had relatively solid financial positions, explain the delay in tackling the problems of the *Cajas*. As a result, the crisis was deeper, longer and costlier to solve.

Therefore, domestic political economy factors were crucial in explaining the delay of the necessary reform of the financial sector. As discussed by Katsikas in his chapter of this volume, strong opposition by public opinion to banking bailouts, together with the influence of vested interests, can block a reform. This was precisely the case in Spain. Only when the problems of some of the larger *Cajas*, especially *Bankia*, threatened the stability of the Eurozone, the European institutions intervened, and the government was forced to apply for an ESM bailout loan, which imposed a strict conditionality. Therefore, the reform was triggered by the severity of the crisis and by its international implications. The key factor that broke the political deadlock that had delayed the Spanish reform was the political pressure by the Troika, which feared an unravelling to the rest of the Eurozone.

In the broader context of this volume, the Spanish case illustrates how a series of governments with sufficient technical capacity to tackle economic reforms, and with the political will and electoral mandate to implement substantial changes in areas as diverse as the pension system, the labour market, taxation and other areas of the economy, in a moment of acute economic crisis, were unable to successfully implement a financial reform that required the use of abundant public funds, without the pressure from external actors, due to domestic political constraints, the power of the financial lobby and the existence of multiple veto players.

The lesson is therefore that public authorities need to act decisively (procrastination only makes things worse) when economic and financial indicators show that risks of default are mounting, and perhaps more importantly, they need to be able and willing to withstand the political pressures that protect the *status quo*. This requires full independence of supervisory and regulatory institutions. Something that did not occur in Spain, as clearly shown by the imputation of the head of supervision at the Bank of Spain, and his immediate subordinates, in relation to the IPO of Bankia, by the Spanish High Court in February 2017 (De Barrón 2017). In hindsight, another lesson is that banking supervision needs to develop several methodologies. Stress tests based on models are certainly necessary, but *in situ* supervision of balance sheets, risk assessments, operations and governance structures should also be a must.

The Spanish case also provides important lessons for the newly created European Banking Union. The first is that regionally fragmented oversight of the financial sector is problematic. One of the biggest problems for the Spanish authorities was to deal with the dual regulatory and supervisory framework that existed in Spain for the private banks and the *Cajas*. Parochial attitudes of defending one's local turf are likely to appear in the European Banking Union as well. Although there is a regulatory rulebook for all the banks operating in the Eurozone, supervision is fragmented between the 130 biggest banks, which are supervised by the ECB through the Single Supervisor Mechanism, and the rest, which are controlled by national or even regional authorities. This might lead to unforeseen difficulties.

The Spanish example shows that sometimes it is the small or savings banks that can bring the greatest problems. Identity politics might also be a problem when it comes to one of the big banks, most of them national champions. The European

Resolution Mechanism remains broadly an intergovernmental construct; hence it has to be seen whether at times of crisis, when public scrutiny is at its highest and nationalistic feelings are running high, a smooth resolution and takeover of a big bank from France and Germany by a rival bank from Italy, for example, would be possible. Therefore, to avoid double standards, lack of information about how the banks are run, parochial attitudes and multiple veto players, regulation, supervision and resolution should be both centralized and fully independent from political pressures.

A second lesson is that a big fiscal backstop is absolutely necessary. In a systemic crisis, the only actor that can stabilize the financial system is the sovereign by using taxpayer's money: the so-called big bazooka. Unfortunately, the euro is still an orphan currency without a state, and this makes it a fragile construct. The European Banking Union is a half-built house. It has a Single Supervisory Mechanism, a common (not a single) Resolution Mechanism and it still lacks a single deposit guarantee scheme. For a considerable number of policy makers in the creditor countries, especially in Germany, the bail-in regime should be enough to withstand future crises. This view seems to overlook the history of finance. The bail-in framework, under which the creditors pay first and the taxpayers pay last, might be working for smaller banks, but for big banks, threatened by the shocks of a systemic crisis, the Eurozone will need to have a larger fiscal backstop. The final lesson, therefore, is that the members of the Eurozone will eventually have to pool their fiscal sovereignty in order to effectively deal with future European banking crises.

Notes

1 Cuñat and Garicano (2009) have shown that *Cajas* with politically connected chief executives with no previous banking experience and no graduate education did substantially worse in the run up to the crisis.
2 Of the 9,000 branches opened by the *Cajas* between 1985 and 2004, almost 70 percent of them were established outside of their original region.
3 TARGET2 is a Eurozone payments system that allows for the settlement of national and cross-border payments in central bank funds.
4 The strategy was based on the so-called 'cold fusions' (*fusiones frías*), a kind of merger by which each *Caja* maintained its name, brand, legal stature and autonomy, but that allowed the 'group' to perform some actions in common, such as raising capital in international markets or centralize costs to increase efficiency.

Bibliography

Bolaños, A. (2011) Los inspectores del Banco de España culparon a Caruana de los problemas de la banca con el 'ladrillo. *El País*. [Online]. Available from: https://economia.elpais.com/economia/2011/02/21/actualidad/1298277177_850215.html.

Calomiris, C. W., and Haber, S. H. (2014) *Fragile By Design: The Political Origins of Banking Crises and Scarce Credit*, Princeton, NJ, Princeton University Press.

Carbó-Valverde, S., Marqués-Ibáñez, D., and Rodríguez Fernández, F. (2011) *Securitization, Bank Lending and Credit Quality: The Case of Spain*. ECB. Working Paper No. 1329.

Cuñat, V., and Garicano, L. (2009) *Did Good Cajas Extend Bad Loans? The Role of Governance and Human Capital in Cajas' Portfolio Decisions.* Monograph FEDEA. [Online]. Available from: www.vicentecunat.com/Cajas.pdf.

De Barrón, I. (2017) Dimite la cúpula de supervisión del Banco de España tras ser imputada (Heads of the Supervision Division of the Bank of Spain Resign After Being Imputated). *El País.* [Online]. Available from: https://economia.elpais.com/economia/2017/02/13/actualidad/1487008751_499826.html.

De Juan, A., Uría, F., and De Barrón, I. (2013) *Anatomía de una Crisis*, Madrid, Deusto.

Expansión (2008) *Zapatero asegura que el sistema financiero español es el más sólido del mundo.* [Online]. Available from: www.expansion.com/2008/09/24/economia-politica/economia/1168531.html.

Fernández de Lis, S., and García-Herrero, A. (2012) *Dynamic Provisioning: A Buffer Rather than a Countercyclical Tool?* BBVA Research. Working Paper No. 12/22.

Frieden, J. (2015) The Political Economy of Adjustment and Rebalancing. *Journal of International Money and Finance*, 52(C), 4–14.

Garicano, L. (2012) *Five Lessons From the Spanish Cajas Debacle for a New Euro-Wide Supervisor.* VoxEU. [Online]. Available from: www.voxeu.org/article/five-lessons-spanish-Cajas-debacle-new-euro-wide-supervisor.

IMF (2014) *Spain: Financial Sector Reform – Final Progress Report.* IMF. Country Report No. 14/59. [Online]. Available from: www.imf.org/external/pubs/ft/scr/2014/cr1459.pdf.

Losada López, R. (2006) *Estructuras de titulización: características e implicaciones para el sistema financier.* Comisión Nacional del Mercado de Valores (CNMV). Monografia No. 14.

Mars, A. (2012) España, duda permanente. *El País.* [Online]. Available from: https://economia.elpais.com/economia/2012/05/18/actualidad/1337372536_133343.html.

Reinhart, C. M., and Rogoff, K. (2009) *This Time is Different: Eight Centuries of Financial Folly*, Princeton, NJ, Princeton University Press.

Royo, S. (2013) *Lessons From the Crisis in Spain*, New York, Palgrave.

Santos, T. (2014) Antes del diluvio: The Spanish Banking System in the First Decade of the Euro. *Conference in Honor of José A. Scheinkman*, New York, March. [Online]. Available from: https://www0.gsb.columbia.edu/mygsb/faculty/research/pubfiles/6162/Santos-March-2014.pdf.

Sarriés Menéndez, N. (2015) *Bankia Confidencial*, Madrid, Deusto.

Woll, C. (2014) *The Power of Inaction: Bank Bailouts in Comparison*, Ithaca, Cornell University Press.

12 Conclusions

Paolo Manasse and Dimitris Katsikas

The chapters of this book have covered the recent experience of southern European countries in dealing with structural reforms during their worst recession period since World War II. The different contributors have covered a wide range of issues in specific countries, from banking reforms in Cyprus (Clerides, Chapter 9), Greece and Portugal (Panagiotarea, Chapter 10) and Spain (Otero-Iglesias and Steinberg, Chapter 11), to labour market reforms in Spain (Cuerpo, Geli and Herrero, Chapter 7) and Portugal (Turrini, Chapter 6), to product market reforms in Greece (Petralias, Anastasatou and Katsikas, Chapter 8). Other authors have taken a multi-country perspective, discussing the effects of structural reforms on the functioning of the labour market (Aksoy and Manasse, Chapter 4) and on the current account (Catao, Chapter 5) and the political issues that arose during the reform effort (Terzi, Chapter 3).

In the introduction to this volume we organized the discussion in two parts, one dealing with the issue of how to design an economically efficient reform programme and one concerned with the political economy of reforms. In trying to draw 'lessons' from the episodes covered in the book, we realize that these two ingredients are a convenient tool for expositional purposes, but are always found mixed up 'in reality'. Reforms in the different markets were introduced in heterogeneous economic, political and institutional conditions, by governments of various degrees of commitment and competence and were implemented by administrations of different technical ability. While the basic ingredients of the policy prescriptions of international institutions were quite similar across countries, they were met by different degrees of resistance by public opinions and organized special interests. And yet we cannot escape two important questions. First, what conditions were conducive to relatively successful implementation of reforms and which were the most difficult obstacles to overcome? Second, what characteristics in their design and implementation improved or undermined their effects?

These questions revolve around a few common issues that were very important in the episodes discussed.

(1) *Delay*. Economic crises may occur over-night, but are typically the results of decades-long imbalances, which myopic policy makers have consistently ignored. Stagnant productivity growth in Portugal and Greece; obsolete

labour market institutions in collective bargaining, and hiring and firing procedures in Portugal, Greece and Spain; high entry barriers in product markets and bureaucratic obstacles for setting up new firms in Greece and Portugal; inefficient supervision, nepotistic corporate governance and political interference in the banking sectors of Cyprus, Greece and Spain; bloated government sectors with high political interference in Greece and Portugal. The list could be much longer. When the government and/or the banking sector suddenly loose access to the international capital market, all these issues suddenly come to the fore and cannot be any longer ignored or postponed. At that time, the longer the delay in reforms, the larger the imbalances become, which makes the recovery lengthier and costlier. In the financial sector, banks' balance sheets deteriorate until NPLs become unsustainable (Portugal and Greece), the cost of recapitalization increases, to such an extent that external intervention becomes necessary to avoid spill-over effects (Spain), and solutions previously thought politically impossible are put forward (Cyprus). In product markets, the positive effects on employment, prices and productivity lag behind the effects of the abrupt adjustment on the demand side and thus fail to support output, or improve competitiveness. More generally, the longer the delay, the larger is the burden of adjustment and the more difficult it becomes to share it among stakeholders: banks, unions and insiders, large corporations, who thrived in the old system.

(2) *Ownership.* Delay has an additional perverse 'cultural' implication: it often generates the illusion in the public opinion that, having endured for decades, obsolete institutions pose no threat, and, more importantly, they are not the culprit of the current hardships: it's reformers who are to blame. In fact, one of the explanations for the (relative) success of Portuguese reforms in the banking sector and of labour market reforms in Portugal and Spain, was that the governments and the public opinions in these countries were well aware of the need for reform, and the countries had an history of partial reforms. In other words, in these cases there was some consensus among political parties, interest groups and public opinion on the need for change. By contrast, in Greece, political polarization and instability prevented any consensus. In Cyprus, the conflict extended to political institutions, with the Central Bank and the Government openly disagreeing on measures to recapitalize the ailing banking sector. In Spain, the financial sector reforms got delayed not because of political conflict, but rather due to inertia, as most players were unwilling to disrupt the status quo, even if that meant a higher cost of restructuring in the future. Finally, ownership may be important not only for implementing reforms, but also for keeping them in place; implementing reforms only under market or institutional pressure may render the reforms short-lived and thus ultimately unsuccessful.

(3) *External Constraints.* The discussion on ownership is closely connected with that of the role of an external constraint. The ability of international institutions to enforce reforms upon recalcitrant governments is limited. Surely,

international creditors can credibly threaten to withdraw or not renew credit lines and liquidity support, as the Troika and the ECB did in Greece. But the credibility of the threat is possibly weaker when made by European institutions to a Eurozone member, compared to when it is made by the IMF. The external scapegoat may relieve some of the domestic political pressure from reform-prone governments, as in the case of Portugal and to some extent Spain, but as the case of banking resolutions in Greece illustrates, there are limits to external interventions. International creditors can successfully initiate a reform process, but implementing reforms is a much longer and more difficult endeavour: in this respect, the external constraint is only a poor substitute of 'ownership'. And yet the cases of Cyprus and Spain provide interesting illustrations of the detrimental effect of the *lack of* external constraint. Initially, the Cyprus authorities explored the possibility of obtaining a loan from Russia, a loan that they hoped would come with no conditionality strings. This only delayed the banking resolutions and made the required adjustment more painful. Similarly, in Spain, it was only when the European institutions intervened and forced a bailout programme for the financial sector that substantial restructuring took place. On the other hand, the attempt by the Troika to make conditionality more stringent by resorting to a hyper-detailed programme, as in the case of Portuguese micro-managed labour market reforms, did not prove to be particularly useful.

(4) *Timing of Reforms.* Are economic crises a catalyst for reforms? The answer suggested by the examples discussed in the book is that 'it depends'. When the economy has deteriorated substantially, achieving political and social consensus on – and not backtracking from – reforms becomes virtually impossible. The case of Greece is a clear example. The international institutions' failure to address the issue of debt restructuring early on, during the first adjustment plan, required a harsh fiscal consolidation programme, which eventually played in the hands of anti-reformers. To a large extent, the international institutions did not understand, or were unwilling to consider, the importance the domestic *political constraint*, which limits the feasibility of fiscal consolidation plans and eventually structural reforms. On the other hand, the examples of the labour market reforms introduced in Portugal and Spain suggest that an incoming crisis can indeed force a consensus on the need of change, particularly if there is a history of public debate on reforms (see the previous point on 'ownership'), and provided the economy has not already deteriorated to such an extent as to make the domestic 'political constraint' binding.

(5) *Balance and Timing of Fiscal Consolidation and Structural Reforms.* The chapters in this book have discussed structural reforms, but, as we saw, the ghost of fiscal consolidation has always hoovered in the background. At least initially, the positive effects of structural reforms in southern Europe were obscured by the depth of the recession. Thus, product market reforms in Greece had positive effects on employment and prices, but these took some time to manifest and were swamped by the short-run recessionary

effects of expenditure cuts and the inflationary effects of tax hikes respectively. Moreover, we saw that improvement in productivity and in unit labour costs occurred in southern European countries, but the current account improvements were mainly led by the collapse of demand. Finally, structural reforms in labour and product markets eventually helped speed up the recovery of unemployment rate, but made employment more sensitive in the short run to output shocks, aggravating job losses. This evidence suggests that the timing of fiscal consolidation and structural reforms should be better coordinated. Structural reforms produce positive and durable effects in the medium term, and therefore fiscal consolidation should be phased in more gradually in order not to compromise their effects, as well as their political support.

(6) *Sequencing of Reforms.* A reasonable sequence of reforms must respect political constraints. The first one is that 'political capital' is a scarce resource for the government. It should be invested in a few crucial reforms that identify the more 'stringent' bottlenecks to economic growth. It is quickly dissipated if invested in across-the-board programmes, and when this happens, reforms back-track. In Portugal for example, the authorities successfully sequenced reforms by starting from the most feasible ones, those in the labour market, whose positive effects improved 'ownership' and their sustainability. However, in the case of Greece the analysis suggests that giving priority to the reforms which apparently present the least resistance, again those of the labour market, rather than starting from those in the product market, which were politically more difficult, eventually backfired. The second constraint is that the economic reforms must be sequenced to minimize the burden of adjustment and possibly imply a 'fair' distribution of the adjustment costs. In Greece, fiscal consolidation and labour market reforms took precedence over product market reforms and privatization. As a result, the fall in aggregate demand was aggravated by the drop in nominal *and* real wages, as prices did not follow wages. Foreign demand did not sufficiently pick up to compensate domestic demand, while the more 'flexible' labour market amplified the fall in employment caused by the recession. Workers and credit-squeezed small enterprise born the entire cost of the adjustment, and then revolted by electing reform-averse parties. Reforms aimed at raising total factor productivity, for example by fostering lower barriers in the product market or by improving the wage bargaining, are very effective in improving current account imbalances. Since they take considerable time displaying their effects, they should be given priority.

Clearly all these features, delay, ownership, external constraints, economic conditions, timing and sequencing of reforms, are not independent variables, but they affect each other. Therefore, reformers should always keep them in check as the success or failure of structural reforms ultimately depends on how they are combined. In this sense, the evidence presented in this book verifies many of the propositions produced by previous research, which however had focused for the most part in underdeveloped and developing parts of the world. The global financial crisis (to a substantial degree) and particularly the Eurozone debt crisis that ensued, are the first major international crises in the post-war period, which were crises of the developed world. The contributions in this book have shown that many of the design issues and political economy preoccupations that plague structural reforms, particularly in times of crisis, are not unique to single countries or even to a group of countries, but tend to manifest repeatedly across countries and time. This is not to say that the issues are *exactly* the same; obviously, the technical issues of reform design are different from country to country, and even more so from developing to developed countries, given the different economic, political and institutional conditions. Indeed, one of the core lessons that comes out of this volume is that structural reforms, especially in times of crisis, should proceed on a case by case basis, taking into account the distinct features of different economies and social and political systems. Having said that, history and experience provide valuable lessons and as the process of reforming the economies of southern European countries is still ongoing (and will be for some time), policy makers would do well to heed these lessons. Hopefully this volume has contributed to this endeavour.

Index

external constraint 3, 11, 18, 30–33, 200, 208, 215–216, 220, 240–241, 242

fair dismissal 121
fiscal conditions 19–20
fiscal consolidation 3, 22, 166, 241–242
fiscal policy 22

general government balance 96
Germany 4
Greece: adjustment policies and structural reforms 170–177; balancing adjustment policies and structural reforms in 162–179; business environment 163–170; current accounts 100, 107; Cypriot banks 199–200; delay in implementing reform 239–240; economic performance 49; effects of structural reforms on unemployment in 78–79; emergence of very large deficits in 89; employment 171–173; external constraints 215–216; financial crisis 4, 61; fiscal adjustment measures 172–173; fiscal consolidation 46, 166; government bonds 193, 196; IMF/EU adjustment programmes 41, 91; inflation 171–173; international competitiveness 163–170; labour market reforms 82; NPLs 207–208, 213–218; origins and handling of crisis 163–170; political economy of NPL management in 216–218; product market reforms 165–170, 172–173, 178, 241; reform measures 49; role of external constraint in implementing reform 241; role of ownership in implementing reform 240; sequencing of reforms 242; timing of reforms 241; unemployment rates 68, 82

honeymoon hypothesis 47, 48, 52

inflation 171–173
initial conditions 8, 18–20, 30, 130, 208, 211, 219
institutional conditions 19
interest groups 7, 18, 25–26, 32, 43, 48, 124, 200, 240
International Monetary Fund (IMF): constraints on democracy 32; distributional costs of policy conditionality 32; IMF/EU adjustment programmes 41, 51, 91, 120; policy design 30–31; political economy 31–33; role in structural reforms 18, 30–33, 61; structural reform objectives 6

Ireland: current accounts 100, 107–108; emergence of very large deficits in 89; financial crisis 61; IMF/EU adjustment programmes 91; macroeconomic adjustment and external pay-offs of 100; ratio of NPLs to total loans 207; reforms and external balances in Southern Europe and 89–109; unemployment rates 68
Italy: effects of structural reforms on unemployment in 79; financial crisis 63; pension reform 51, 53; ratio of NPLs to total loans 207; unemployment rates 82

Juncker dilemma 43
Juncker, Jean-Claude 43

labour markets: active policies in Portugal 119; developments in Portugal 114–116; institutions in persistence/resilience trade-off 71–78; institutions in Portugal 116–119; reforms 3, 64–65, 82, 179; reforms during economic crisis in Spain 141–159; reforms in Portugal 119–129
lobbies 25–26
Luxembourg 68

Maastricht treaty 73
macroeconomic adjustment 9, 46, 91, 100–107
macroeconomic conditions 19–20
Malta 68
monetary policy 22

Netherlands 68
New Zealand 45
'non–accelerating (wage) – inflation unemployment rate (NAWRU)' 66
non-performing loans (NPLs): Greece 213–220; political economy of 207–209; Portugal 209–213, 218–220

Okun Law 63, 65–71
output gap 96–97
Outright Monetary Transactions (OMT) 46
ownership 9, 11, 30, 32, 72, 123, 130, 130–131, 159, 210, 217, 219–220, 240, 240–242

policy conditionality 32–33
policy design 30–31, 129–131
political constraint 241
political economy: of Cyprus crisis 200–202; of NPL management in Greece 216–218; of reform 207–220; of reform in Europe's

For Product Safety Concerns and Information please contact our EU
representative GPSR@taylorandfrancis.com
Taylor & Francis Verlag GmbH, Kaufingerstraße 24, 80331 München, Germany

www.ingramcontent.com/pod-product-compliance
Ingram Content Group UK Ltd.
Pitfield, Milton Keynes, MK11 3LW, UK
UKHW021616240425
457818UK00018B/597

* 9 7 8 0 3 6 7 6 6 7 3 0 6 *